CHALLENGING REALITY explores changes in five key 'facets of reality' past, present and future. In its quest to rediscover the passion of past human wonders, it also predicts a 'Future Mindset' for achieving long-term business success.

Dilemmas for the Future Organization

What will be the structure of the Future Organization? How will the role of management change in an Age of Imagination in which the majority may labour as free agents? And which activities will add most value when information, like air, becomes so widespread a resource that it is worthless?

From the Pyramids to the Digital Age

Hold tight for a rollercoaster ride from the Pyramids to the Digital Age, from ancient hieroglyphics to metamedia, and from early rural communities to the global marketplace. By examining cutting-edge technologies, innovative social structures, and revolutionary past events, *CHALLENGING REALITY* provides you with a unique perspective upon the bold and bleak new realities of the future.

Christopher Barnatt has written three previous books on computing and organizations, and is currently a Lecturer in Organizational Behaviour, Computers and Management at the University of Nottingham. *CHALLENGING REALITY* is the second volume in his Future Trilogy, and the first sequel to *CYBER BUSINESS*.

T0318304

Also by the author from John Wiley & Sons:
Cyber Business: Mindsets for a Wired Age

Challenging Reality

In Search of the Future Organization

CHRISTOPHER BARNATT

JOHN WILEY & SONS
Chichester • New York • Weinheim • Brisbane • Singapore • Toronto

Copyright © 1997 by John Wiley & Sons Ltd,
Baffins Lane, Chichester,
West Sussex PO19 1UD, England

National   01243 779777
International (+44) 1243 779777
e-mail (for orders and customer service enquiries): cs-books@wiley.co.uk
or http://www.wiley.com

Other Wiley Editorial Offices

John Wiley & Sons, Inc., 605 Third Avenue,
New York, NY 10158-0012, USA

VCH Verlagsgesellschaft mbH, Pappelallee 3,
D-69469 Weinheim, Germany

Jacaranda Wiley Ltd, 33 Park Road, Milton,
Queensland 4064, Australia

John Wiley & Sons (Asia) Pte Ltd, 2 Clementi Loop #02-01,
Jin Xing Distripark, Singapore 129809

John Wiley & Sons (Canada) Ltd, 22 Worcester Road,
Rexdale, Ontario M9W 1L1, Canada

Library of Congress Cataloging-in-Publication Data

Barnatt, Christopher: 1967–
    Challenging reality : in search of the future organization / Christopher Barnatt.
        p.   cm.
    Includes bibliographical references and index.
    ISBN 0-471-97072-7 (pbk)
    1. Organization. 2. Management. I. Title
    HF31.B3682   1997
    658—dc21   96-39899
                                                       CIP

British Library Cataloguing in Publication Data

A catalogue record for this book is available from the British Library

ISBN 0-471-97072-7

Produced from camera-ready copy supplied by the author

To my parents—for making me think, and for encouraging me to continue to do so . . .

Contents

Preface

REALITY IS THAT WHICH is taken to be real. Frequently this implies that 'reality' is simply that in which the majority choose to believe. Recently, advances in computing have led to the development of artificial graphics worlds. Such 'virtual' realities provide excellent arenas for training, product development, and simulation testing. Virtual reality interfaces will soon also permit far less daunting interactions with computers. Additionally, when the hardware required to immerse a human being within the electronic domain of 'cyberspace' becomes less cumbersome, more robust, and less expensive, virtual reality will become a widely-utilized playspace. Indeed, there are already those who believe that virtual worlds will one day become the most common domains for human interaction.[1]

The development of computer-generated virtual realities is still largely a technical concern. However, the capability of human beings to create alternative forms of reality within computers is stirring far wider debate concerning the nature of 'reality' itself. Computer scientists are certainly not the only group of wizards capable of conjuring up virtual worlds. Entrepreneurs, scientists, religious leaders, and artists across history, have always been adept at creating alternative realities. The notion of virtual reality is older than science fiction. Indeed, the art of reality manipulation stems from prehistoric campfire enactments, Greek theatre, and a host of ancient performance rituals intended to heighten human experience via dramatic, multisensory stimulation.[2]

This book investigates the technological and social metamorphosis which has constantly redefined the limits of human endeavour. In doing so, *Challenging Reality* explores the fluid boundaries of organizational achievement past, present and future.

Since the dawn of humankind, organizations have been the most common mechanisms used to alter the limits of possibility. Indeed, without its evolution into a cooperative species, the human race would never have survived its early days. Nor would those before us have constructed great buildings, harnessed science, breathed life into the arts, or set foot upon the Moon.

In order to predict the characteristics of the 'Future Organization', *Challenging Reality* specifically examines how five key 'facets' of reality have evolved in irregular and often giant steps since the dawn of human civilization. Granted, tomorrow will not turn out to be a basic continuation of today. However, this need not imply that we cannot learn from the past and from the present.

History, like youth, is wasted on the young. Youthful minds simply have nothing to compare previous events with; no possible internal point of reference between a 'then' and a 'now'. It is therefore a pity that the vast majority of the population are only educated in history within their very early years. The value of our heritage as an organizational resource is demeaned and largely ignored as a result. However, only from the achievements and failures of our ancestors can we hope to learn to cope proactively, rather than reactively, with changes that will alter our lives. Already new technologies and social expectations are altering the rules for the Future Organization. We are at present only paddling in the shallows of an incoming sea of change. The cosy reality of the present will soon be no more and like it or not we will have to move beyond.

Christopher Barnatt

Acknowledgements

LISTS OF ACKNOWLEDGEMENTS HAVE a habit of becoming too long. For those of you eager to read every word in this book I will therefore keep at least this section brief!

Firstly thanks must go to Sarah Brown, Geoff Farrell, Alison Mead, Claire Plimmer, and Diane Taylor, at John Wiley & Sons, for their assistance in bringing *Challenging Reality* to press. Secondly I would like to thank Allen Barnatt, Chatsworth Television, Mark Daintree, Michael Downey, the Millennium Group, Norman Powell, and Mick Rowlinson, for supplying background information or for providing a forum within which to develop some of my ideas. Thanks also go Richard Davey for doing such a wonderful job as copy editor. I would also like to thank Pauline O'Sullivan, Steve Toms, and everyone at the Nottingham Writers' Contact, for providing feedback upon specific chapters or sections thereof. Lastly, and of course by no means least, many thanks go to Sue Tempest for reading, commenting upon—and often debating!—the content of the entire manuscript over the course of 1996. With no dogs, cats, budgies or even goldfish left to mention, we are now quite free to get on with the rest of the book.

Prologue
Sunrise in the Desert

REACHING THE SUMMIT OF the dune, he paused to behold the golden aura and the coolness of the dawn. Before him, the sun was slowly creeping from behind the mighty bulk of the rising tomb. Couched in long, dark shadows, carved stone blocks and mounds of rubble lay scattered across the sand as far as the human eye could see. Indeed, it was only the Gods who could truly comprehend the scale of the greatness upon which his people laboured. And it was to the Pharaohs of the Heavens to whom they had all entrusted their destiny.

Although only half completed, the building upon which they were working was already magnificent and a focus of great reverence and pride. Eight seasons before it had begun to rival the earlier glories of Dahshur and of Saqqara. By now there could be no question that it would become the greatest ever construction of any land or any time. It was rumoured that the height of the king's final dwelling would be that of over one hundred slaves. The outer limestone casing was also being ground far more smoothly, and being set far more accurately, than that of any previous tomb.

Slowly the site was coming alive. Soon it would be crawling with masons, architects and labourers. With the fields flooded, it was not a time when men could work upon the land, and there were many ramps to be built in order to move more of the completed stones up into position.

Raising a smile, he took the first of many sliding steps down the sands towards the coming labours of the day. As usual he would arrive early—not due to the threat of the whip, but out of respect for Ra, Horus and Osiris. As the architect had bid them all understand so many dawns ago, even if some of them travelled to the Other World before the tomb was completed, their endeavours would still be preserved forever within Eternity. There was a glory to be achieved in this place far greater than that of any mortal man.

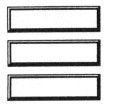

1
Prelude

When such thoughts crossed his mind, it seemed as if the structure of reality trembled for an instant, and that behind the world of the senses he caught a glimpse of another and totally different universe . . .

Arthur C. Clarke
The City and the Stars[3]

TURMOIL, UNCERTAINTY AND TRANSITION have become dominant characteristics of the late-20th century. Indeed, we are increasingly witness to the erosion of the great castles of tradition. Empowered via new computing and information technologies, *global connectivity* is fast being achieved across the markets and economics of modern business. An ethos of cocooned individualism is also sweeping the societies and organizations of the West. Family units are getting smaller and smaller, whilst more people live alone than ever before. New planetary-wide economic and political networks are also emerging under the control of global business organizations rather than national governments. In addition, the human race faces looming environmental problems, physical and mental resource constraints, and the increasing burdens of overpopulation. In a very 'real' sense, as the promise of a new millennium draws near, the very cornerstones of common reality are crumbling before our tired eyes.

There is, however, little need to be overly pessimistic. Many times in the past the human race has faced monumental social, cultural, technological—and hence organizational—turmoil *and has won*. The late-20th century is far from the only period in history to be leading its children into an uncertain future. History itself is characterized by change. Men and women are linear beings who in the main enjoy the challenge of the unknown. Or as Alvin Toffler once observed, change is life itself.[4]

CHALLENGING REALITY

This book invites you on a journey across time—across reality—on a quest to discover the organizations of the future. During the voyage we will gather together resources from the past, and from the present, in order to enable us to better cope with the many challenges of the early-21st century and beyond.

UK management guru Charles Handy has argued that we must not let 'our past, however glorious, get in the way of our future'.[5] In one sense this may be correct. The past is certainly not a place in which we can afford to dwell. However, we must be equally careful not to dismiss the past, as it represents a very valuable resource for times ahead. Granted, the Pharaohs of ancient Egypt, Victorian railway engineers, 1960s space scientists, and a host of other powerful historical mentors, did not contend with the downsized, outsourced, networked-organic-tangle of modern organizational evolution. However, what they did do was to overcome great *organizational* adversity. The future has been termed the 'undiscovered country'. In contrast, the past is a largely known resource from which we still have much to learn.

The previous book in this Future Trilogy—*Cyber Business*—explored the organizational implications of new computing and communications technologies.[6] Several of my colleagues have expressed some surprise that I am now in part looking back to the past in order to further my analysis of things to come. However, no longer will embracing the computing technologies of 'cyberspace' provide a sufficient recipe for medium- and long-term business success.

Most managers now appreciate the importance of embracing new and continual developments in information technology. However, what is still largely ignored is how reality itself is changing as new technologies, novel working practices, and fresh organizational forms, come to be adopted. To cope with the tools of the Digital Age we must not only contend with their immediate hardware and software. In addition, we need to embrace the new realities which revolutionary technologies and social transformations empower and create.

HISTORY & ORGANIZATION

Organizations provide the physical, social and cultural infrastructure essential for the survival of humanity. The word organization is taken from the Greek 'organon', meaning a tool or an instrument. As tools or instruments, organizations are devices for accomplishing goals.[7] And as tools which fashion human beings into patterns of collective activity, organizations are effectively social machines. Hence, to truly understand how organizations are to evolve into the next century, we need to study the likely metamorphosis of human society. In particular, it seems wise to examine how some of our ancestors coped with previous periods of near-overwhelming change.

The present century has undoubtedly proved almost totally different from the earlier span of human history which preceded it. Automated assembly lines, industrial cities, electronic telecommunications, computers, and global markets, are all children of the past one hundred years. What's more, none of the aforementioned 'new' developments have yet to run the full course of their evolution. The age of electronic interconnection—the *Knowledge Age* wherein human beings will work in tandem with smart machines—is only just beginning. In parallel, the heyday of mass production and industrial concentration is now drawing to a close.

A NEW MINDSET

The most common problem encountered when trying to derive value from history—particularly in a business context—is of trying to learn from *yesterday*, rather than from previous *periods of change*. Therefore, whilst *Challenging Reality* may detail some specific historical undertakings, it only does so in order to provide icons of past achievement from which we may chart clear evolutionary progressions. The future will certainly not, as believed throughout many recent decades, prove to be a bigger and better continuation of the present. The Age of Certainty is most definitely over.[8] Future business success will therefore depend upon the adoption of a new 'mindset' for continual change, rather than any particular new set of skills.

A mindset may be defined as a broad mental framework for guiding forward-looking strategies and actions. Mindsets are becoming increasingly important as sets of skills deteriorate with increasingly regularity in a world of constant change. Today, only ways of thinking, rather than means of doing, exhibit any longevity. The primary aim of this book is therefore to develop some fresh mental frameworks. Details of many innovative technologies and working practices happen to be included along the way. However, these are intended to illustrate trends, rather than to suggest specific, catch-all future solutions. Indeed, the final conclusions from this book are presented within a ten-point Future Mindset framework within **chapter 17**.

Embracing a new mindset—and in particular clearing out the mental space to let it on board—quite possibly constitutes the greatest challenge that any individual may face. This said, across history it has been those individuals who have dared to think differently from the masses who have instigated our greatest acts of achievement. Great changes—great reality shifts—always start with single, free-thinking individuals, not organizations. Indeed, many surveys have now shown how committees only ever vote for incremental change rather than radical transformation. Scale inhibits novelty. So called 'groupthink' hence resists those new realities which so often result from the labours and dreams of the lone, imaginative, and risk-hungry mind.

CAGES & MEMES

One way to think of reality is as the ultimate group or team perception. Reality is nothing, after all, if not collective. In broader terms, reality may be defined as the consensus of the masses concerning the boundaries of what is right, what is wrong, and what may be achieved. Or, as Timothy Leary so nicely puts it, reality designing is a team sport.[9] However, we should also remember that reality has often been imposed *upon* the masses by visionaries, scientists, politicians, religious overlords, and other members of the dominant and defining managerial clan.

We may also think of reality as a cage of thin elastic. If you run up against the walls of this cage they stretch a little and send you flying. However, if you leap at the walls of reality hard enough and fast enough, then they snap and permit escape. Moreover, once the bounds of the elastic cage have been ruptured, the mass populace soon follows through into the larger and more complex world beyond. By breaking out of the elastic cage, individuals empower themselves as new leaders—as definers of reality, rather than as passive acceptors of its bounds.

Within his fascinating best-seller *The Selfish Gene*, Richard Dawkins introduced the noun 'meme' as the unit of cultural transmission.[10] According to Dawkins, memes may be tunes or ideas, catch-phrases or fashions, ways of making pots or of building arches. In other words, memes are icons of current reality which may be passed across and down generations. Memes are the essence of what it is, was, and will be, to be human. Or as Dawkins contends, 'just as genes propagate themselves in the gene pool by leaping from body to body via sperm or eggs, so memes propagate themselves in the meme pool by leaping from brain to brain'.[11]

Memes are carriers of our greatest achievements and cultures. As such, memes are replicable carriers of the very *spirit* of our organizations past, present and future.

In order to more easily identify how the memes of organizations and their members have shifted across time, I have chosen to define five reality 'facets'. The five subsequent Parts of this book will each deal with the transformation of just one of these attributes of reality.

Obviously the number of reality facets isolated is arbitrary and open to debate. However, my sole intention in cleaving out my chosen 'reality set' is to provide a clear framework within which to study what would otherwise prove an over-complex set of transitions. To this end, I hope that readers will at least find the five facets defined herein clearly distinct, readily identifiable, and of immediate significance to the Future Organization. **Figure 1.1** illustrates the five facets of reality, and hence the headings of Parts I through V of *Challenging Reality*. Whilst each reality facet and its accompanying memes are detailed within these Parts, the following section also provides brief, introductory definitions.

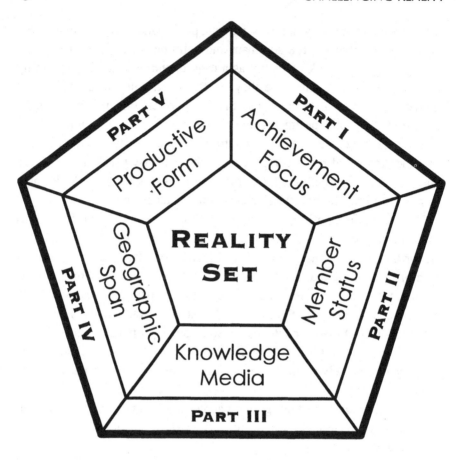

Figure 1.1 The Facets of Reality

THE REALITY FACETS

The first reality facet—*achievement focus*—is almost certainly the least tangible. Yet it is arguably the most important and the most interesting. Achievement focus is a measure of the kind of accomplishments individuals and their organizations strive towards. For example, it may be that some societies concentrate upon building armies, whilst others focus upon crafting religious monuments. Yet others may make the advancement of science their primary objective, or even the creation of artistic works of unrelenting beauty.

In essence, achievement focus encapsulates the key characteristics of those overwhelming accomplishments that manage to inspire widespread pride, reverence or majesty. As a result, achievement focus also happens to reflect that for which any culture, society, or organization, is likely to be most remembered. In a nutshell, achievement focus is about what inspires wonder.

Reality facet two—*member status*—is far easier to define. Member status provides a measure of the types of roles held by most ordinary individuals within their societies, cultures and organizations. For example, the member status of the majority may be that of slavery, or of being the machine-line employees of an industrial bureaucracy.

Knowledge media, the third reality facet, indicates the means used to replicate ideas over distance and time. Knowledge media therefore encapsulate all of those technologies and conventions—from ancient hieroglyphics to the telephone or television—which may be involved in the communication and/or the storage of memes.

The fourth reality facet of *geographic span* concerns the physical area across which any society or organization may achieve dominance. In part, geographic span is therefore limited by the third facet of knowledge media. For without adequate communications, broad empires may not be maintained. However, in addition, geographic span is also constrained by the available technologies and infrastructures for individual travel and physical trade.

Finally, the facet of *productive form* concerns the dominant structure of work and its organization within any particular reality set. Productive form is therefore influenced by all of the other reality facets. In particular, there tend to be interactive tensions between the reality facets of productive form, achievement focus, and member status. The reality facets of knowledge media and of geographic span then additionally impinge upon the type of organizational arrangements most likely to evolve. By studying such tensions and constraints in Part V, we will find ourselves able to reach many conclusions concerning the characteristics of future organizational forms.

HISTORY IN THREES

Each Part of this book is divided into three chapters. Each chapter then investigates a specific facet of reality in either the past, the present, or the future. Of course, in order to adopt such a structure, we clearly need definitions of when 'the past', 'the present' and 'the future' will be taken to be.

Many writers have argued that we are now entering a third phase of human advancement. For example, in 1980 futurist Alvin Toffler wrote of the pending 'future shock' of the coming *Third Wave*.[12] Such a 'post-industrial age' will be characterized by the mass-adoption of information technology. It has therefore often been labelled the 'Information Age'. In contrast, the two ages or 'waves' to precede the third were those of mass-agriculture and then mass-industrial production.

In 1984 Charles Piore and Michael Sabel published a book about industrial transition within which they contended that clear 'industrial divides' were apparent between eras with common paradigms of production.[13] Specifically, Piore and Sabel labelled the period of transition from agriculture to mass production as the first industrial divide. They then labelled our current period of social and organizational upheaval as the second industrial divide. In common with many other analysts, Piore and Sabel contended that this current period hailed the death of bureaucratic, large-scale organizations tooled for standardized mass production.

Challenging Reality's division of human history into three simplistic frames of time is roughly in line with those models put forward by Toffler and by Piore and Sabel. Herein 'the past' will be taken to correspond to that vast period of history spanning from the very dawn of human civilization right up until the mid- to late-19th century. In other words, the term 'the past' will be used within *Challenging Reality* to refer to the entire era of pre-industrial history before the rise of large-scale business organizations.

Defining when 'the present' takes place clearly has the potential to prove somewhat problematic. For our purposes, the present will be taken to encompass the heyday era of industrial mass-production. This period of time is generally agreed to span from the mid- to late-19th century to around the end of the 20th. The present, then, is the period of Toffler's

'Second Wave'—or that timespan bounded between the first and second industrial divides.

By definition, 'the future' has to begin where the present ends. Herein, the turn of the millennium will be taken to cleave the present from the future. By the early-21st century we should have finally crossed the second industrial divide to have embraced the spirit of the New Age. Many academics have labelled this dawning period of history as 'post-modern'. Discussions of 'post-modernity' subsequently now consume many pages of high-brow, academic debate. However, within this book the concept of post-modernism will not be discussed. Indeed, my intention from the start is to avoid getting caught up within any ivory-towered, sociological drama.

THE CHAPTER MATRIX

By imposing the timeframes of the past, the present, and the future, against a listing of our five reality facets, a route map indicating the structure of the following fifteen chapters is revealed. **Table 1.1** illustrates this chapter matrix. It also highlights the key factor upon which each facet of reality has been, is, or is likely to be focused. The contribution of each chapter to the final presentation of the Future Mindset in **chapter 17** is also identified as a result.

As can be seen from the table, Part I's concentration upon achievement focus—upon accomplishments, dreams and aspirations—sees a shift from an age of awe, to one championing ingenuity, through to a coming period of time which will most value imagination. In terms of member status, Part II then tracks the progression of the majority of human beings from being serfs or slaves, to being cooperative employees, and in future to being free agents with few organizational allegiances. In Part III, we see a shift away from single channel knowledge media (based upon the spoken or written word), towards today's multi-channel or 'multimedia' modes of sound-and-vision electronic communication. Future 'meta-channel' knowledge media are then predicted. These will utilize new technologies—such as computer-generated virtual reality—to permit the sharing of synthetic human experiences both in the flesh, as well as remotely across the electronic domain of cyberspace.

REALITY FACET			TIMEFRAME
	Past	Present	Future
Achievement	Awe	Ingenuity	Imagination
Focus	[chapter 2]	[chapter 3]	[chapter 4]
Member	Serfs & Slaves	Employees	Free Agents
Status	[chapter 5]	[chapter 6]	[chapter 7]
Knowledge	Single Channel	Multi-channel	Metachannel
Media	[chapter 8]	[chapter 9]	[chapter 10]
Geographic	Constrained	Relaxed	Unlimited
Span	[chapter 11]	[chapter 12]	[chapter 13]
Productive	Feudal/Craft	Bureaucratic	Organic
Form	[chapter 14]	[chapter 15]	[chapter 16]

Table 1.1 *Challenging Reality*—**Chapter Matrix**

The three chapters of Part IV next set out to explore the broadening geographic spans which have been controlled by humankind across history. Discussion within these chapters initially focuses upon the expansion of trade between regions and nations. Globalization, and in particular the lingering 'death' of the nation state as a key economic region, are then detailed. Some possibilities for the geographic expansion of humanity beyond the confines of the Earth are also included within **chapter 13**.

Finally, Part V analyses the shift across time from feudal/craft to bureaucratic to organic productive structures. As the mass-production methods of the industrial era increasingly fail, these chapters look forward towards more flexible and even 'virtual' patterns of organization for the 21st century. Our analysis of the progression of the other four reality facets is also drawn together within Part V as we predict the characteristics of the Future Organization.

It is important that none of my past–present–future progressions be treated too literally as exclusive scales. Quite to the contrary, some overlaps will clearly exist over each three-phase progression. Across history, different members of society will not have always suffered or enjoyed quite exactly the same member status. Similarly, a wide variety of different knowledge media will have been used for communications. Differing regions, nations and organizations across time have also exhibited a wide variety of achievement foci, geographic spans, and productive forms.

The above noted, simple structural overlays often prove extremely useful when attempting to clarify broad, historical transitions. And although simplistic in some respects, the five three-point-scale reality facet progressions are solely intended as analytical tools in this light. Indeed, to analogize, if we were to isolate a progression concerning the technologies used by authors, then we would sensibly chart an advancement from pen and paper to typewriter to personal computer. However, such a progression would not imply that pen or paper are now totally obsolete, nor that all typewriters have been scrapped. In a similar fashion, it is important that the past–present–future progressions listed within **table 1.1** are viewed as guides for furthering debate, rather than as pigeonholes into which many phases of historical revolution are to be squashed.

* * *

A PERSONAL CRUSADE

Ultimately, my personal intention in writing this book is to explore some of the most significant watersheds in the organization of humanity in the past, in the present, and in the future. To this end, *Challenging Reality* is concerned with charting and exploring the *visions* which have, do, and will continue, to empower our race's greatest feats of economic and social engineering.

Perhaps the only unlimited yet still largely untouched business resource is collective human imagination. Within the following chapters, every attempt is therefore made to capture the very *essence* of those 'awe factors' which have occasionally managed to capture the hearts of a generation, and which have subsequently catapulted humankind along a fresh road of invention, imagination and success.

When, in the mid-5th century BC, Phidias sculpted his forty-foot high statue of Zeus, the Greek Gods became empowered with a physical as well as a mythical presence.[14] When, in the early-16th century, Nicolaus Copernicus theorized that the Earth rotated around the Sun (and not the other way around) the place and prominence of Man and Woman in the Universe changed.[15] And when, on the 12th of April 1961, Yuri Gagarin became the first man in space, our species ceased to be a resident of a planet and instead became a native of the wider galaxy beyond.[16] Such moments in history are significant. They shaped and nurtured our very development. Further, they may also provide us with vital clues for our continuing evolution.

Lyricist Gary Osborne once wrote that 'Man is born in freedom but he soon becomes a slave . . . [caught] . . . in cages of convention from the cradle to the grave'.[17] Across the following sixteen chapters, the means—physical, social, cultural and psychological—used to metamorph individuals into the cogs of organizational convention are detailed from a wide range of perspectives.

People specialize within modern societies not only in order to survive most comfortably, but in addition to build legacies in the hope of finding purpose within their short lives. Frustrating laws and bureaucracies are accepted for the common good, whilst inequalities are tolerated for social and economic stability. Just occasionally, injustices are also condoned in the name of progress—or apathy—or as an 'inevitable' consequence of the politics and policies of glancing-aside non-interference. Yet we are also at a turning point. With 'downsizing', 'flexibility' and 'outsourcing' the present key-words of the business community, resources rapidly depleting, and population expansion out of control, centuries-old veneers of cosy civilization are facing turmoil. And it is no longer to monarchs, to dictators, or to governments, to whom the populations of the world may turn in the hope of gaining some reassurance as to the journey ahead. Rather, it is mighty global corporations which now govern the destiny of humanity. We therefore need to study the evolution of the Future Organization in order to best determine the roots of the future.

Across history, men and women have become more capable than any other Earth-bound species of engaging in acts of long-term cooperation. Such acts have usually relied upon our ability to communicate not just information, but also knowledge and visions of future accomplishment, across the boundaries of both geography and time. Keyboard-hungry technoholics today are removed by thousands of years of evolution from their ancient ancestors. However, they may still derive meaning from finger paintings on age-old cave walls. Some people today can also decipher faded lettering scrawled upon scrolls of yellowed papyrus. Similarly, the golden death mask of ancient Egyptian Pharaoh Tutankhamen remains a slightly-disturbing icon of the past for millions around the globe.[18]

With men and women long dead capable of influencing the thoughts of their descendants, it is but folly to hope to investigate the organizational challenges of the present, and of the future, without some appreciation of the great organizational accomplishments of the past. The concept of a well-managed, organizational machine is certainly not one which was first conceived by the business gurus of the 20th century. Similarly, visionary intensity is not solely an icon of the New Age to which many writers claim we are now witness. In looking to the future we would therefore be wise to also look back to the past. Only our ancestors have faced and overcome changes in the nature of the realities in which they have lived. Only from them can we therefore muster any practical knowledge of how to most successfully contend with fresh realities to come.

Finally before we commence our journey, I would like to ask for just a little patience. As I constantly seek to explain to many of the aspirant business hopefuls within my MBA class at Nottingham, we must seek firm foundations before forging too quickly ahead. In order to learn anything from historical transition we first need to share some common foundations in the past. Inevitably, therefore, the focus of *Challenging Reality* tends to shift from the historical to the business orientated. Earlier Parts and chapters hence serve as broad resources for those that follow.

In particular, it should be noted that the following two chapters (addressing humanity's achievement focus in the past and the present), focus in some depth upon the building of the Pyramids of Egypt, and then upon the US moonlandings programme. Some business readers seeking answers rather than questions may therefore prefer to skip **chapter 2** and **chapter 3**. Indeed, those really pressed for time may decide to read only the final, future-focused chapters of each Part of this book![19] However, whilst valid in some respects, such a strategy misses much of the point of *Challenging Reality*. Ultimately, this book is about *atmosphere*—about human progression—and about putting the startling novelty and promise of the third millennium into a broad and very *human* context. So please, be open-minded as we journey back to the banks of the Nile and on to the wastes of the Moon and beyond. Until we have smelt the roses of the past, we will remain hampered in judging the scent, fair or foul, of the future.

PART I
ACHIEVEMENT FOCUS

2
An Archaeology of Wonder

THE PYRAMIDS OF EGYPT and the Hanging Gardens of Babylon. The ivory and gold Statue of Zeus in Olympia, the pillared Temple of Artemis, and the gigantic Mausoleum of Halicarnassus. The Pharos lighthouse at Alexandria and the statue of the Colossus which watched over the harbour at Rhodes. Together, the aforementioned monuments comprise the Seven Ancient Wonders of the World.[20]

Most people have heard of the Seven Wonders, even if few are aware of actual contents of the ancient list. However, since only the Pyramids of Egypt have survived to this day, such a lack of specific knowledge is hardly surprising.[21] Indeed, some of the Seven Wonders existed as no more than seafarers' tales or myths even when the great list was first being written over 2000 years ago.

Regardless of their individual histories and characteristics, what the Seven Wonders collectively embody are a set of qualities, struggles and achievements which may be admired to this day. The Seven Wonders were once all awe inspiring constructions of great might. They therefore provide an ideal starting point for our exploration of the achievement focus of humanity. Indeed, lingering hints of the most marvellous monuments of antiquity still haunt the modern world.[22]

The list of the Seven Wonders was completed at a time when human beings were starting to ask not what they could do for the Gods, but rather what great civilizations could accomplish for themselves. The list's purpose was therefore to showcase the very finest achievements in history. In doing so, the list also served to demonstrate the unbounded ability of humankind to defeat nature and to alter the limits of reality. Every entry on the list represented an epic volume of achievement that, even when only described rather than seen, still carried with it an overwhelming aura of greatness long after its creators had ceased to exist. The Seven Wonders hence bestowed immortality upon those who had produced them. Or as the Greek scribe who first wrote out the 'dazzling list' himself noted, the Seven Wonders were sights that, once seen in the mind's eye, could never be destroyed.[23]

AWE, INGENUITY & IMAGINATION

The purpose of the next three chapters is to make you think about the visions, the labours, and the dreams, that have driven some of the greatest ever feats of human accomplishment. My contention is that, in reflecting upon the awe and the wonderment associated with previous great achievements, we may discover a spirit and a passion of value to the Future Organization.

There can be little doubt that people are any organization's greatest asset. On the brink of the 21st century, no longer are significant accomplishments achieved via the application of brute force and artistry in the fashioning of huge monuments of stone. However, today's most talented employees and entrepreneurs do on occasions engage in the creation of modern wonders which in some ways rival the legacy of those of the past. Perhaps most often, wonders of the 20th century have been achieved via the clever invention and application of new forms of technology. As just two examples, the development and mass-adoption of the internal combustion engine and the microchip have radically altered our lives. As will be discussed in **chapter 3**, the last one hundred years may well be remembered as the century of technological ingenuity and innovation.

How future wonders will be created inevitably remains somewhat uncertain. However, it is likely that the most overwhelming accomplishments of the 21st century will be those capitalizing upon great leaps of imagination. We have already noted how many of the boundaries which constrain our lives exist solely within our minds. Yet such mental barriers usually prove the most difficult to overcome. One only has to recall the relatively slow take-up of personal computers as office tools in the 1980s to be reminded of the resistance of most people and organizations to radical change.

As science and technology continue to progress, we may soon enter an age within which any dream will be able to realized in some form of reality. However, whether most of the achievements of which we will be capable will have any meaning or any value will be quite another matter. Imagination is therefore likely to become the key achievement focus of the future, as will be detailed in the final chapter of Part I.

FEARED BY TIME ITSELF

There is something almost magical about any accomplishment which has stood the test of time. As celluloid archaeologist Indiana Jones was once reminded when threatening to destroy an ancient relic, 'Indiana, we are simply passing through history. This—this *is* history'.[24] In a world where products, organizations, and their managers, rise and decline with increasing regularity, such a quotation can only count as double with respect to the Pyramids of ancient Egypt. Or as this sentiment is expressed in an old Arab proverb, 'Man fears Time, yet Time itself fears the Pyramids'.

The Pyramids remain some of the largest and most awe-inspiring constructions of any age. Just as importantly, the Pyramids also represent the culmination of some of the greatest ever feats of physical and social engineering. The Pyramids may be products of very simple technologies. Yet they were also the result of an immense organizational complexity capable of empowering and impoverishing an entire nation in pursuit of a single vision.

Over the next few pages we will examine some of the characteristics of ancient Egyptian civilization. In particular we will focus upon the construction of its most awe inspiring tombs. As our exploration progresses, I would ask you to think—to *really think*—about the processes which went into the Pyramids' creation. Time is a great barrier to empathy. However, for a few minutes try to imagine the labour and the organization of those who moved literally *millions* of stone blocks across the desert. Or perhaps even consider what it might have been like to crawl down a dark, narrow, sloping corridor in order to sculpt hiero-glyphics deep within a tomb. However told, the story of the Pyramids is not just a tale of ancient history. Rather, it is a legacy of who we are—of what we have so sadly lost—and of the latent potential once again remaining to be tapped from the pool of humanity in the future.

THE INHABITANTS OF THE NILE

The modern myth of the ancient Egyptians is of a morose and gloomy people obsessed with death. Such an impression arises from the fact that many of the tombs and burial artifacts of their great civilization have survived, whilst most ancient Egyptian towns, palaces and houses have long disappeared.[25] However, in contrast to the popularist view, those who inhabited the fertile valley of the Nile for some 3000 years were actually a people of great gaiety and good living. In fact, the ancient Egyptians loved life so much that they could hardly conceive of it ending. Whilst other ancient peoples feared an afterlife of darkness and misery, the Egyptians thought of the 'Other World' as a happy place of eternal banquets, dancing girls and 'every good thing'.[26]

For the Egyptians, death was a transition to a place with none of the sorrows, pains or unpleasantnesses of the mortal plane. That the Pyramids and other mastaba tombs[27] of Egypt have survived is therefore a tribute to their builders' obsession with *life* rather than with death. Indeed, the papyrus scrolls of spells buried within mummy cases, and now known collectively as the *Book of the Dead*, were in fact known to the Egyptians as *The Chapters of the Coming Forth by Day*. Far from being dark and macabre, the contents of these documents were concerned with the maintenance of a satisfying and pleasurable existence in the Other World. The ancient Egyptian psyche—unlike that of modern Western civiliza-tion—was one of art and culture; of an optimism and a positive vitality for life eternal.[28]

IMMORTALIZED IN THE DESERT

Whether the monarchs of the Nile did ascend to a pleasurable eternal plane is a subject to be left to theologists and other champions of religion.

However, whether they achieved immortality is in little doubt. Probably beyond the wildest expectations of their architects, the desert tombs of the early Pharaohs[29] have already managed to withstand the eroding onslaughts of time for well over four millennia.

Whereas even vague memories of so many peoples, times and places have been lost in the deep chasms of history, the monarchs of the Nile are still remembered around the globe. Indeed, even if the Pyramids, sarcophaguses and golden death masks of ancient Egypt do now crumble, their image will continue to survive. The ancient Egyptians have managed to live on into a digital age which will preserve their majesty forever. Today, we may find visual remnants of the Pharaohs not just within buildings, books and television documentaries. In addition, images and writings of ancient Egyptian civilization are now encoded inside multimedia encyclopedias copied in their tens of millions for less than a dollar. It does seem, however, that the price of immortality is to have the words 'copyright Microsoft Corporation' emblazoned upon every eternal portrayal.[30]

The first pyramidal structure—the Step Pyramid of King Djoser at Saqqara—was also the first building to be constructed entirely out of stone. Previous tombs, temples and dwellings, not just in Egypt but also in other ancient Empires such as those of Mesopotamia, had been built largely from mud bricks. Stone had only been utilized in earlier constructions to form lintels and thresholds. Indeed, before the Step Pyramid was erected, people had been hesitant to trust stone as a reliable building material. Daring to be different was King Djoser's architect Imhotep. He alone of his generation had the vision to accept the strength of stone for building purposes. He was later even deified as a result. And perhaps even more significantly, Imhotep's 'leap of faith' construction which began the modern building age is still standing after 4500 years.[31]

THE GREATEST OF WONDERS

As its name implies, the Step Pyramid was constructed without smoothly sloping sides. Four successions after Djoser, it was therefore a Pharaoh named Snefru who became responsible for the first two 'true' Pyramids. Built at Dahshur, these have become known as the Red and the Bent

Pyramids.[32] However, it was Snefru's successor Khufu[33] who oversaw the construction of the most famous pyramid. Built at Giza,[34] Khufu's Great Pyramid rises a staggering 481 feet above the desert and has sides measuring 750 feet in length. The Great Pyramid is constructed from around 2.3 million blocks of stone, each of which has an average weight of over 2.5 tons. Each block was also moved across the desert and up into position without the aid of a pulley or other lifting device. Most probably, this feat was achieved by using rubble to build gently sloping ramps up against the sides of the Pyramid. Stone blocks could then be manhandled up these temporary constructions and into position with the aid of ropes and levers. To reduce friction, surfaces across which the stones were to be moved are believed to have been coated with mud.

The Great Pyramid remains one of the most accurate buildings in the world. Despite the fact that its builders did not possess a compass, their mighty creation is almost perfectly aligned on its North–South axis. The difference between the Great Pyramid's longest and shortest sides is also only eight inches (an error of less than one tenth of one per cent).

Within the Great Pyramid's massive superstructure an entrance corridor opens out into a rising corbel vault some 150 feet long and 26 feet high. This passage in turn leads to the King's granite-lined burial chamber. At the very heart of the Pyramid, the King's Chamber features two eight-inch square shafts which slope up for hundreds of feet until they reach the outer surface. Over the years, these shafts have become a source of intrigue for many Egyptologists due to their precise alignment with major stars.[35]

Further adding to the Great Pyramid's mystique is the fact that the entrance to the King's Chamber is one inch *narrower* than the stone sarcophagus held within. Most probably this was intended as a defence against tomb robbers (and indeed the sarcophagus is all that remains of the contents of the burial chamber), although it does present some interesting questions as to how such an apparently 'magical' feat of engineering was achieved. The Greek scholar Herodotus once recorded that 100,000 men were involved in constructing the Great Pyramid over a period of 20 years. Such figures are almost certainly somewhat of an exaggeration. However, it is likely that there were times when every Egyptian citizen not required to be toiling upon the land was engaged in pyramid construction.[36]

Skipping one succession from Khufu, King Khaefre built a second and almost equally massive pyramid on the Giza site. The Great Sphinx also occupies the same location, perhaps crafted around a spur of rock left over from quarrying activities.[37] Alternatively, it is now thought by some analysts that the Sphinx may be a relic of a far older civilization which was simply re-faced with an Egyptian likeness.[38] A third, final and far smaller Giza pyramid was built by Khaefre's immediate successor Menkaure. Later Pharaohs of the Fifth and Sixth Dynasties also opted for pyramid tombs, though none of these were nearly so large and imposing as the two giants of the Giza trio.[39]

ADDING TO THE FUTURE

The achievements in architecture and construction engineering realized by the architects of the Pharaohs were mighty indeed. However, just as awe-inspiring must have been the ideas and pronouncements which led to their construction. Imagine waking up one morning and being told that you were to build a 500 foot monument in the desert! Up with the boldest business gurus of today, one can certainly not deny that the Pharaohs possessed extraordinary vision.

It is also worth noting that, for the Egyptian people, the Pyramids were far more than royal tombs. In addition, they also constituted markers in time which dominated not just skylines but human minds. The Pyramids became icons of how man could add to his future. Or, as prehistorian Grahame Clark so nicely puts it, 'no Egyptian could have passed [through] his brief existence without being made aware that he lived in a community consecrated by history'.[40]

The lives of most ancient peoples consisted of endless cycles. Every year rivers like the Nile would flood and ebb carrying mud and silt to fertilize the land. And just as the nights would grow shorter and then longer again in a constant repetition of the seasons, so religious festivals would arrive on an annual basis, always to be conducted in an identical, timeless fashion. Children would come of age, form relationships, bear offspring, and would eventually die, always with the knowledge that the cycles of life would perpetuate unbroken. For the ancients across the world there was change but no novelty. Time itself was a cyclical eternity. People would progress through cycle after cycle, life after life, but their participation in events would not impact upon subsequent generations. A son could wish to be like his father—a daughter to be like her mother—yet neither could expect their actions to alter the environment and the cycles to be experienced by their children or great grandchildren generations down their line. The past had been, the present was, and the future (synonymous for many ancient cultures with the end of the world) was beyond humanity. The actions of human beings could therefore have no possible consequence in time. However, in building the Pyramids, the ancient Egyptians became one of the first civilizations capable of rising above such constraints in the reality of time itself.

Whether they toiled as architects, masons, or even as humble labourers, those who worked upon the Pyramids were empowered to add to the future. In crafting a tomb for their King, the mass populace could win for itself a place within Eternity outside of the endless cycles of daily life. For the first time, the labours of a parent could result in a creation whose majesty would be revered by his or her offspring for generation after generation. Time subsequently ceased to be perceived as an eternal cycle, and instead became a linear stream of events capable of being shaped by human action. As illustrated in **figure 2.1**, a progressive link hence came to be identified between the past, the present, and the future.

THE BIRTH OF MODERNITY

Moments in history wherein perceptions of time change from the cyclical to the linear have been labelled periods of modernity.[41] Naturally it is during such periods when the bounds of reality are most readily exploded. The construction of the Pyramids and other monuments of ancient Egypt led its people to conceive the world as something which could be changed by the labours of individual human beings. Throughout later periods of antiquity, through the Middle Ages—and indeed up until the 19th century—such a perception was sadly repressed.[42] The ancient Egyptians were not just at awe with their creations of stone. They were also inspired by the fact that their monuments gave them a definite place within a new

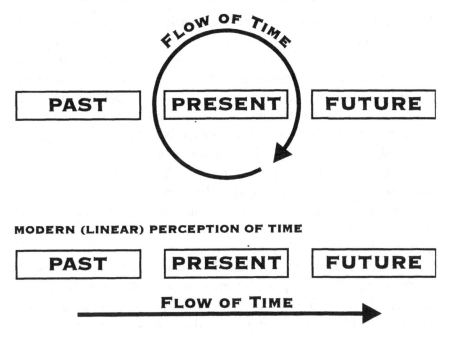

Figure 2.1 Cyclical verses Linear Perceptions of Time

reality of time. Such feelings were undoubtedly the true source of ancient wonder. What's more, it is surely such a concept of awe which we need to recapture in order to create successful Future Organizations.

Today, far too many people—and in particular far too many employees—see their careers, their products, and their markets, as given and unyielding. Too few individuals therefore make any attempt to add to the future, and hence to immortalize themselves beyond the genetic reproduction of the flesh. Sadly only a handful of humanity really attempt to engineer and to propagate radically fresh memes. Yet as Richard Dawkins contends, 'we should not seek immortality in reproduction'.[43] We should also remember that it is not just the Pharaohs whom the Pyramids are keeping alive. In addition, they also embody the labours and the very souls of *every* person who slaved in their realization.

CATHEDRALS IN ETERNITY

It would be foolhardy to suggest that the ancient Egyptians were the sole champions of past awe and wonder. There were, after all, seven wonders of the ancient world. What's more some—such as the Pharos light-house—served a more useful function than the Egyptian tombs. Indeed the Pyramids, although created to protect the bodies and treasures of the Pharaohs, failed completely in this task. It is in fact for this very reason that later Pharaohs reverted to less elaborate mastaba tombs, such as that of Tutankhamen which lay undiscovered for several millennia. However, as we have seen, works of awe—accomplishments of wonder—cannot really be judged only with respect to their physical practicality.

Like the Pyramids, the cathedrals of medieval Europe were not built purely to satisfy material needs. Rather, they had the greater human purpose of freeing entire societies from the confines of the present.[44] Like churches, mosques, temples, chapels and synagogues around the world, cathedrals once provided entire communities with hope, with guidance, with learning, with art, as well as with a spiritual focus. It is therefore not that difficult to comprehend why so many poor people gave of so much in the building of magnificent places of worship. Masons would labour all of their lives sculpting detail upon buildings which they knew they themselves, nor their children, nor even their *grandchildren*, would ever see completed. Yet they laboured with pride knowing that their patience would one day be rewarded. The mason's descendants would behold the results of their craft and dedication, even if their immediate offspring could not.

LIVING FOR TODAY & BUILDING FOR THE FUTURE

There can be little doubt that in days gone by many people accepted the need to take part in momentous projects which consumed decades, let alone multiple human lifespans. In contrast, in the blinkered, short-term-dominated world of today, we are lucky if even the largest of organiz-ations are looking more than a decade ahead. How, then, can we hope to overcome some of our greatest challenges? The only answer can be that we need to foster a new mindset—a new meme—towards restoring pride in projects which may not be realized in the blinkered profit horizons of the here-and-now. Reality can be changed, but only if we again come to take pride in accomplishments beyond the capabilities of individuals and small groups within the short-term.

The ancient Egyptians embraced modernity, as did all those who crafted the wonders (ancient or otherwise) of our past. Granted, as many managers today argue, we cannot live and work solely for great goals and horizons far ahead. Year end performances and quarterly results may not simply be ignored. If they were, then many companies would risk going out of business. The answer? Perhaps *to live for today* (there is, after all, always that unseen bus to consider), *to plan for tomorrow* (in order to survive), but most importantly *to build for the future*. This idea hopefully constitutes one of our first memes for long-term future success. Indeed, it will form one element of the Future Mindset to be presented in **chapter 17**.

A DARKLY BEAUTIFUL WOMAN

Within this chapter we have begun to explore the ability of some of our forebears to realize great visions requiring forward-looking patterns of organization. In the next, we will contrast their labours with those of the near-present day. Inevitably—perhaps thankfully—constraints of space have led our investigations of past wonders to focus in the main upon a single civilization and its famous tombs. Yet in this I do not think that we have been cheated. For men and women around the globe, the magic of ancient Egypt continues to transcend much of what we today perceive as so solid and so 'real'. Encapsulated in stone in the desert, the ghosts of one of the first truly great civilizations still have the power to make our present world seem more than a little temporary and synthetic.[45]

When setting out to write this chapter, I hoped to capture the awe of times in the desert so long ago and so far away. Fortunately, in my quest I came across the writings of Joseph Kaster. To cite the introduction to his splendid work upon the wisdom of the monarchs of the Nile:

> Ancient Egypt is like one of those darkly beautiful women who seem to exude an aura of deep and awesome mystery and in whose languid eyes there lurk nameless secrets and desires. She is sometimes radiant with

splendid majesty, sometimes shimmering with undulating gleams of languorous sensuality, always glamorous, always entrancing men with the unearthly magic of her fascination.[46]

To Kaster's poetic introduction there can be little left to add. Save, that is, for the fact that the ancient Egyptians did not choose to distinguish between the mythic and the real.[47] Maybe that's why their civilization still endures in our race memory. Perhaps it also explains why we face so much difficulty nowadays in creating achievements capable of demanding awe and of inviting reverence. And in that there may just be another of our many lessons for the future.

3
The Age
of Invention

History will remember the twentieth century for two technological developments: atomic energy and space flight. One threatened the extinction of society, one offered a survival possibility . . .

Neil Armstrong[48]

IN 1958 EGON LARSEN published a book entitled *Atomic Energy: The Layman's Guide to the Nuclear Age*.[49] In spite of the holocaustic mushroom cloud featured upon its cover, this hopeful tome did not contain any material relating to the development of nuclear weapons. Rather, its controlled scientific prose concentrated upon the most likely peaceful applications for nuclear power.

Included within Larson's book were schematics for nuclear power stations capable of generating the extremely low cost electricity due to end 'poverty, starvation, cold and discomfort'.[50] *The Nuclear Age* also confidently predicted that nuclear power would become 'the norm for marine propulsion within a quarter of a century'.[51] The development of atomic aeroplanes was also assured, once certain reliability and weight problems had been overcome.[52] Analysis even extended to the possibilities for nuclear automobiles. This said, the development of atomic cars was thought to be unlikely due to the vast energy savings soon to be reaped in so many other spheres.[53]

I do not mention Egon Larson's book in order to poke ridicule at scientific predictions which have failed to become a reality. Rather, I refer to his optimistic work of once-science-fact to draw attention to the achievement focus of humanity within the Present Age. Larsen's predictions were based upon a faith, common for the period, in the sheer cleverness of science and technology. For many decades there was a definite belief that, whatever problems humanity faced, sooner or later they would all be overcome by a dedicated army of white-coated backroom boffins. After all, whatever else you may think about nuclear physics, one surely has to respect the ingenuity behind any science that plays with the very components of atoms. The past one hundred or so years (the period of time that we are taking within this book to equate to 'the present') has undoubtedly been a period of radical and almost universally applauded technological innovation.

THE CHANGING FACE OF WONDER

In the past, most lasting achievements involved the construction of a physical structure of such magnificence that it inspired awe and reverence. Past wonders were physical creations of might. However, across the Present Age, it has usually been the *cleverness* of fellow human beings which has most inspired and amazed other members of the population. Granted, in the 20th century, numerous achievements in science and technology have led to the creation of many incredible products, communications media, and new means of transportation. Such creations have also greatly improved many people's standards of living. However, notwithstanding this fact, it has largely been the ingenuity *behind* the invention and application of new forms of power, manufacture and communication which has most inspired wonder.

With new principles—or new *means* of doing things—applauded to such a high status, scientists and inventors have become the dominant meme-setters of the Present Age. The very act of invention itself has become something to be respected and admired. Indeed, one of the most significant features of modern Western civilization has been the 'invention of invention'; of the establishment of legal and social systems and structures supportive of inventors and their ideas.[54]

Archaeologist John Romer once stated that, since ancient times, the very *nature* of wonder has changed. As he explains:

It's not the hardware any more—it's not the buildings. It's the software that designs them. It's not great statues any more, it's the pill. It's the telephone—the thing that joins all the buildings in the world—not just one building. It's *process*.[55]

As detailed in **chapter 2**, the great legacy of the ancient Egyptian architect Imhotep is his Step Pyramid at Saqqara. In contrast, Thomas Alva Edison is remembered for *inventing* electric light and sound recording, rather than for any individual incandescent filament lamp or phonograph device.[56] In championing electricity, Edison gave the world a new *source* of power, together with several new *means* of illumination and new *forms* of entertainment. It is therefore Edison's *acts* of ingenuity (and their subsequent consequences) which remain wondrous to this day. And it is a celebration of human ingenuity—of accomplishments wherein the tangible output of the act of achievement is secondary to the act itself—which is undertaken within this chapter.

ACHIEVEMENTS OF THE PRESENT

Ingenious accomplishments have taken place in such multitude in recent times that it would be difficult to list them all herein, let alone discuss their individual significances. As illustrated in **table 3.1**, a great many of the technologies and processes which we take for granted today have been the product of the past 120 years. As a consequence, we live very different lives from those of most of our ancestors.

Without the development of the internal combustion engine and petrochemicals we would not now enjoy the personal freedom of the motor car, nor the luxury of powered flight. Without the telephone we could not be in instantaneous contact with others around the globe. Without magnetic recording, movies, and television, we would have to change many of our educational and leisure activities, not to mention working practices. Without the xerox process, fax machines, and computers, we would now struggle to cope with the complexity of current business functioning. And without reliable electricity supply networks—be they fed

TECHNOLOGY / PROCESS	YEAR
Telephone	1876
Sound recording	1877
Electric light bulb	1879
Petrol driven automobile	1885
Cinema	1895
Powered flight	1903
Moving assembly line	1913
Quick-frozen food	1925
Television	1926
Penicillin	1928
Jet aircraft	1939
Xerox copying	1942
Colour television	1950
Videotape recording	1956
Communications satellite	1958
Birth control pill	1960
Pocket calculator	1972
Fibre optics	1975
Compact discs	1979
IBM Personal Computer	1981

* Whilst the above lists the generally-accepted date for the invention of the process or technology named, it should be appreciated that the majority of the above took many years —and in some instances many decades—to enter common application. For example, most homes did not have mains electricity (and hence electric lighting) until well into the 20th century. Other electrical domestic appliances—such as washing machines and refrigerators—were also not owned by many until after WWII. Colour television was not common until the 1970s, whilst home video recording remained a novelty until the 1980s.

Table 3.1 **Wonders of the Present Age**

from coal, oil, nuclear or hydroelectric sources of power generation—all modern economies would rapidly grind to a halt. Yet when most people's great-grandparents were born, *none* of the aforementioned wonders existed, let alone could they be found in common application. Indeed, in stark contrast to the eternal, repetitive cycles of life experienced by most of our ancestors since antiquity, the novelty of contemporary experience can only be described as astonishing.[57]

Just as we used the construction of the Pyramids as a past icon of awe in the last chapter, so now we will focus upon a single great project to highlight the achievement focus of ingenuity within the Present Age. As already cited, there are many, many wonders whose stories could be investigated. Indeed, many developments in communications media, physical transportation, and means of manufacturing, will be detailed in later chapters. However, over the next few pages we will consider what has to be the greatest ever feat of technical and organizational engineering as yet undertaken by humanity. It may be over twenty-five years since Neil Armstrong stepped from the ladder of the *Eagle*. However, his footfall surely remains the greatest leap forward ever to have been taken by humankind.

THE POLITICS OF SPACE

By the late-1950s, the fledgling sciences of electronics and digital computing had progressed to a point where the control and communications systems necessary for space travel could become a reality. Multi-stage rockets capable of flight in the vacuum of space had also been developed. The key technologies necessary for exploration beyond the Earth were therefore in existence. However, it took the Cold War between the United States and the former Soviet Union to kick-start the quest for human beings to reach out beyond their first planet.

In order to demonstrate their superiority, both the Russians and the Americans wanted to be ahead in any race to further new technologies. In particular, dominance in rocket engineering was seen as crucial, as it was rocket technologies which would permit the development of intercontinental ballistic missiles (ICBMs) capable of militarily crushing any opponent. Hence, when on the 4th of October 1957, the Russians succeeded in launching Sputnik[58]—the first man-made satellite—the Americans had to rise to the challenge. However, before the United States managed to successfully launch its own Explorer 1, the Soviets had put a dog (Lakia) into orbit to become the first living creature in space. A third space first in a row was then won by the Russians when, on the 12th of April 1961, cosmonaut Yuri Gagarin became the first man in space.

Three weeks after Gagarin's flight, the United States successfully launched its first astronaut.[59] However, there could be no denying that the Russians had taken the lead in space exploration. Other Cold War developments were also going badly for the United States.[60] The Americans therefore needed to take swift and decisive action if they were to restore their battered international pride and superpower reputation. As Senate Leader Lyndon Johnson contended, there was a risk that, just as the Roman Empire had controlled its roads and the British Empire the oceans, so the Soviet empire could end up dominating the new territory of space.[61]

NOT BECAUSE IT WAS EASY

In order to beat the Russians, the Americans needed a target sufficiently far enough ahead that they would not be disadvantaged in its attainment by early Soviet space success. On the 25th of May 1961 President John F. Kennedy therefore announced the national goal of setting an American upon the Moon by the end of the decade.[62] As he continued within his historic address to Congress:

> No single space project in this period will be more impressive to mankind—or more important for the exploration of space—and none will be so difficult or expensive to accomplish . . . . We choose to go to the Moon in this decade and do the other things not because they are easy, but because they are hard. We set sail on this new sea because there is new knowledge to be gained, and new rights to be won, and they must be won and used for the progress of all mankind.

With the above invitation, Kennedy gave the American people the wondrous challenge of conquering the final great frontier. However, many of the top scientists at the National Aeronautics and Space Administration (NASA) did not believe that Kennedy's goal could be achieved. The programme to send a man to the Moon was very much instigated upon political grounds. Actual technological capabilities had very little to do with it.[63] In 1961, travelling to the Moon—let alone attempting a landing—*was impossible.* Neither the Americans nor the Russians had walked in space, manoeuvred ships outside of the atmosphere, or attempted any kind of spacecraft docking. Yet all of these skills and more would be needed in order to set a human being upon the surface of the Moon over 250,000 miles away. Technical and organizational ingenuity were called for in the extreme. Hardly surprisingly, the project was therefore to prove as difficult and as expensive as President Kennedy had predicted.

The initial $1.7bn allocated to NASA to kick-start the moonlandings programme would prove to be just the tip of the iceberg. Overall, the final cost of sending Americans to the Moon amounted to around $24bn—or the equivalent of $120 a year from every US citizen for the nine year duration of the programme.[64] Human resource commitments were equally great. Indeed, NASA had to engage a staggering 20,000 industrial contractors and 400,000 technicians, engineers, managers and administrators.[65] However, in distributing contracts, NASA was at least careful to ensure that work upon the space programme was spread as evenly as possible across all US states.

CHARIOTS OF THE GODS

The moonlandings programme progressed through three distinct phases. Firstly there came the Mercury missions, which carried a single astronaut into space.[66] These largely automatic flights continued until the May of 1963, by which time NASA boasted fifteen astronauts upon its payroll.

Following Mercury came Gemini. Weighing three and a half tons, Gemini capsules were far larger than their predecessors. They were also designed to carry two astronauts, and to be far more manoeuvrable than any previous Russian or American spacecraft. Ten manned Gemini flights took place between March 1965 and January 1966. Every mission accumulated more and more of the technical and human expertise vital for future lunar missions.[67] Indeed, by the time the Gemini programme was completed, the Americans had finally started to pull ahead of the Soviets in the accomplishment of critical space procedures. It is therefore little wonder that Gemini came to be affectionately known as the 'little spaceship that could'.

The third and final phase of the moonlandings programme was Apollo. However, after Gemini's success, its initial progress proved to be disappointing and slow. Deadlines were continually missed due to a range of technical and design problems. Indeed, in a press conference in late 1966, NASA freely admitted to having experienced over 25,000 failures of one kind or another.[68] Events were also to turn from bad to worse. On the 27th of January 1967 a launchpad rehearsal ended in disaster. Pressurized with 100% oxygen to test its hull integrity, Apollo 1 experienced a cabin fire caused by an electrical short circuit. None of those aboard stood a chance, and astronauts Gus Grissom, Ed White, and Roger Chaffe, were asphyxiated in a mere eight and a half seconds.[69]

As a result of the accident, further delays were inevitable. There was also a very real possibility that the entire programme would be cancelled. A team of 1500 people investigated the charred remains of the horrific fire, and delivered a damning 3300 page report. Management structures at NASA were quickly overhauled, whilst there was a $0.5bn redesign of both the Apollo capsule and of the lunar module intended to carry men to the Moon's surface. Both craft had to be absolutely free from any risk of fire. Speaking years later, NASA Flight Director Chris Kraft recalled the Apollo 1 accident as 'unforgivable'. However, he also noted that the tragedy instigated 'a new resolve and a strengthened commitment to get the job done', without which many of the problems which plagued Apollo's systems might never have been overcome.[70]

Confidence in Apollo did not start to return until the first Saturn V rocket successfully carried an unmanned Apollo craft and lunar module into earth orbit in the November of 1967. Towering over 350 feet high, loaded with over 500,000 gallons of fuel, and capable of delivering 7.5 million pounds of thrust, Saturn V launch vehicles were mighty beasts indeed. On the 1st of October 1968, a smaller Saturn 1B carried the first manned Apollo capsule into space.[71] Over two and a half years since the previous US manned space mission, this flight finally exorcized the lingering ghosts of Apollo 1, with the newly designed craft performing to perfection.

THE GREATEST GAMBLE

In the fall of 1968, time was growing thin to achieve the goal of setting a man upon the Moon by the end of the decade. All future flights had to go perfectly, and there were rumours that the Russians were about to get there first. Indeed, in September 1968, a Soviet Zond craft had flown around the Moon with a cargo of tortoises, flies and worms which had been successfully returned to the Earth.[72] The Americans had to do something and fast.

Despite the fact that there had only been one manned Apollo flight, in the late December of 1968 NASA decided that the next Apollo mission should take its crew into lunar orbit. Almost certainly this was the greatest ever gamble of the US space programme. Fortunately it paid off. Over half a billion people followed Apollo 8's progress. All listened intently to live telecasts as some of the first 'poets in space suits' described the distant Earth as a 'grand oasis in the big vastness of space'. Both the confines and the majesty of our parent planet could never be quite the same again.

Apollo 8's crew made a safe return home a few days later. Apollos' 9 and 10 then flew two further test flights to practise lunar module docking procedures in orbit around the Earth and subsequently around the Moon. With both of these missions successful, the stage came to be set for the launch of Neil Armstrong, Edwin (Buzz) Aldrin and Michael Collins aboard Apollo 11 upon the 16th of July 1969.

THE FINAL STEP

By the 20th of July Apollo 11 was in lunar orbit, and Neil Armstrong and Buzz Aldrin had transferred into their lunar module—the *Eagle*—for their historic journey down to the surface. However, their descent was not to be quite as uneventful as planned. For a start, the *Eagle*'s computer soon signalled that it was overloading. A slight navigation error had also thrown the lunar module off course. Tensions mounted as Armstrong was forced to manoeuvre his tiny craft clear of a perilous landing site strewn with large boulders. With only sixteen seconds of fuel remaining before an abort would have been inevitable, the lunar module's three landing pads touched solid ground. As Armstrong reported to the nail-bitten population of a nervous planet 250,000 miles away across space, the *Eagle* had landed.

On the morning of the 21st of July 1969—eight years after Kennedy's promise to his nation—Neil Armstrong opened the *Eagle*'s hatch and clambered down the ladder. As he dropped the final three feet from the bottom rung to the Moon's surface, he spoke those words now etched into history: 'That's one small step for man, one giant leap for mankind'. The great dream of the decade had finally become a reality.

Armstrong and Aldrin spent about two hours exploring the 'magnificent desolation' of the lunar terrain. They also collected soil and rock samples and planted an American flag.[73] Time was even found for the astronauts to take 'the most historic phone call ever made' from President Nixon. During all of these activities, a world-wide television audience looked on courtesy of a live black-and-white television camera placed sixty feet from the lunar module. As with all other phases of the Apollo programme, NASA had made sure that each historic event would be witnessed from as wide a range of viewpoints as possible.[74]

After Neil and Buzz had safely blasted-off to rendezvous with their command module for their return to Earth, the Moon was once again a lifeless satellite. However, it did retain the discarded descent stage of its visitors' lunar module. The side of this abandoned craft also bore a plaque with the simple message:

HERE MEN FROM THE PLANET EARTH
FIRST SET FOOT UPON THE MOON
JULY 1969, A. D.

Armstrong, Aldrin and Collins (who had remained in lunar orbit to pilot the command module) returned to the Earth as heroes. Nine Apollo missions were planned to follow them to the Moon. However, this number was cut to six after Apollo 13 suffered an explosion 200,000 miles out in space and very nearly failed to return its crew safely back to the Earth.[75]

By the time that the moonlandings programme came to an end in the December of 1972, astronauts were no longer mythical figures. Indeed, moonshots had almost become run-of-the-mill. A total of twenty-four astronauts had managed to travel to the Moon (some twice), with twelve men having been granted the privilege of walking upon its surface. 'Old' Apollo and Saturn rocket hardware flew again in 1973 and 1974 with the brief establishment of the Skylab space station.[76] A final Apollo flight occurred in the July of 1975 in a joint US/Soviet mission in which an Apollo and a Soyuz spacecraft docked in Earth orbit. This link up was one of the first acts of superpower cooperation to signal the ending of the Cold War—the political conflict whose rivalry had fuelled the race to the Moon in the first place.

THE PRICE OF ADVENTURE

Ever since manned space flights began in the early 1960s, there have been those who have questioned their worth. After all, even with research and development costs excluded, the price tag for a single Apollo moonshot amounted to over $400 million. Clearly a case can be made that such money could have been better spent upon the poor and the starving here on Earth. After all, what did Americans really gain by setting foot upon the Moon? Simply some expensive national prestige coupled with a little political capital for whoever happened to be in the White House? Almost certainly not. The US moonlandings programme gave the world, let alone the United States, far, far more than that.

Some proponents of manned space flight point to the value of technological innovations that resulted from programmes such as Apollo in order to justify their cause. Perhaps most notably, the development of microelectronics was radically advanced. Teflon—the non-stick coating now found adorning most frying pans—was also a by-product of the space race. So were velcro fastening strips. However, it is unlikely that the moonlandings budget could ever have been justified purely as a catalyst for technological development. Indeed, President Kennedy said nothing of the advancement of science or technology—nor did he even promise any military or commercial benefits—when he committed America to the space race.[77]

A level up from direct scientific and technological returns, the moonlandings programme was about demonstrating the feasibility of new forms of transportation. As Werner von Braun, NASA's chief rocket scientist, once argued, Apollo was about opening up the new frontier of space. As he analogized, when Charles Lindbergh made the first non-stop solo flight across the Atlantic, nobody believed that his sole purpose was to get to Paris. Rather, Lindbergh had set out to prove the feasibility of trans-oceanic air travel.[78] In a similar vein, the Apollo programme set out to empower a new reality in exploration and transportation by using a common goal (the Moon) as its target, or as 'its Paris'.[79] However, even this argument, whilst powerful, does not explain the true value of the Apollo programme.

Rather than being physical and technological, the real triumphs of the race to the Moon—the real rewards—were and remain psychological. The whole programme was about leaping new mental frontiers rather than proving humanity's ability to overcome technological hurdles. It was therefore the very act of achievement which left the greatest of marks. For as Buzz Aldrin, the second man to walk upon the Moon, later noted:

> To me the most important part of the mission was what happened in the minds of the people who witnessed that event. They will never forget that. We [the astronauts] won't either. But something very important happened and it wasn't up on the Moon.[80]

TOWARDS IMAGINATION

Setting a man upon the Moon almost certainly remains the most ingenious wonder of the Present Age. Around 20,000 companies and 400,000 people all dedicated towards one footfall 250,000 miles away which changed the way we think about ourselves. However, for many the question remains of why we did not attempt to further capitalize upon Apollo's triumph. As the NASA Flight Director who watched over Apollo 11 from Earth, and who believes that achievements like the moonlandings are what 'life is all about', once commented:

> God we were there. Why the heck did we surrender? Why did we not go back? Why have we become so complacent about exploration? Why do we

not continue to pursue every opportunity to delve into the unknown, to unlock the mysteries? Why are we not sending our explorers not just to the Moon, but on to Mars? It's really frustrating to see us *there*, then all of a sudden to just sit back and say 'it's all over'.[81]

Perhaps the answer to the above lies in the fact that we now know that of which we are capable. Ingenious acts by themselves are no longer enough to satisfy our lust. We certainly *could* continue to go to the Moon. However, to do so we would first need to be presented with another and powerful 'why'. For the moment we shall leave any such 'why' unexplored. However, its necessity will be raised again within **chapter 13**.

It took less than 100 years to progress from the invention of the first light bulb to the first microprocessor.[82] The means by which human beings may dominate nature have indeed come a very long way in a very short space of time. And so, perhaps, as a race we have become more than a little tired of ingenuity and of invention. In the place of a youthful desire to blindly create, a realization is now dawning that more than ever it is *why* we choose to do things, rather than *how* we come to achieve them, or exactly *what* physical products may result from our actions, which ought to demand the greatest significance and respect.

Today, an increasingly number of the population are beginning to question just exactly what constitutes 'progress', and hence the most sensible road ahead. No longer do students successfully completing MBAs or other business degrees always foster earnings maximization as their primary objective. More and more, potential 'high flyers' are now opting for less demanding and less stressful career activities which will permit a better quality of life. In fact across the West, for those in work the talk is now as much of reducing stress and of clawing back lost leisure time as it is of gathering in greater financial rewards. What we perceive as *progress*—as *achievement*—is coming to be questioned once again. In future it will not even be *process* which constitutes wonder. It will be the ideas behind ingenious acts. It will be *imagination*.

At an individual as well as national level, there is now a subtle shift afoot in our achievement focus from the *what* to the *how* to the *why*. In order to cope with this change, Future Organizations will require radically new goals, new mindsets, and maybe even new dreams. What's more, with the *what* and the *how* now achieved in many quarters, Future

Organizations will also need to capitalize upon creativity more than in any other age if they are to avoid stagnation and decay.

4
Creativity
& Decay

IN 1975 MOVIE DIRECTOR George Lucas formed a company named Industrial Light and Magic (ILM) to create the spectacular space battles for his film *Star Wars*. Since the ending of the studio system, the Hollywood special effects industry had been in decline. However, with the formation of ILM, Lucas managed to reverse this trend. Working not only upon Lucas' *Star Wars* and *Indiana Jones* trilogies, but in addition upon several other blockbusters of the period, ILM came to paint celluloid visions the like of which had never been seen before. Whether it was flying space vehicles, assisting archaeologists in swashbuckling escapes, or even conjuring forth the wrath of God, ILM became the undisputed champion of movie fantasy.

Just as amazing as ILM's fictional creations were the models, computerized camera control systems, and composite optical printers, which its technicians created in order to render magic upon the big screen. By the time ILM was working upon *Return of the Jedi* in the early 1980s, some of its extraordinary models were costing tens of thousands of dollars to produce. Occasionally, miniatures were having to be formed from a nickel plating just one 15,000th of an inch thick. Other models, cast in fibreglass over aluminium, boasted such powerful internal lighting systems that they required compressed air cooling to prevent them from melting before the cameras.[83] There were also instances where seventy or more separately filmed elements were being optically composited together within some action sequences.

In order to realize its technical marvels, ILM boasted artists and innovators skilled in electrical and electronic engineering, as well as in the fashioning of all types of metals, resins, mould-making compounds, and plastics. A decade ago there was nothing that ILM could not create by either building a model or by painting upon glass and then placing the result before a camera. Every element of each special effects composite was an ingenious and painstakingly crafted work of art in its own right.

Today, whilst George Lucas' technicians remain at the top of the special effects business, the ILM model shop has all but disappeared. In place of metals, plastics and glass—camera tape, human sweat, and finely oiled gearing—most of the company's magical creations are now built within computers. Space ships, and the lights that illuminate them, are now virtual, not 'real'. In a similar fashion, you can no longer buy painted cells from the latest Disney animations, because these too now only exist as bit-patterns within computer memory.

Undoubtably, the quality and the range of movie effects which may now be created has increased. Yet there has been a human cost. As ILM animator Phil Tippett bemoans, computers have 'short circuited' a lot of careers. No longer is it economically viable for model makers to craft physical works of art with their hands. In fact, non-computer technologies are no longer even considered good enough to 'get the slickness required' for a $60 million movie.[84]

With computers, *anything* that may be dreamed can now become a movie reality. Physical technical skills are simply no longer a constraint. As special effects has 'gone bitmap', so the only remaining limit to movie magic is the director's imagination. During a restructuring in 1993, it was therefore hardly a surprise that ILM was reorganized to become a division of Lucas Digital Limited.[85]

FROM INGENUITY TO IMAGINATION

The changing face of movie special effects reflects a widespread and radical evolution in the way in which human beings have begun to produce goods and services, to communicate, and to trade. Digital technologies are now flooding many industrial sectors, with few organizations likely to remain untouched by the binary tide. As this trend continues, tactile wonders are becoming more of a rarity. And, as the case of ILM illustrates, no longer are achievements crafted within the 'real world' always the most wondrous.

Increasingly, synthetic, electronic creations are likely to prove 'better' (or at least more cost-effective) than the real thing. Like it or not, the Age of Ingenuity is coming to an end. In its place, the Imagination Age is beginning to dawn. In the future, it will be the *idea* behind most great achievements that will be most wondrous, rather than the skills employed in any act of realization, or the physical fabric of any end product. As noted at the end of the last chapter, the achievement focus of humanity has switched away from the *what* or the *how* and towards the *why*.

CHALLENGES AHEAD

After thousands of years struggling to overcome nature, the human race is finally reaching a plateau from which it will be capable of constructing any future reality it so chooses to create. Granted, as I hear some critics quickly contend, we are still a long way from being able to build a *Star Trek* style matter transporter. Nor will human beings soon be able to travel freely within outer space or abreast the endless rivers of time. However, with rapidly converging developments in computing, genetic engineering, and a host of other technologies, many of the barriers which once constrained human accomplishment will soon be no more. Unfortunately, this turn of events will place two serious dilemmas before the Future Organization.

Firstly, as we enter an age in which anything will be possible, there will be the very real danger that fewer and fewer human achievements will actually come to *mean* anything. Eventual omnipotence over nature may be judged a two-edged sword. Bad ideas will become just as technically feasible as good ones. It will therefore become extremely difficult to identify truly innovatory products and services whose eventual production will actually add value to an organization. Any product will be capable of being computerized, of being smart, and of being tailored by programmable plant to individual customer specification. With technological and knowledge barriers receding on all fronts, in future choosing which markets to target will become even more difficult than it is today.

Our second future dilemma concerns the fact that, whilst technologies will certainly be available to reshape both physical and mental realities towards any human whim, they will also be increasingly resource intensive. In other words, the price of custom realities will be high. Even if a future Utopia exists, it will certainly not be on offer for the majority. Indeed, there are already disturbing signs that society will increasingly segment. At one extreme, there may well emerge a technologically-empowered 'overclass' keen to realize its elite and 'selfish' desires in plush isolation. At the other end of the spectrum, there will be those now labelled as the 'underclass'. This majority group of have-nots will be impoverished due to the rape of scarce resources by those who hide away from reality behind paranoic barriers of concrete, knowledge and digital electronics. In the long-term, such a sorry state of affairs is likely to prove very bad news for the Future Organization. After all, the larger the underclass/overclass rift becomes, and the longer it is perpetuated, the more likely it will be that advanced economies and financial systems will be destabilized, and that sooner or later their great organizations will fall.

The above two dilemmas leave us with two key challenges ahead. On the one hand, future managers will need to be capable of separating purpose from purposelessness. On the other, Future Organizations (some of whom will be what we currently label as 'governments') will also need to find means of formulating visions and of realizing wonders across increasingly disparate social and economic stratospheres. A tall order on both counts. However, as we have begun to witness within the previous two chapters, incredible accomplishments have already become the hallmark of humanity. Indeed, both as a race and as individuals, we invariably function most effectively when desperation looms large and the chips are down.[86]

TECHNOLOGICAL VISIONS

To take on board the above challenges it is important to have an appreciation of some current key areas of cutting-edge technological development. It may at first seem strange to focus upon any new technologies in a chapter about the rising power of imagination as the key achievement focus of the future. However, it is paradoxically because future technologies will be so incredibly *powerful* that their *perceived significance* in the accomplishment of great future achievements is likely to diminish. To demonstrate this point, we need only consider how the value of some 'amazing' technologies is ignored even today. For example, the global telephone network is now taken for granted. The value of an apparently limitless electrical energy supply is also hardly given a second thought.

Like many other critical technologies, telephones and electrical power have become a part of the ubiquitous nervous system of contemporary humanity. Their added value is therefore beyond common perception and hence conscious appreciation. As with food or water, most people today would only appreciate the true value of phones or electricity in their prolonged absence. Indeed, as most technologies develop and become more powerful, we simply build on top of them. Their use thereby becomes transparent.

By developing technologies we develop our environment, and hence our current perception of reality. In studying a future achievement focus of imagination, we therefore need some appreciation of the likely capabilities of currently cutting-edge technologies which will soon become ubiquitous within our lives, and which will hence soon be taken for granted. Today we may turn on a light, or call a friend in Australia, without a second thought as to the technology involved. Similarly, in future we are likely to accept conversing with computers in natural spoken languages, designer genetics, and even meeting with 'remote' individuals in virtual reality, as little more than run-of-the-mill.

Many futurists have grouped together specific sets of technological innovations which they think likely to play a key role in the decades ahead. Some such forward-gazers are business analysts; their concerns primarily focused upon new means of product and service manufacture and distribution. One such individual is Daniel Burrus. Within his very readable book *Techno Trends*, Burrus cites a list of 'technologies that will revolutionize our lives' (and whose adoption may hence increase business competitiveness). Specifically, Burrus' list includes genetic engineering and biochemistry, digital electronics and advanced computing, optical data storage, artificial intelligence, lasers and fibre optics, advanced satellites, micromechanics, new polymers, high-tech ceramics, superconductors, and molecular designing.[87]

As distinct from business technology watchers, a second group of futurists may be labelled as the 'transhumanists'. This collection of individuals is dedicated to the advancement of technologies which may permit a proactive hand to be exercised within human evolution. Transhumanists believe that humanity is destined to advance beyond the flesh. They are therefore interested in all practices and systems likely to be of assistance in the continuation of life beyond the body. These include developments in cybernetics, cryogenic freezing, and direct neural-computer links for 'uploading' human minds.[88]

A third category of future gazers, and one which boasts both business analysts and transhumanists amongst its ranks, may be termed the 'cyberians'. This powerful and wide-ranging classification of futurists believe that the electronic information domain of 'cyberspace' holds the key to our advancement. In particular, cyberians advocate the many technologies which may enable virtual reality (VR) cyberspace access as the most critical future social and business tools.[89]

Several proponents of VR have claimed that soon many people will play out large proportions of both their business and personal lives within virtual graphics worlds. Such predictions have led to the publication of a plethora of books.[90] They have also instigated numerous heated debates regarding the benefits, drawbacks, and likelihood, of future VR development. Many of these arguments are both important and wide ranging. The future role of virtual reality within business and leisure activities is therefore explored in comparative isolation from other debates within **chapter 10**.

From the above it should be apparent that providing a simple, concise, yet comprehensive coverage of all of the technological developments likely to transparently empower future human achievement is nigh-on impossible. Just two key areas of progress will therefore be chosen for closer scrutiny within this chapter. Firstly, there will be some further analysis of the increasing trend towards digitization. Secondly, we will scrape the surface of the science of genetic engineering. Whilst we are only going to focus upon developments within these two key fields, the message to be gained should be clear enough: when it comes to techno-logical advancement, the best (or worst) is yet to come.

DIGITIZATION & THE DIGITAL AGE

Digitization is the encoding of previously physical products and information media into an electronic format which may be stored and processed within computers. As already noted with the case of Industrial Light and Magic, the trend to go digital has already begun to transform some business organizations. What's more, no longer are computers only employed to process and to store data converted into digital patterns. Just as importantly, computers are now also becoming globally interconnected to serve as our primary business communications network. As explored within my previous book *Cyber Business*, the emergent 'global hardware platform' of information technology systems so interlinked is already presenting organizations with a challenging new frontier across which to market, to sell, and to distribute their wares.[91]

One of the many analysts enthusing about the trend for digitization is Nicholas Negroponte. The director of the Media Laboratory at the Massachusetts Institute of Technology (MIT), Negroponte contends that business functioning is starting to shift away from the production and the transportation of *atoms*. In place of such an 'atom-focus', businesses are instead starting to concentrate their activities upon the production and the communication of intangible *bits* of computer data.[92]

The bit—or the binary digit represented by either a '1' or a '0' (an 'on' or an 'off')—looks destined to become the future unit of world trade. Granted, as Negroponte admits, the shift from atoms to bits will not be able to transform every industry. Food produce, clothing and shelter will certainly remain physical in nature for a very long time to come. However, we can certainly not ignore the impact of digital technologies upon the productive outputs of either individual human beings or their wider organizations. As artificial reality guru Myron Krueger reminds us, interfacing with computer technology has now become a permanent aspect of the human condition.[93]

PATENTS, COPYRIGHT & DIGITAL COPIES

As the world goes digital, there will no longer be any such thing as a 'final product' or a 'definitive copy'. Once encoded into binary patterns, *any* creation—be it a drawing, a movie, a novel or even a future VR holiday resort—may be replicated an infinite number of times over without any fidelity being lost. 'Originals' will no longer have any more value than copies. Rather, the two will simply be identical. The value of digital products is therefore likely to decay rapidly if new copyright laws and/or data protection systems are not introduced.

The achievements of the inventors and entrepreneurs of the Present Age have in general been well protected. This has been because patent legislation has enjoyed both widespread enforcement and public respect. Indeed, in the 19th century, many new processes came to be developed purely because of the need for inventors to avoid the infringement of the patent rights of other parties.[94] Alarmingly, however, the copyright laws needed to safeguard the value of many future products of the Imagination Age are nowhere near so strong. Indeed, there are already hundreds of thousands of illegally made digital copies of texts, images, sounds and video clips paraded with no shame upon the Internet's world-wide web.[95]

In schools, children are actively encouraged to cut-and-paste text and images from multimedia reference sources. Students in colleges and universities are also applauded for 'surfing the Net' in order to locate (and then to copy?) the latest on-line information. Will such individuals leave their electronic collage mentality behind when they transfer into the business world? Probably not. Indeed, it is their digital cut-and-paste skills which are likely to be their most valued abilities. Bill Gates' company Corbis may be digitally stockpiling a million or more images in order to reap future royalty payments. Media conglomerates may be rubbing their corporate hands with glee in contemplation of the value of their film and video programme archives. Publishers and authors may also be looking forward to a spate of new royalty payments resulting from digital copies of their books. Yet all are likely to face mass piracy of their digital wares. The trouble is, stealing digital product is not only already widespread around the globe, *it isn't even perceived as 'wrong'*.

As the cyberpunk ethic states, 'information wants to be free'. Unless drastic measures are taken (which at present seem somewhat unlikely) we are therefore at risk of forging an economy based upon intangible outputs which will have less property protection than any other unit of trade ever known. The Japanese have predicted that thirty per cent of their gross domestic product will be derived over computer network links by the year 2020.[96] That's an awful a lot of added value to be floating around in cyberspace.

In future, ideas will more than ever before become a primary business resource. However, any value which may cling to resultant digital products will rapidly disseminate. The real business implication of 'being digital' may therefore not be the shift in trade from atoms to bits. Rather, far more significant may be the shift from a society and an economy in which key human and organizational achievements were well protected (by patents), to one in which they become barely protected (by inadequate and ignored copyright laws).[97] As Esther Dyson of EDventure Holdings of New York suggests, in future it will be those services which *transform* bits, rather than those that simply provide them, that will render most value added.[98] As a result, traditional forms of intellectual property (like copyrights) will decline in significance. In parallel, 'uncopiable' service/transformation processes will become the true value engines of the Future Organization.

CREATING THE DIGITAL HIVE

Furnishing digital lives represents a $5 trillion market opportunity.[99] However, to reap such rewards, organizations will have to convince their customers to move indoors so that they may live out their lives in a 'digital hive' wherein every human being will be electronically inter-linked. Once again we are witness to the possibility that the Age of Imagination may not be a Utopian age. To truly go digital—to accept products and services in binary abstraction—humankind has to retreat from its roots within the natural world. Unlikely? Almost certainly not. Some people already treat a telephone conversation as just as 'real' an encounter as one which commences with a handshake in the flesh. Electronic social exchanges are no longer the 'next best thing'. And this is before widespread video and VR-conferencing arrive en masse. As the proponents of global connectivity contend, in the New Age people will never be alone: they'll be wired. So just how long will it be before we are reading of the first person to be fitted with a surgically-implanted mobile phone? What's more, will the availability of such a prosthesis be reported as nightmare or as the realization of a yuppie dream?

Digitization itself arguably constitutes a form of future wonder. Already, every fact that can be digitized now is.[100] The entirety of human media output may now be made available for all current and future generations. All of our art and science may be communicated near-instantly anywhere around the globe. The embryonic and much-hyped 'information superhighway'[101] may become a focal force for uniting humanity. Alternatively, global connectivity may evolve into a negative influence; one solely used to empower a minority and élite overclass. Once again we have to weigh the balance; creativity or decay?

Many day-to-day implications of digital technologies will also be enormous. Once any product boasts electronic circuitry, it is potentially capable of becoming programmable and even 'smart'.[102] In the fairly near future, household devices will communicate with each other, entertainment systems will learn to automatically record the programmes which their owners most enjoy, and stolen cars will phone home to inform us of their location. Developments in computing and digital technology are accruing almost exponentially, and faster than even experts like Nicholas Negroponte can believe.[103] Indeed, as the *Being Digital* guru contends, 'you can expect to have on your wrist tomorrow what you have on your desk today, and what filled a room yesterday'.[104]

As we will discuss further across **chapters 10, 13** and **16**, digitization is a powerful force for both harmonization and empowerment. Ultimately, digitization will also globalize geography whilst decentralizing many modes of organization. As has been the case throughout history, artists (like those recently at Lucas Digital) have shown us the way.[105] However, it is the champions of more traditional industries who will carry digital technologies to their ultimate heights.

GAMES WITH LIFE

Bits of information are not only the primary constituents of an increasing number of products and services. Information is also the primary constituent of life. Computer data is at present processed, stored and transmitted by electronic, magnetic and optical means. In contrast, the biological information which defines the characteristics of different species, individuals, and their traits, is chemically encoded within each organism's genes. Hardly surprisingly, the decoding, recording and manipulation of the basic nature of living organisms is therefore known as genetic engineering.

In some instances, genetic engineering involves changing the inherent characteristics of microorganisms such as bacteria or viruses. Such changes may be undertaken in order to make the former microorganisms yield useful chemical products, or to adapt them to new and hostile environments. For example, the gene for insulin has now been isolated and can be introduced into certain bacteria cells. The genetically altered bacteria that results may then be grown in large quantities in order to produce a synthetic (or 'recombinant') insulin for the treatment of diabetes. Genetic engineering has also been used to produce a recombinant version of Factor VIII—the blood clotting agent required by haemophiliacs. As well as being available in potentially-infinite quantities, genetically synthesized drugs also involve none of the contamination risks that may be associated with compounds derived from 'natural' sources.[106]

Genetic engineering is now also being applied in the generation of vaccines and in the production of pharmaceutical compounds within the milk of animals. In future, the manufacture and the biochemical make-up of an increasing number of chemical compounds is likely to be influenced by genetic manipulation of one form or another. Used in combination with other technologies for molecular designing,[107] genetic engineering will permit any substance to be given any property we require, and to become available at any time and in any quantity.

DESIGNER GENES

As well as assisting in the creation and adaptation of drugs and other chemical compounds, genetic engineering now also includes the practice of gene therapy. This involves the manipulation of the DNA[108] of a living organism in order to correct or to prevent a particular trait, genetic disorder or ailment. Gene therapy has already been applied to engineer crops which are resistant to specific diseases. Farm animals have also been genetically manipulated in order to optimize their yields of milk or meat.

Gene therapy can be divided into two types. The first involves the alteration of 'germ cells'—ie sperm or eggs—in order to introduce a permanent change into an organism *as well as into its subsequent generations*. At present, such 'gene line therapy' is not considered ethical within humans. However, gene line therapy has been used to alter the hereditary traits of certain species of plants and animals.

Whilst human gene line therapy is currently banned, geneticists are at present legally permitted to engage in more specific 'somatic cell therapy'. In such instances, a sample of tissue is removed from a patient and its genetic make-up adjusted. The reengineered tissue is then returned to the 'donor' in the hope that its altered cells will spread and multiply. If successful, the new cells come to 'reprogram' the patient's original genetic material. There is currently the prospect that a wide range of medical conditions will be able to be treated by somatic cell therapy. These include cancer, heart problems, blood disorders, and even Alzheimer's disease. Indeed, clinical trials in the treatment of certain cancers by somatic cell therapy have already begun. However, whilst their work is potentially of enormous value, scientists in this area are at present proceeding with caution (and under strict governmental regulation), as there is always the risk that unforeseen medical problems could actually be *created* if their experiments do not turn out as planned.

In order to engage in any form of human gene therapy, it is important for scientists to understand as large a proportion of our genetic make-up as possible. Towards this end, a fifteen-year investigation entitled the Human Genome Project is being undertaken. Officially launched in the United States in 1988, the goal of this mammoth international project is to chart the chemical sequences of the three billion nucleotide base pairs which comprise the human genome (or in other words human DNA).[109]

Enormous ethical concerns are likely to arise as the Human Genome Project nears completion. Success, after all, will make it possible to both test for, and in future to 'correct', any genetic disease or characteristic. 'Designer human beings' and 'designer babies' will become a very real *technical* possibility in the medium- to long-term. Genetic science is also one day likely to make it possible to clone both human beings and other animals. Indeed, advancements in cloning research continue to shock and surprise. As just one example, in the March of 1996 researchers at the Roslin Institute near Edinburgh in Scotland announced that they had successfully cloned two sheep. Developed from eggs 'reprogrammed' in the lab with DNA grown in a culture of nutrient solution, the two lambs were identical twins born of different mothers.[110]

The potential implications of genetic engineering may be even greater than those of computer-based digitization. Digital and genetic technologies will each permit us to reengineer the environments in which we live. However, developments in genetic engineering will also enable us to reengineer ourselves. We are also in future likely to see the convergence of digital and genetic research. As reported in the New York Times in 1995, scientists are already planning the development of organic computer systems which will be many times faster than today's silicon-based counterparts. One proposal is for a memory bank containing a pound or more of DNA suspended in around 1000 quarts of fluid in a tank around a yard square. Such a memory bank would, in theory, be more capacious than all of the conventional computer memory ever made. It could therefore store the sum total of human knowledge.[111]

As the level of miniaturization in digital electronics increases, electronic and genetic engineering look increasingly natural partners. A whole new arena of manufacturing possibilities is likely to be opened up when they finally marry. As Negroponte only half-jokes, in the future 'computer displays may be sold by the gallon and painted on, CD-ROMs may be edible, and parallel processors may be applied like suntan lotion'.[112]

THE CURSE OF DOMINATION

It will not be long before currently dumb objects all around us are 'electrified with smartness' and living organisms (ourselves included) are 'hacked' to the latest fashion. As technosceptic Mark Slouka sadly predicts, soon the couch will shrink out of your way to stop you skinning your shins, whilst the cat will have a patent number.[113] Technology will become our new environment. Our new reality. No longer a wonder, technology will constitute the backcloth of the 'artificial' environment against which we all play out our short lives.

In **chapter 2** we noted how, in ancient times, significant events repeated around humanity in endless cycles. For the ancients there was therefore *change but no novelty*. However, as the divide between technology and nature—between that which we can control and that which we have to accept—becomes increasingly blurred, it may well be that future societies come to know *novelty but no change*. Time will be neither a linear nor a cyclical stream of different events. Instead, with a distinct lack of diverse experiences to be beheld across its progression, time may eventually appear to have been put on hold altogether. As Francis Fukuyama contends, we may therefore fast be approaching the end of history itself.[114]

Already in today's global world of cohesively intermeshed economies, humanity has become a master of the seasons. The temperatures of our offices and homes may be set to any reasonable level we desire. We may also consume whatever agricultural produce we wish at any time of the year. The changing climate of local seasons no longer has any major impact upon the diet of the industrialized world. With advancements in computing and digital communications, time also no longer plays a dominant role in the way in which we structure our work, nor in determining when our work is undertaken. As wired individuals within the digital hive we may add value any time we so choose.

Modern entertainment also knows no time boundaries. Using video recorders to 'timeshift' television programmes is a commonplace activity. Popular programmes are therefore no longer watched in social unison by their millions of fans. Future 'video on demand' cable systems will take the timeshifting of information and entertainment one stage further, with consumers able to decide the timing of their own, individual broadcast schedules.

As technological sociologist Allucquère Rosanne Stone contends, human physical and cultural evolution are now 'falling out of step'.[115] The more technology empowers human creativity, the more organizations may push their employees to use technology to create. Individuals are thereby likely to become more and more stressed—their fresh ideas and creative solutions demanded faster and faster in an lightspeed world which refuses to slow down, but within which people themselves seem to be getting nowhere. It is therefore hardly surprising that 'achievement for achievement's sake' is being questioned in so many quarters.

Even for those who do still strive to create great modern wonders, the struggles involved are increasingly political and financial rather than physical and technological. Once political and financial blessing have been achieved, almost any plan may now be realized. Acts of accomplishment have almost been made too easy by new technologies. Indeed, already there is almost too little to be gained from realizing even the best of ideas in actuality. We also now live in a world which, largely due to an overly-open and 'free' media, gleefully celebrates failure and decay, whilst only finding the time to pick fault with creativity and success.

* * *

OUR SUNSET ON CLEVERNESS

Last Christmas my father was given a pair of socks. Nothing very surprising in that. Fathers have been receiving socks for Christmas for generations. However, when the ankles of these particular garments were rubbed together, they emitted an electronic chime that mimicked the ringing of a telephone.

The aforementioned items of footwear caused my family some brief merriment over the Christmas period. However, in ancient times, socks capable of making a noise would have been physical wonders. Each magical pair would have constituted an amazing achievement in its own right. Even ten or twenty years ago, and most people would have marvelled at the creation of a low-cost microelectronic sounding device capable of imitating a telephone and of being hidden within a slender woolly ankle. Inhabitants of the 1970s would probably also have worried about how one could change the battery.

Today, of course, we know that the above socks were simply designed to be thrown away once their novelty had diminished.[116] In our disposable society of soundbites and aesthetic whims, power cell replacement is therefore simply not an issue. In fact, the only thing remotely wonderful or astonishing about chiming socks is the fact that anybody actually dreamt up such a product in the first place.

The above tale nicely encapsulates our progression from an achievement focus of *awe* to one of *ingenuity* through to that of *imagination*. Being capable of physically altering their surroundings has been a vital survival skill for successful human civilizations since ancient times. Applying scientific ingenuity in harnessing and in altering nature has also been of paramount importance within modern economies since the industrial revolution. However, today our perception of wonder—of great feats of accomplishment—is moving on again.

Ingenious wonders of the Present Age have included numerous devices capable of destroying the world several times over. The technological fruits of contemporary invention are also at least partly responsible for the increasingly apparent segmentation of society into a knowledge-empowered overclass and a far larger underclass of rapidly decreasing prosperity. In future, we may well reach a point beyond which further technological innovation may not either be wise or socially acceptable. Man is fast becoming the Lord of Nature which he has so long aspired to be crowned. However, having fostered cultures, sciences and technologies for thousands of years, we may finally be inflicted with the old curse of 'what we wished for'.

As I was fairly recently informed by a senior television executive, his trade internationally is now as much in formats and scripts as it is in finished programmes. A situation comedy or a game show may now be easily and comparatively cheaply remade to suit the requirements of any particular domestic market. That's the easy bit. It's the format—the idea—that's the real key to any programme's success. Television companies are therefore shifting away from trading in products and ingenuity to trading in imagination. In a similar vein, most challenges ahead are now mental, not physical. The quest before the Future Organization is therefore to unlock the largely untapped reservoir of the human spirit. As we will explore across Part II, the question is not whether our achievement focus has altered; of whether a Digital Age in which we will program both life and objects will emerge. Rather, all we may realistically contemplate is the likely impact which such unstoppable changes may have upon human beings as members of organizations, and hence upon their individual status within either a bright or a dark New Age.

From the deserts of the ancient Nile to the wastes of the lunar plains, humankind has long laboured in the pursuit of wonder. Such a spirit of curiosity still lingers within us to this day. As one of Microsoft's slogans tempts computer users, 'where do you want to go today?' What this simple question clearly infers is that we now have the tools and the technologies—the *what* and the *how*—to empower any future achievement. Hence, all that is left to be discovered is the *why*. The question should therefore really be, 'where do all of us want to go tomorrow?'

PART II
MEMBER STATUS

5
Tools that
Talked

A COLLEAGUE ONCE RECOUNTED the tale of a Roman Emperor who wished to confirm whether physical exercise hindered the human digestive process. The Emperor subsequently called in two slaves and served each of them a hearty meal. One slave was then set to work labouring, whilst the other was allowed to rest. After some time had elapsed, both slaves were slaughtered, sliced open, and the contents of their stomachs examined. To the Emperor's delight, the food within the stomach of the labouring slave was found to be in a lesser state of digestion than that recovered from the innards of his equally-unfortunate comrade. The Emperor could therefore be certain that physical exercise was indeed an impediment to rapid digestion.

The above tale horrifically demonstrates how some human beings once treated fellow men and women as property. Slaves were possessions just like jewellery, houses, pottery, or any other attribute of wealth. There was therefore nothing 'wrong' in utilizing slaves in any way in which a master saw fit. Indeed, the citizens of the ancient hellenistic city of Pergamon referred to their slaves as 'tools that talked'.[117] In stark contrast to the present, the citizens of this great cultural metropolis existed for a thousand years without developing any technology that might have risked upsetting the social structures of their 'idyllic' society.[118]

Those fortunate enough to be cast as the masters of the hellenistic Mediterranean saw physical work as a degrading activity to be feared. Fortunately for them, slaves were in plentiful supply, and each of Pergamon's leisurely citizens owned between eight and ten personal servants.[119] Citizens of Pergamon thereby came to have no interest in work, nor in advancing any machinery that would have permitted their city and its spectacular theatres and gymnasiums, its great library and its culture, to be enjoyed by the majority.

DOMINANT RELATIONSHIPS

Slavery, or systems of serfdom wherein peoples become 'unfreely' tied to an overlord, have been nearly universal institutions since the beginning of human history.[120] All ancient civilizations were built upon the pillars of slavery or of serfdom, as these alone provided the means of mass labour organization. Today, in most countries, slavery is no longer either legally or morally acceptable. This said, slave labourers may still be found working in some of the most impoverished regions of the world.[121]

Whilst in the main slavery no longer exists, systems still need to be in place which are capable of mobilizing human beings into mass activity in order to support the infrastructure of society. None of us who desire the fruits of living within an advanced human collective can ever possibly be 'free'. A minority of human beings will always need to be in command of a 'suppressed' majority. Since the Industrial Revolution, such a command structure has largely been dependent upon employment systems wherein individuals come to be contractually obligated to behave according to the wishes of 'their' organization in return for monetary reward. In addition, certain status and job security rights have also become codified as parts of the so called 'psychological contract' that has grown up between companies and their workers.[122] In the place of slaves and masters, or of serfs and overlords, the Present Age has therefore been built upon a work/command structure based around employees and employers as its key social and legal entities. Over the course of the 20th century, even if most workers have gained no more freedoms than slaves, most have at least come to possess some wealth of employment rights.

Whilst solid lines of responsibility and accountability between employees and employers have provided the backbone for the Present Age, the foundations of such concrete role sets are now clearly starting

Timeframe	Majority Member Status	Command Minority
Past	Slaves/Serfs	Owners (masters)
Present	Employees	Employers
Future	Free Agents	Organizational Broker Cores

Table 5.1 Changes in the Dominant Work/Command Relationship

to falter. Since the mid-1980s, many organizations have sought to be more flexible in order to become more competitive and cost effective. Towards this goal, many organizations have attempted (often with success) to alter their relationships with their workers. As a result, stable patterns of employment with a single organization for long periods will not prove to be the model for many future work/command structures. Rather, Future Organizations will increasingly expect single individuals to offer a portfolio of services as 'free agents'. The contents of such individual worker portfolios will then be drawn upon by organizational 'broker' cores within the human resource marketplace only as and when required.[123] Future workers may therefore lose employment rights in 'return' for greater (if not necessarily desired) individual freedoms. As illustrated in **table 5.1**, we may therefore chart three very different forms of dominant work/command relationship in the past, in the present, and in the future.

We are already witness to the commencement of a change in working relationships which is likely to be as radical as that which occurred when slaves became employees and those in command ceased to own people outright. The objective of Part II of *Challenging Reality* is to explore this change in the dominant *member status* of society. Initially, this chapter will examine the practices of human ownership upon which the vast majority of organizational history has been based. **Chapter 6** will then detail the changing role of the employee within the Present Age. Finally, **chapter 7** will reflect upon the economic and social and changes likely to empower free individual agents as the dominant workers of the 21st century.

THE TECHNOLOGY OF THE ANCIENTS

It is simply not true to claim that the civilizations of ancient times did not utilize a great deal of technology. They did. It just happened to be that ancient methods of agriculture, manufacture, and communication, were based upon the exploitation of human muscle power rather than inorganic machinery. As my old economics teacher was so found of preaching, most large tasks may be undertaken with either great pools of labour, or with just a few human beings operating a large number of powerful machines. It has perhaps only been the relatively limited labour force available within the Western economies over the past couple of centuries that has led to their mass industrialization. In the developing world, no more so than in China today, the alternative of using a mass labour supply in the place of metal-and-plastic technology continues to be demonstrated to great effect.

Slavery constituted the technology of ancients. Indeed, without it none of their great achievements in architecture, agriculture or commerce could have been realized. Just some of the ancient empires built upon the backs of slaves included those of ancient Egypt, Mesopotamia, China, India, Greece, Rome, and Central America. However, so different were ancient times from those of today that it is difficult for citizens of the West at the end of the 20th century to impartially judge the previous importance of the slave as a key productive resource. This is not to suggest that slavery could or should now be condoned as acceptable. However, as historian J.M. Roberts notes:

> The ancient world rested civilization on a great exploitation of man by man; if it was not felt to be very cruel, this is only to say that no other possible way of running things was conceivable.[124]

Quite possibly, the origin of slavery lay in conquest. Certainly slavery was the fate which awaited the losers of any of the many wars of ancient times. However, by the days of the early Babylonian empires, regular slave markets were taking place. There therefore must have been a frequent trade in slaves as personal property rather than solely as the spoils of war.[125]

The ancient empires most usually associated with slavery are those of ancient Greece and ancient Rome. In Athens circa 330 BC around 100,000 slaves were owned by the other 200,000 members of the population.[126] Large-scale plantation slavery is thought to have been less common in Greece than in other empires, with most Greek slaves engaged in personal or domestic service. Greek slaves are also thought to have been treated fairly humanely, even if many of the great philosophers of the period raised no objection to slavery on moral grounds. This said, Aristotle suggested that some slaves should be allowed to earn their freedom in return for loyal service, and indeed some Greek slaves did eventually become free citizens.

Slavery in ancient Rome was more severe than in ancient Greece, with masters having (in law) the absolute power of life or death over their servant property. The sprawling cities, country homes, and imperial conquests, of Rome placed a great deal of strain upon the native Roman workforce. The Roman Empire was therefore far more dependent upon slavery than that of ancient Greece. With so many workers needed, a great many Roman slaves were foreign prisoners and convicted criminals. Hardly surprisingly, slave revolts were not uncommon. Indeed, the great slave revolt of 73 BC was only crushed after three years of military campaigning and some 6000 crucifixions.[127] Ultimately, a reliance on a harsh slave regime is thought to have contributed to the eventual downfall of Rome.

LORD & MASTER

In the Middle Ages, with Christianity rising and the Roman Empire in decline, conditions for slaves tended to improve. A transformation towards a system of serfdom also occurred across much of Europe. Although not owned as property like slaves, serfs were legally bound to live and to work upon the land owned by their lord and master. Some masters were corporations, such as monasteries, cathedral chapters, or royal estates.

When the land upon which they worked was sold, serf tenants were transferred with it to the new owner. Serfs were permitted to cultivate some individual land to support themselves. However, they also had to make payments to their landowner in the form of either produce or taxes. Local customs and traditions of equity tended to govern serfdom as much as legal deeds. Some degree of mutual independence also existed between landowners and their peasant tenant human 'property' up until the dawning of the Industrial Revolution.

By the 18th century serfdom had largely disappeared. This was due in part to growing labour shortages, as well as to an increasing monetary- rather than commodity-based economy. Serfdom was also eliminated across much of Europe by the French Revolution of 1789. However, in parts of Russia, serfdom persisted until its final abolition in 1861 by the 'Liberator Tzar' Alexander II.

TRADE & ABOLITION

Whilst serfdom was on the wain, a modern, intercontinental slave trade had been growing up following explorations of Africa and the coloniz- ation of the Americas by the Europeans in the 15th and 16th centuries. Portugal effectively began the African slave trade when, in 1441, a sailor named Antam Goncalves seized ten Africans near Cape Bojador.[128] Not long after, the Portuguese set up a permanent slave trading station in Black Africa. The Spanish, the Dutch, and the French, in addition to the British Empire and its American colonies, soon also entered the slave trade. Conditions aboard slave ships were atrocious, with mortality rates of ten per cent per voyage being typical to low. Altogether, between nine and ten million African slaves were captured and transported to the Western hemisphere. Some six million people were kidnapped and shipped from their homelands in the 18th century alone.[129]

Slavery quickly became of fundamental importance to the workings of the American colonies. As well as being employed in domestic service, slaves were also utilized in great numbers upon agricultural plantations such as those which produced cotton. By 1800 the number of slaves in the then United States of America[130] numbered over 800,000.

It was not until the early-19th century that the African slave trade, and then slavery in general, came to be outlawed. The British Empire abolished the African slave trade in 1807, and was followed in 1808 by the United States. The Ashburton Treaty between the two nations in 1842 subsequently set up squadrons on the African coasts to enforce the prohibition.

Whilst the slave *trade* from Africa was prohibited in 1808, slavery itself was still widespread *and growing* within many Southern American states until well into the mid-19th century. Indeed, there were a staggering four million slaves reported within the US census of 1860, mainly within the Southern cotton growing plantation territories. However, in the Northern states, several churches,[131] together with politicians such as Abraham Lincoln, were increasingly campaigning for slavery's abolition. The issue divided the American Union on a clear North/South basis. When Lincoln was elected as President by the Northern and Pacific Coast states in 1860, South Carolina decided to leave the Union in protest.[132] Six other Southern states soon followed, and together with South Carolina formed the Confederate States of America. The American Civil War ensued. However, with the Union eventually victorious over the Confederacy, slavery was finally abolished within the once-more United States with the ratification of the 13th Amendment to its Constitution in 1865.[133]

A MORAL SHIFT?

In common with the spread of human rights, the emancipation of women, the rise of democracy, and the breakdown of class boundaries, the abolition of slavery is often argued to have been a matter of social 'choice'. However, all such reality shifts can only really be understood as inevitable consequences of humankind's continual technological, economic and organizational development.

As the social analyst Gregory Stock reminds us, up until less than a few centuries ago slavery was accepted as inevitable and even 'natural'. As Stock continues, it was the changing nature of human endeavour which caused slavery to be abolished, not a shift in mass humanity's morals or ethical codes.[134] Indeed, we are kidding ourselves if we believe that many of our ancestors were morally inferior in comparison with ourselves.

Across Europe, and then the United States, it was the coming of the Industrial Revolution which more than anything else drove human societies and organizations away from systems wherein masters owned their workers. With the utilization of machinery and fossil fuels, it was no longer most effective for great organizations to be supported by a large holding of human property as their primary 'technology base'. The more complex industrial jobs became, the more training workers required, and the less likely it was that slaves could be forced to use their own initiative in the name of their owner. Systems of employment based upon monetary payment also started to prove far cheaper than the ownership of slave labour. Workers in early textile mills, for example, were paid pitifully low wages which cost their employers far less than the purchase, feeding and care of slaves. As another example, in America in the mid-1800s, Irish labourers were frequently paid to do jobs which were considered too dangerous to be undertaken by precious slave workers.[135]

It only became economically (and hence politically) possible to abolish slavery once technological and monetary systems had advanced enough to shoulder the burdens of civilizations once supported by slaves. With the rise of capitalism, it also became essential for the vast majority to be paid for their labours so that they would have money to spend upon the fruits of new, industrial economies. The decline of slavery is therefore far more strongly associated with the rise of modern economic systems than with any particular 'moral crusade'. Indeed, the dawn of an ethic of universal human equity almost certainly *followed*, rather than *led*, technological and in some cases organizational advancement. What's more, in some senses, whilst living standards have dramatically increased across the Western world since slavery's abolition, patterns of human subjugation have only been altered, rather than erased. Today, it is quite possible to compare organizations to the slave masters and overlords of olden times. Both dominate human minds and bodies to fulfil their will alone. As Gareth Morgan explains:

> . . . over the ages much has changed. The conscription and slavery that provided much of the labour power required to build pyramids and empires has given way to the use of paid employment where employees have the right to leave. Slave drivers have given way to managers. And employees now typically work in the interests of shareholders rather than pharaohs, emperors, or absolute monarchs. However, in all cases, pursuit of the goals of the few through the work and labour of the many continues. Organization [itself], in this view, is best understood as a process of domination.[136]

Perhaps inevitably, there will always be a divide between the commanders and the agents of society—between those charged with managing, and those who labour in pursuit of another's aspirations. However, before we proceed to explore contemporary employment relationships within the next chapter, we ought perhaps to highlight one final observation concerning events of the past. Whilst we tend to associate human servitude with the ancients, we ought not to forget that the amendment to the American Constitution abolishing slavery *was only ratified in 1865*. Yet in an organizational context we usually only associate the late 1800s with revolutionary technologies and new working processes. To remember that our great-grandparents did not have electric light serves as an indication of the incredible progress of technology in recent times. However, to recall that some of our great-grandparents were slaves in the United States is a social recollection which polite society is more than happy to sweep under the fading carpet of history.

As we blindly career ahead in a profit-flung technoaddiction, it may transpire that the last years of the current century cloak an equally-radical social watershed behind the digital gloss of contemporary technological advancement. As the last century drew to a close, its underclass/overclass divide may have been massive. Yet at least its social chasm was beginning to lessen, with most men (if not most women) destined to become 'free'. In the late-19th century individual rights were starting to be enshrined in law, if not in deed and common action.

Today, however, the rights and the power of the underclass—of the majority who lack the skills and knowledge to compete as free agents within the Wired Age—are already starting to diminish. Slavery and serfdom may be no more. However, a potentially massive social shift in the member status of the majority may again be being catalysed by technological forces, organizational transition, and economic change.

Slavery and its derivative systems of human ownership disappeared when the overlords of society demanded paid employees to fill roles within their rising bureaucracies of mass industrialization. However, as we shall discuss in later chapters, today the bureaucracies of mass industrialization may well be in their final throes. As organizations evolve, so they may not in future demand a large number of long-term, full-time, paid employees. In fact, many indicators suggest that the number of people which many Future Organizations may actually *need* at their core may be very small indeed. And so, alarmingly, the past 150 years may merely have been a phase of worker transition away from slavery and towards economic and organizational structures to be reliant upon freelance workers and inorganic machines. Almost certainly, rights in long-term employment are now on the wain. The real change in member status may therefore be yet to come.

6
Willing Cogs
in the Machine?

WHEN THE BBC DECIDED to chart the history of the 1900s, they chose the title of *People's Century*. Their intention in doing so was to highlight how an enormous variety of economic, technological and political forces had enabled a very large number of people to play an active role in shaping the previous 100 years.

As we have already witnessed in **chapter 3**, innovations of the present have resulted in many great and empowering technological wonders. Moreover, the 20th century has also been the first span of civilization to be heavily influenced by democracy, by widespread literacy and education, and by mass market forces. In short, the 20th century has been the first period of mass participation.[137]

In the mid- to late-19th century, society centred around the privileges of the controlling few and the obedience of the working majority. However, as the 20th century dawned, a new industrial class was already swelling beneath this apparently stable veneer.[138] Whilst lords and masters still boasted most of the wealth, spreading industrialization was creating a new demand for factory workers, clerks and labourers. People were increasingly becoming employed by large business organizations. And the wages they began to earn started to render the majority a previously unknown economic leverage.

This is not to say that most workers in the early decades of the 20th century were affluent. To the contrary, most were poor. However, in aggregate, the incomes of the rising industrial class at this time gave employees a previously unknown influence over what economies demanded and supplied. As capitalist structures spread, so payment in return for labour quickly became the dominant means of acquiring and controlling a workforce. Rather than being under the influence of a lord or master, workers therefore became enslaved to the coins and notes of a free currency of exchange. Economists and industrial engineers hence started to consider human beings as rational economic machines who would only work in exchange for monetary reward, and who would work harder and harder the more they were paid.[139]

This chapter will tell the story of the evolving relationship between employees and employers across the Present Age. At the dawn of this period, the writhing tail-end of the Industrial Revolution was still requiring vast numbers of workers to move from agriculture into manufacturing. The powerful industrial logic of mass production was also starting to emerge.[140] As we shall see, for many decades organizations demanded employees who could be trained to complete only a few tasks, and who would work effectively as *components* within great industrial machines. However, in more recent times, a changing economic climate, smart and programmable productive capacity, shortening product lifecycles, a growing service sector, and the trend towards globalization, have placed great strains upon this previously sound work/command relationship.

Employment rights (not least in terms of job security) hard-won in the first half of the 20th century have been eroded as the 21st has loomed closer. As indicated within the last chapter, it may well be that the 'traditional' employee–employer paradigm which has dominated most of our working lives is no longer suitable for the Future Organization. The wholesale purchase of labours, loyalties and lifetimes in exchange for wages or salaries may have served organizations well for around a century. However, as the following history will begin to demonstrate, the long-term purchase of human beings to serve as unquestioning components may not enable organizations to most effectively survive within the imagination economy of the future.

MOVING ALONG

As mass consumer markets began to emerge in the early decades of the 20th century, factories grew both in size and complexity. However, as a consequence, the skills which organizations demanded from their workers came to be reduced. There were in essence two reasons behind his trend. The first was the introduction of the moving assembly line. The second involved new 'scientific' techniques for rational worker specialization.

Moving assembly lines were a logical development of previous techniques for standardized mass production. In the early-20th century, firearms, sewing machines, bicycles, automobiles, railway engines, and other machines, were already being assembled in large numbers from standardized components. However, particularly when they were charged with constructing complex products like automobiles, a great many factory workers had to be skilled or semi-skilled craftsmen trained to perform a wide range of assembly operations. Moving assembly lines were to change all this, as they only required workers capable of performing a narrow range of activities.

In 1913 automobile manufacturer Henry Ford had already witnessed the movement of animal carcasses along a chain of hooks within Chicago's slaughterhouses. It did not take long before he began experiments with moving manufacturing lines. To demonstrate his concept, Ford arranged for one of his workers to pull a car chassis past a line of mechanics who each fitted various parts. Only a year later, Ford introduced his first operational automated assembly line. Transforming his Highland Park Factory, the moving line paraded an endless stream of car chassis past employees who each performed only a very few assembly operations. In a stroke, the value of widespread craft skills disappeared. In their place, the new skill demanded from workers was speed.[141]

Assembly line manufacturing had an incredible impact upon output. When craftsmen had moved from car to car within Ford's Highland Park factory, each vehicle had taken around twelve-and-a-half hours to produce. In contrast, cars built upon Ford's first assembly line were completed in just ninety minutes. Hardly surprisingly, other manufacturers quickly followed Ford's example, and moving assembly lines soon became a feature of factories around the world. Progress, however, was not without its price. Employees of the line soon discovered that their new rhythm of work was almost unbearable. As one employee upon a French assembly line later commented:

You had to assemble so many parts per hour . . . . No sooner had you
finished one part than the next arrived. No stopping allowed. The workman
was just part of the machine. At the flick of a switch the machine went into
action and you had to keep pace with it. It was worse than hard labour . . .
it was no better than being a galley-slave.[142]

With work on the line so arduous, many workers did not want to
remain. Ford's response was to double his employees' pay and to include
them in a scheme to share in the huge profits being reaped from assembly
line manufacture. In 1914, Ford's previously unthinkable 'five dollar day'
had workers flocking to his employment. The work was still tiring and
mindlessly repetitive, but the money made it tolerable. Capitalizing on his
employees' intense monetary motivation, Ford bought bodies and minds
for eight hours a day, although he used only the former. Ten years later,
and over ten million Model 'T' cars had been produced within Ford's
factories.

BRAWN NOT BRAINS

Henry Ford was far from the only manager keen to exploit a desire for
high wages in return for the employment of a workforce which would
unquestioningly undertake repetitive activities. Another great exponent of
the cause was Frederick Winslow Taylor. Fascinated by the
'inefficiencies' of many manual working practices, Taylor championed his
own system of work rationalization which he christened *Scientific
Management*. Whilst Ford mainly concentrated upon improving complex
manufacturing processes, Taylor was far more concerned with increasing
the productivity of individual workers in the completion of fairly basic
manual tasks. Taylor saw labourers as 'stupid', and hence considered
them incapable of understanding the 'science' required to perform their
jobs most effectively. He also considered workers to be inherently lazy.
Taylor was therefore keen to identify working methods which would 'stop
the loafing' (or the 'systematic soldiering') of employees in order that
their productivity would be improved.[143]

Specifically, Taylor's Scientific Management involved introducing
optimal methods for task execution, employee selection, and managerial
specialization. Key to Taylor's analysis was his belief that there was 'one

best way' to do any job. By developing time and motion study techniques,[144] Taylor discovered this one best way for each of the tasks which he set out to optimize. He then went about scientifically selecting and training employees to work in this one best way.[145]

Invariably, Taylor's methods led to working routines heavily governed by preset principles and rules. Specialization was not only applied to the physicalities of the job in hand, but in addition to the allocation of managerial responsibility. Taylor was convinced that work and responsibility should be divided and then 'dovetailed'—with employees trained to unquestioningly carry out tasks according to the precise instructions of their supervisors.[146] In justifying such an approach, Taylor explained that he was in search of true workplace harmony. He also proposed that workers were of such a limited intellectual capacity that the sole rewards that they would be seeking from their jobs would be financial. Workers would therefore be happy to cooperate with scientific working methods so long as they received a 'fair day's pay'.

Many of Taylor's experiments and triumphs took place at the Bethlehem Steel Corporation in the late-19th and early-20th centuries. In perhaps the most famous instance, Taylor studied a group of labourers who were employed to lift and carry 92 lb 'pigs' of iron. Before Taylor started his experiments, pig-iron handlers loaded an average of 12.5 tons per day. By the time that Taylor had trained each worker to work in his one best way, some were loading as much as 47 tons in the same period, and for only 60 per cent higher wages. After this success, Taylor went on to calculate optimal shovel sizes for employees shovelling different grades of coal. Eventually, as a result of all of Taylor's experiments, the Bethlehem steel works was able to reduce its workforce from around 600 to just 140, with the remaining men paid 60 per cent higher wages.[147]

GROWING UNREST

In common with Ford, Taylor and the many other managers who employed his methods were criticized for being 'inhuman'. They were also accused of exploiting their workers as machines.[148] By the time that the Great Depression started in October 1929,[149] worker unrest was rife. However, with unemployment levels steeply rising, employers who remained in business chose to remain oblivious to employee complaints and to any demands to recognize trade unions. Employers like Ford had promised work to thousands, yet now there was little to be had. However, huge crowds of people desperately looking for employment still gathered outside factories around the world. In this climate, managers and foremen had the absolute power to fire dissenting employees by the minute. They were, after all, always safe in the knowledge that plenty more prospective workers were waiting just outside the gates.

Into the 1930s, production lines were driven faster and faster. In parallel, the hunger, denial, disease and unemployment of the Depression only grew.[150] Eventually people had had enough. In 1932, 80,000 men at Ford's prestigious River Rouge plant brought the assembly lines to a halt. Ford's promises of work for any man who wanted to be employed were not being fulfilled, and they all felt betrayed. Soon a march began towards the Ford headquarters. A cordon of armed police met the crowds and unleashed bullets and water hoses in the freezing cold. Four protesters were killed. As one of the marchers later remembered, 'Instead of getting jobs, we got lead, we got bullets and blood'.[151] But their protest did signal a turning point for assembly line workers across the United States and beyond.

In Detroit, the United Auto Worker's Union (UAW) began to recruit employees from several car plants—even if many men joined in secret and in fear of strong-arm company security men. As the Depression began to lift from the mid-1930s onwards, the economy once more began to prosper and employment levels rose. So too did worker dissent around the world. In France, frustrations snapped in 1936 when there were a series of strikes and factory occupations by workers fed up with being treated like machines. Social and industrial reforms soon followed, with workers awarded a statutory 40-hour week and paid holidays.

In 1937 in the United States, a UAW sit-down strike at General Motors resulted in the Company finally recognizing the union. Henry Ford resisted such change until July 1941, when a strike finally forced him to grant his employees union recognition, health insurance, pensions, and a seniority system. In other words, Ford gave his people back some of their human dignity.

Across the world, union membership was rising and increasing employment rights were being gained. By 1935 there were four million union members in Britain, and by 1945 almost fifteen million union members in the United States (equating to more than 35 per cent of the non-agricultural workforce).[152] Power began to be vested on both sides of the employee–employer work/command relationship. Granted, employees were still tiny cogs within great mass-production machines. However, individuals strong in coalition were demanding and obtaining many rights in addition to pay in order to function in such a manner. Employee–employer cooperation (and with it productivity) improved as a result. As the Hawthorne Experiments at the Western Electric Company had shown from 1924–1932, people worked better when they were treated with respect and consideration as human individuals, rather than as homogeneous flesh components.[153]

THE RISE OF FLEXIBILITY

Utilized in amalgamation, the legacies of Henry Ford and of F.W. Taylor became the foundations for industrial success for well over half a century. So long as consumers demanded standardized, mass-produced products, dedicated assembly lines and rationalized working practices continued to prove most effective. Throughout the post-war boom years, and for several decades afterwards, profits remained cosily high in industrialized economies which, as Harold Macmillan so famously noted, 'had never had it so good'.

It was not until the early-1980s that the dominance of the traditional employee–employer work/command relationship came to be challenged. Many companies had been hit hard by the recession of this period. Substantial redundancies had therefore been inevitable as firms had fought to reduce costs in order to stay in business. Within organizations on both sides of the Atlantic, the boom-decades fat of overmanning had been trimmed right back to the bone.

Even when the recession began to lift, many firms were reluctant to return to their previous permanent manning levels. Rather, as demand grew for their products, companies instead chose to utilize temporary, part-time, and sub-contractual personnel. Such workers granted firms far more flexibility in their employment costs and obligations. As the *Sunday Times* explained in November 1985, employers who had made substantial redundancies during the recession did not want to risk re-employing vast numbers of their old workforces again as better times appeared.[154] The early-1980s recession had therefore led organizations to perceive a need for a permanent reduction in their labour commitments. And with unions weak after a period of high unemployment, employers were effectively granted a free hand in introducing any radical changes they desired.

In addition to a new risk aversion concerning any expansion of their permanent workforce, there were several other factors that drove organizations in the 1980s towards more flexible employment strategies.[155] For a start, most markets were proving to be far more competitive than those which had preceded them. Market volatility and uncertainty also seemed to be increasing. Certainly product lifecycles were rapidly shortening as marketeers became extremely adept at persuading consumers that their tastes and needs were now constantly in flux. Indeed, even more than the 1950s and 1960s, the 1980s became a decade to be totally dominated by the me-first fashions, doubts and whims that remain the stock-in-trade of the advertising industry to this day.

Technological change was also a major factor driving organizations towards more flexible manning requirements. Unlike those set up by Ford at the beginning of the century, new assembly lines began to include programmable machine tools and robots capable of producing *different* and *customized* outputs according to fresh customer demands. As we shall explore further in **chapters 15** and **16**, the value of mass production as the dominant organizational paradigm thereby came to be challenged.

No longer was rationalization and standardization always the most effective business strategy. Organizations therefore sought employees with a variety of skills. Subsequently, demarcations between different categories of worker were no longer tolerated. With patterns of employment based upon rigidly standardized skillsets under close scrutiny, many industries came to be decimated and then reborn in a new mould. For example, in newspaper publishing there were bitter industrial disputes as craftskilled typesetters and their unions resisted attempts to introduce new technologies and working practices. Eventually, however, computer-based imagesetting systems operated by workers with a wide range of new skills did transform newspaper production. And after equally arduous industrial turmoil in the television industry, no longer could a scene shifter refuse to move a cable simply because he was 'not an electrician'.[156] In a brave, new workplace brimming with an ever-present drive for cost reduction, practices for flexible manning simply had to be accepted as the norm.

DIVIDED WE FALL

As firms took on more and more temporary, part-time and sub-contractual workers, a definite chasm started to open up between those permanently employed at the 'core' of the organization, and those who enjoyed far fewer rights in more periphery employment. John Atkinson proposed that a new model was emerging, which he entitled the *Flexible Firm*.[157] **Figure 6.1** illustrates the key elements of Atkinson's model. In particular it highlights the likely distinction between 'core' and 'periphery' employees within many a modern organization.

Key to Atkinson's model is the notion that, in order to enjoy a wide range of flexibility options, organizations will seek different modes of manpower flexibility from different groups of workers. Specifically, the contention is that the permanent, full-time workers at an organization's core will offer it *functional flexibility*. In other words, core workers will be multiskilled. Organizations will therefore be rendered the flexibility of being able to move their core workers between activities as and when required.[158] Task-based job demarcations are therefore very unlikely to exist within the core of the Flexible Firm.

In return for their functional flexibility, core workers receive the security of a permanent job. They are also likely to enjoy other 'traditional' employment benefits such as paid holidays, sick-pay, a pension scheme, and a health care plan.

By engaging temporary, part-time, sub-contractual and self-employed workers as a periphery labourforce around its core, organizations may also obtain *numerical flexibility*. Agency and other temporary staff paid by the hour or by the day may be employed or removed from service at very short notice. Alternatively, by employing part-time staff, organizations may be able to iron out uneven manpower requirements during the working day. For example, extra canteen staff may only need to be employed around lunchtime, whilst cleaners may only be required in the early morning or evening.

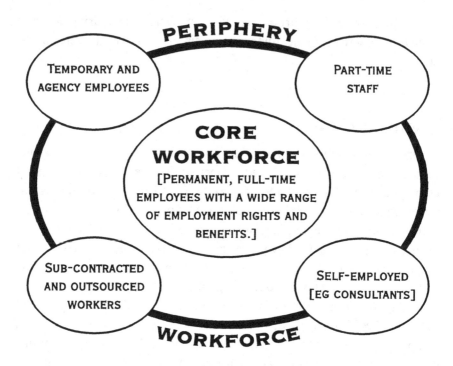

Figure 6.1 Core and Periphery Employment in the Flexible Firm
[Adapted from the work of John Atkinson—see note 157.]

By sub-contracting (or 'outsourcing') tasks to workers employed by a third party (or by engaging self-employed staff), organizations may also be able to obtain longer-term numerical flexibility. Construction firms, for example, may only take on carpenters, bricklayers, electricians, and plasterers, as the services of each worker category come to be required upon each particular project. Flexibility in the number of people an organization employs (or in the number of hours worked by those people), may therefore be bought in a great variety of mixes. By splitting their workload between different types of periphery worker, organizations will also gain some *financial flexibility*, as different workers will be able to be paid on upon different wage, salary, piece-rate, project-specific or bonus criteria.

Most people working within an organization's periphery labourpool have little or no job security. They also tend to obtain few employment rights or benefits aside from direct monetary reward. It is therefore hardly surprising that clear shifts towards Flexible Firm models of organization have not been met with delight in some quarters. In 1985, the Trades Union Congress Economic Review reported that flexible manning practices ought to be considered as 'dangerous'. The Review went on to suggest that where workers saw the word 'flexibility' they should substitute the word 'fragmentation'; and that where they came across the term 'incentives' they should instead read 'exploitation'.

Unquestionably the Flexible Firm model could only have arisen under depressed labourmarket conditions within which the collective voice of unions held little sway. What's more, now that a clear distinction (and indeed fragmentation) between core and periphery employees is increasingly apparent, it is difficult to see how mass unionization will ever return. It is therefore becoming less and less likely that a voice will emerge strong enough to restore some, if not all, of the employment rights which many periphery workers have already lost.

A LABOUR SUPERMARKET

Few Future Organizations will exist as cohesive wholes with a substantial full-time, permanent employee base. Rather, most organizations in times ahead are likely to evolve into amalgams of a relatively small core staff, coupled with a constantly shifting periphery labourforce. Such two-tier models will offer organizations a wide range of manpower flexibility options. These models will hence enable organizations to keep their costs down and to remain in business. Unfortunately, the cost for many single individuals is likely to be high.

For forty to fifty years the employee–employer relationship remained remarkably concrete. Almost the only changes which occurred resulted in actual *improvements* in employee rights and benefits. However, across the past decade-and-a-half, everything has started to change once again.

For workers remaining at the core of an organization, times are still often rosy. In contrast, for workers looking in from the labour periphery, life is not so sweet. Rather than being bought wholesale as dedicated, organization components, periphery workers are now increasingly having to sell their services from the stacked shelves of a labour supermarket within which many organizational cores are free to pick-and-mix from the latest low-price offers. Dehumanization at work is therefore no longer limited to being treated as a component within an organizational machine. In addition, a new generation of underclass is also having to constantly worry about how long any organization will want their services for—be this period of time measured in years, months, weeks, or even just days. Like it or not, at present we are witness to a shockingly-competitive labour economy in which the core may thrive only by throwing scraps to its periphery neighbour. Many of those workers caught around the edge are therefore having to struggle just as hard to survive as their employee cousins back in the factories of the early-20th century.

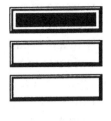

7
Totally Free to Fly & Totally Free to Fall

THE TITLE OF THIS chapter is taken from the narration of a recent television documentary series entitled *Visions of Heaven & Hell*.[159] The goal of this series was to weigh arguments for and against the increased adoption of new technology. Specifically, in Programme II we were told of revolutionary, technology-empowered working practices within advertising agency Chiat-Day. As narrator Tilda Swinton hauntingly explained as the camera trucked through a colourful, sprawling, and free-for-all open-plan work area:

> . . . as free agents [people] roam in a place designed to give them the tools to make work easy, but never the objects to tie them down. They are always on line and never off duty. Totally free to fly and totally free to fall.[160]

At Chiat-Day workers are no longer defined by objects or possessions. Whilst lockers are provided for personal property, nobody has their own desk nor designated work area. There are also no set working hours. Instead, workers arrive and depart from the office as they please. They also use whichever computer workstations and meeting spaces are available as they see fit. All that matters is that their job gets done. People are judged upon the ideas they contribute—the value which they add to the organization—rather than the hours they spend in a particular location. As Laurie Coots, the Senior Vice President in charge of Administration and Business Development at Chiat-Day explains, 'work is [now] something you do, not somewhere you go'.[161]

The minimalist office as a common but not obligatory resource at Chiat-Day serves as a chilling yet powerfully imaginative icon for future organizational functioning. As already noted within our discussion of the rise of the periphery workforce at the end of the last chapter, the relationship between workers and organizations is currently in a nervous state of flux. Less and less will organizations purchase individuals to be trained and enmeshed as long-term organizational components. More and more, worker skills and expertise will simply be bought off-the-rack only as and when required by business alliances charged with realizing specific short- and medium-term objectives.

Clearly such a radical change represents another watershed in the member status of common organizational reality. We are starting to evolve away from a labour market based around times and places towards one focused upon tasks and results in terms of value added. The transition will be as dramatic as that from slave and serf worker to employee; the involved social changes equally as great.

In ancient times, masters traded in people as property. Within the Present Age, organizations have bought a proportion of an employee's time and loyalty in exchange for monetary reward and various other obligations. However, in the future, many people will both own themselves and trade themselves in a market of increasingly-free individual agents. If successful, the rewards to be reaped by individuals as free agents within this market will be great. However, failure in the new economy of labour is likely to be harsh and absolute. What's more, even those who find success as free agents may miss having a long-term organizational parent with which they may share loyalties, and to which they will come to belong. Few individuals like the idea of being corporate property. However, in the long-term, most recognize that membership of an organization may provide them with a strong sense of self-worth and personal identity.

FORCES FOR CHANGE

It is always difficult for futurists to sell ideas which at first seem to be heavily abstracted from reality. And suggesting that we are soon to witness a radical change in the work/command relationship currently enjoyed or at least tolerated by the majority serves as a good example of this problem.

Current employment practices based upon one organization for each individual seem so natural and so *obvious*. It can therefore be hard to accept that, in perhaps only a quarter of a century, currently traditional employee–employer work/command relationships will no longer be the norm. Of course, some people may consider twenty-five years a very long time. However, for those charting future manpower requirements, two-and-a-half decades is not that distant an horizon. It is therefore important for managers and organizations today to try and comprehend at least the *forces* which are driving the greatest transition in the work/command relationship for well over a century.

In **chapter 6** we noted how the initial decision to utilize the services of a greater and greater number of periphery workers was in part based upon a risk aversion to take on permanent or 'core' staff in the early- to mid-1980s. The increasingly competitive market conditions and favourable industrial relations climate of the period also played an important role in the rise of the expanding periphery workforce.

Since the mid-1980s, markets have continued to grow more cut-throat. Any business aversion to taking on too many permanent employees has therefore, if anything, only increased. However, today it is almost certainly three other key factors which are most keenly driving changes ahead in the member status of our labour relationships.

The first of these factors concerns the fairly recent development of new digital technologies. Many of these are permitting the adoption of radically new working practices. The second factor then relates to changing worker expectations. Today, quality of life is becoming more important than organizational advancement for many individuals. Many people are also starting to question the role which may be played within their lives by any government or welfare state. Finally, the third factor driving us towards a more free-agent-biased labour market arises from the shifting achievement focus of humanity.

The remainder of this chapter will initially focus in turn upon each of the above three factors and their significance for labour market evolution. It will then become possible to highlight some of the dilemmas likely to be faced when traditional employees are no longer the dominant worker group within the Future Organization.

FREE AGENTS IN THE DIGITAL AGE

Within the after words to his thesis *Being Digital*, Nicholas Negroponte contends that, by the year 2020, the largest employer in the developed world will be 'self'.[162] This prediction stems from observing the increased interlinking of more and more computers into global networks which will soon make the world one 'seamless digital workplace'.[163] With many organizations transforming into software representations within the new business domain of cyberspace, so in future anybody (*in theory at least*) will be able to work for any organization, any time and anywhere.[164]

In future, organizations as well as people may be judged primarily upon value added. The divide between free agent individuals and organizations will therefore diminish. And across computer network links, free agents and organizations may appear identical. As Negroponte puts it, 'today three people in three different cities can form a company and access a global marketplace'.[165]

The technologies which now enable single individuals to work as sophisticated free agents have advanced rapidly in the mid-1990s. Even fairly basic personal computers (PCs) running standard office packages may greatly empower individuals as free agents. One of Microsoft's recent TV adverts concerns the surprise of a temp who discovers how her self-employed boss can, with modern PC software, handle a workload which would have previously required an entire team. Whilst this advert certainly involves some marketing hype, in essence its message is the truth. As Peter Cochrane, the Head of Future Technology Research at British Telecom similarly enthuses:

> My father's generation had a working life of 100,000 hours. With the technology to hand I can now do all of the work that he completed in a mere 10,000 hours. With the technology that's coming my children will be able to do all the work that I can do in less than 1000 hours.[166]

Coupled with powerful and low-cost desktop or portable computers, groupware communications systems such as electronic mail (e-mail) prove critical digital tools for empowering individuals as free agents. Via e-mail, an individual may send a message (for example an electronic mailshot offering their services) to 1000 recipients just as easily as to a single individual. Electronic mail can also be collected *from* anywhere, allowing individuals working alone to be constantly in touch even when out in the field. Individuals are also just as capable as large organizations of establishing an impressive 'corporate identity' upon the Internet's point-and-click world-wide web. A far broader discussion of the new communications media of the Digital Age takes place within **chapter 9** and **chapter 10**.

As more and more business comes to be conducted across the information economy of cyberspace, so maintaining a plush office and a large staff are no longer prerequisites for business success. Indeed, such assets may even become a hindrance. Whilst many individuals are now seeking to work for themselves over computer network links, so many organizations are equally *encouraging* their people to labour in such a fashion. Employees who are rarely in the office prove far cheaper than real-estate-hungry souls. Indeed, those offering services as totally freelance agents accrue no traditional employment costs at all.

'Teleworking'—whereby individuals work either at home upon a computer, or from a terminal in a local, communal 'telecottage'—is becoming more and more commonplace. According to recent market research, in the United States there are already between seven and nine million teleworkers.[167] Even in the more geographically condensed United Kingdom, there are around 400,000 reported teleworkers. The European Community also has a target for ten million teleworkers by the year 2000.[168] With increased flexibility offered to both workers and organizations, and cost savings for the latter considerable, teleworking has already proved its worth as a mutually-beneficial new working practice.[169] With video links and/or telecottage associations now also available to help ease any involved problems of social isolation, teleworking looks set to become very common indeed.

PORTFOLIO LIVES

Aside from the tools of the Digital Age, new social shifts are also responsible for a Western workforce increasingly keen to be responsible for its own destiny. After WWII, governments in the United States and across Europe championed welfare state systems to provide pensions, healthcare, education, and benefits, to all those in need of them. Unfortunately, as the 21st century dawns, sustaining such systems will prove impossible. Already most of us in work, and with over half of our expected lifespans remaining, realize that the state will not be able to look after us in retirement. As a result, private pensions, in addition to plans for private nursing care in old age, are a boom industry. More and more people are also opting for private healthcare, critical injury insurance, unemployment income protection, and schemes to pay for private schooling for their children. Hence, it is becoming less important to remain employed long-term by a large organization in order to be guaranteed welfare rewards in old age. Whether traditionally employed or not, today more and more people are purchasing their own, individual welfare portfolios. Their reliance upon a work organization for tangible rewards other than direct salary or wage payment has therefore decreased.

Today, a free agent *state of mind* has already been bred into a significant proportion of the population by those who have allowed them to buy-out of the welfare state.[170] Once so many individuals have begun to relish such control over their own affairs, it is hardly surprising that a fair proportion are already determined to set their own agendas as free agents with the labour market. People who have purchased their own welfare portfolios are additionally increasingly likely to want to sell their own skills.

As Charles Handy contends, modern workers (and in particular modern college leavers) are seeking to become 'portfolio people'. Many are recognizing that 'time and talent' are now the labour resources most in demand, and that these are the property of each individual, not of their organization.[171] 'Careers' will therefore take on new meanings, as people come to manage their own skillsets and mindsets and welfare schemes. In Handy's words:

> The fact remains that for the good and ill the portfolio life is for most of us the life of the future. Organizations are never again going to stockpile people. The employee society is on the wane.[172]

Even some of those people apparently content to remain working as traditional employees are starting to adopt a free-agent mindset. In part this is demonstrated by the 'downshifting' trend. Downshifting is said to occur when employees choose to place their own quality of life before advances in work and pay. Rather than taking on better, more stressful jobs that may leave less time for families and hobbies, employees who downshift trade monetary rewards and any improved organizational status for better home lives and fewer work-related worries.

As noted in a recent Mintel report, organizations such as British Airways, Marks & Spencer, and the United Kingdom Civil Service, are already adapting to demands from some workers to downshift by offering new flexible employment packages.[173] Workers may, for example, be able to take long periods of unpaid leave in order to cope with a domestic crisis without losing pension rights and holiday entitlements. With a third of all workers now claiming that their family life is affected by long working hours,[174] the emergence of downshifting signals how individuals are demanding more of a free-agent status even within traditional modes of employment. Organizations are therefore having to learn that forces and desires for increased employee flexibility must now be allowed to flow in both directions.

MINDS, NOT BODIES

As the achievement focus of humanity has shifted from awe through ingenuity and towards imagination, so the demands placed upon workers by organizations have also changed. Future Organizations within most industrial sectors will not rely heavily upon the physical capabilities of human beings in order to produce their outputs. Instead, most will become dependent upon complex and programmable digital manufacturing systems.[175]

Even many routine *mental* activities are now becoming totally automated. Most large retail chains possess electronic data interchange (EDI) links with their suppliers. These are usually programmed so that fresh orders will be generated and dispatched automatically (without human intervention) when goods within the warehouse fall to pre-determined stock levels. The market for 'intelligent software agents' capable of acting as computerized credit authorizers, portfolio managers, researchers, and even as travel agents, is also soon to boom.[176]

Consequently, Future Organizations will not be engaging workers purely to purchase their physical strength, nor even to acquire routine mental capacities. As noted in Part I, imagination will become the key organizational resource of the future.

The key attributes to be purchased from a great many future workers will be their creative minds rather than their physical bodies. Indeed, the future chasm between overclass and underclass is likely to distinguish extremely harshly between those who are capable of adding value by rendering creative services, and those who may only trade in physical or routine mental capabilities. What's more, those of us in the West have to realize that digital technologies are now permitting more and more organizations to shift all of their routine production *and service* operations to geographic regions with far lower labour costs. Already, many major multinationals have moved entire service departments—like accounts, customer booking, and even computer programming—to countries such as India, Russia or China.

Only decades hence, those Americans and Europeans who have priced themselves out of the routine labour market, yet who do not possess the skills to surf the labourpool as creative free agents, will be landed in a very sorry state indeed. Future Organizations and their worker overclass *may* choose to provide a welfare state to support such an 'affluent society' underclass. Then again, they may not. From an individual as well as an organizational perspective, the need to learn to function as a free agent worker outside of traditional employment allegiances has to be very great indeed. Western societies need to develop economies based upon portfolio individuals *and fast*.

SYMBIOTIC RELATIONSHIPS

The shift away from a work/command structure based around employees and employers, and towards one focused upon free-agent workers and core organizational brokers, will present many management challenges. Perhaps most significantly, perceptions of the power relationship between worker and organization will need to change. Far less frequently will managers be able to exert control in their old 'I'm the boss and you are the underling who must obey' fashion. In theory, of course, few if any modern managers operate with such a mindset. In practice, as we all know only too well, many still rely heavily upon the bureaucratic omnipotence of their role.

To break the 'you're lucky to be here' mentality of many managers may take decades. However, stick-in-the-muds will be increasingly likely to encounter future workers who will retort that an organization is lucky to be enjoying their services. A *symbiotic relationship* between worker and organization will in future be required: a relationship across which both worker and organization perceive and accrue synergistic benefits through mutual cooperation. Granted, shoddy workers who do not deliver on quality will be lucky to gain employment. Yet strong, creative labour talent will be like gold. New models of worker–organization relationship will be needed. Indeed, in some quarters they have already arrived.

Cavendish Management Resources (CMR) is a UK company with an investor base in excess of £200 million. Run by Harvard graduate Mike Downey, the company has also been operating as a model for many a Future Organization since 1984. Despite its size and range of activities, CMR only employs a couple of secretarial employees at its central office in London's Harley Street. However, around this core, over 150 free agents provide national and international expertise in fields ranging from intellectual property protection and licensing, through to corporate recovery and executive training.

Each of CMR's free agents (or 'members') pays a monthly fee in order to be linked to the core. Whilst this payment does not guarantee any work, it does enable members to capitalize upon CMR's image, client list and reputation. Members of CMR also gain access to the expertise of all other members. In addition, they may distribute 'individual' workloads across the organization. This helps to alleviate the problems of under- or of over-trading which plague many an individual businessman. Newsletters and regional dinners, together with a skills database, keep CMR members in touch. Within the organization, loyalty and mutual respect are a completely two-way street. For CMR needs talented members just as much as its free agents value their attachment to its fluid but united whole.

Unencumbered by the shackles of traditional employment relationships, CMR provides a fresh model for human resource management. Enjoying ultimate manpower flexibility, the organization is empowered to provide the very best for its customers. Individual CMR members also enjoy widespread flexibility as they are free to trade outside of the CMR alliance. As a trail-blazer for worker and organization married in a new state of symbiosis, we are certain to witness many more organizations like CMR in the future.

A QUESTION OF IDENTITY

Shifts towards more flexible and free-agent-based working practices are inevitably creating tensions for those worried about long-term job security. The sense of identity derived from being part of something greater than oneself is also being threatened by the rising trend for periphery or free agent working patterns. Sensitivities towards both of these very *human* concerns are likely to separate the 'good' (and hence successful) Future Organizations from the bad. With worker allegiances to single organizational parents already decreasing, it will be increasingly important for Future Organizations to demonstrate how much they really *care*.

Worries regarding job security have now moved high up many political agendas. Some political parties—such as New Labour in the United Kingdom—are even claiming that they are capable of *solving* the problem of increased job insecurity. Unfortunately, they are not. For better or for worse, the world has moved on. Over the coming decades, more and more people will find themselves a part of an expanding periphery workforce. Indeed, any industry or organization (let alone government) claiming to offer secure employment now needs to be viewed with great suspicion. After all, such a claim can only really be made by those ignoring the labour flexibilities now essential to remain competitive. Few people may like the new and harsh realities of labour markets to come. However, they are realities that are not going to go away. The question should therefore not be how we may 'cure' the affliction of job insecurity, but rather how we may best cope with the heartaches to which this modern dilemma of economics gives rise.

As highlighted by Tom Peters and Robert Waterman within *In Search of Excellence*,[177] many companies may in part attribute their success to their strong 'corporate culture'. Within many organizations, such cultures have created a 'family-style' atmosphere which has fostered strong bonds between the workforce and the organization. People need something work-related to belong to, especially if they do not enjoy strong family or community bonds. And an organization with a strong corporate identity can for many fit the bill. However, cultures focused around a common workplace and its 'way of doing things' are not the only kind capable of providing people with the sense of self associated with belonging to a unified collective. Aside from those rooted in particular roles, tasks and/or locations, cultures at work may also be centred around personal skillsets or trades.[178]

Most professions have evolved strong cultural attributes that provide a unity of identity for their members. Accountants, architects, doctors, engineers, and solicitors, are just some of the professional groups that huddle under a strong cultural umbrella. Workers from within these groups may therefore prove to be most suited to the new free-agent, portfolio-style working arrangements of the future. Even if people from within such groups lose their organizational ties as long-term employees, they still maintain a strong sense of *professional* identity. Future Organizations keen for a content and productive workforce must therefore encourage people to become involved with professional bodies, trade associations, and their like. In the past, hard-won educational qualifications fostered strong professional loyalties in skilled employment, whilst trades unions were the extra-organizational bodies to which other workers belonged. Yet now, more and more people need advanced skills training, whilst unions hold less and less of an attraction as the labourpool fragments. Professional and/or skills-based identities are therefore likely to be of increasing importance for both individuals and their organizations in the years ahead.

CORE OR PERIPHERY?

Already in the UK, about half of employed women (around 5.5 million) and one quarter of employed men (about 3 million) are located in flexible jobs within the employment periphery.[179] The number of full-time 'core' jobs is also declining rapidly. More and more part-time positions are also being created. Similar periphery/core employment ratios may be cited for the United States.

It is against the above scenario that we need to assess manpower strategies and priorities for the Future Organization. That the future workforce will be segmented into 'core' and 'periphery' elements is in little doubt. That periphery work opportunities will continue to expand at the expense of more traditional core employment relationships is also fairly certain. Given these two facts, and bearing in mind the free-agent mentality and welfare flexibility of many technologically-empowered individuals, any successful Future Organization's manpower strategy *has* to include plans for engaging the services of free individuals trading their own skill portfolios.

It is simply not the case that some firms will be able to step aside to offer 'secure' core employment to all of their workers as one big, happy family. Adapting to make the best use of the expanding periphery marketplace of free agent workers is a matter of economics rather than morality. Indeed, it is worth remembering that business overlords and organizations over a century ago came to switch from owning serfs and slaves to employing early factory employees on economic rather than moralistic grounds.

Some employment analysts have argued that shifts towards increased periphery employment do not bode well for the future, and that as economies begin to boom in the next millennium the core workforce will expand once more. I do not believe this to be the case for two reasons. Firstly, our experiences of the post-recession 1980s do not support this hypothesis. Quite to the contrary, they suggest that it is peripheral, free-agent labour markets which will expand in times of future boom, rather than those of the core. Secondly, we have to ask ourselves where the most talented future workers will place themselves. And this is likely to be within the expanding periphery. As demonstrated by the downshifting trend, people as well as organizations are now demanding increased flexibility.

The best Future Workers will strive to provide themselves with the skills, the personal welfare schemes, as well as the *mindsets*, to trade themselves as free agents. Indeed, the art of being a free agent is already that of adopting a new state of mind. Why should gifted individuals want to remain as pegs hammered into the holes of organizational bureaucracies, when they may enjoy the variety of working for many different organizations? Conversely, why should the best Future Organizations want to employ their key personnel as core workers, when free agents will possess a far wider range of experiences and may hence be able to offer a greater range of creative opportunities?

A shift in perceptions is on the near horizon. In ten years time it will not be periphery workers who are second class citizens in comparison with the pampered long-term employees of the core. Periphery workers will almost certainly have the potential to be no more 'disadvantaged' than the majority of today's core workers, as both groups will be forced to purchase their own non-pay welfare provision as state systems collapse. Indeed, the 'stigma' of the future may be to be a core rather than a periphery worker—to be a person who does not 'live on the edge' and who only works for one organization.

A THREE-WAY DIVIDE?

A three-way social divide may soon emerge. Most fortunate will be an overclass of free agents who live portfolio lives. In the middle there will be an underclass of far less flexible workers who are paid more and more meagre amounts as their non-creative skills base degrades at the core. Finally, there will be an even more impoverished group who will find little or no work to sustain their existence.

Such a three-tiered model containing a significant number of 'disposable' people (as Handy terms them)[180] is not a future state of affairs to be relished by society in general. Indeed, over time it is only likely to result in increased social disparity and unrest. However, forecasting from work/command relationship trends across a considerable frame of time, such a balance of citizenship does unfortunately look extremely likely. The reign of the job-for-life, high-status employee will soon be over (if indeed it has not already ended). The future instead belongs to those individuals talented and tough enough to survive on their own, and to those organizations who will most keenly offer the flexible and dynamic work/command relationships that these individuals will demand.

PURCHASING ORGANIZATIONS

Around the time of the launch of the prequel to this volume, I found myself at the London International Bookfair for a meeting with the marketing and editorial staff from my publisher, John Wiley & Sons. Once the business of bringing the book to an unsuspecting marketplace had been conducted, we managed to win one of the few tables around the outskirts of the sprawling exhibition in order to grab some plastic-encapsulated sandwiches. Aware that I had designed and typeset *Cyber Business*, my marketing manager asked why I was not publishing the book myself. My reply concerned my wish for my work to be backed and marketed by a large and reputable organization.

In deciding to sell my book to John Wiley & Sons, I had resolved that I wanted to utilize the reputation and expertise of a pre-existing mix of people and capital resources for my own profit. In this sense, I was as much *purchasing* an organization to perform the marketing functions which I desired, as I was *selling* John Wiley an input to one of their productive processes. When this revelation finally hit me several months after the bookfair, it changed my entire perception not just of publishing, but of evolving labour market conditions.

Not everybody publishes books. However, as individuals with free agent mentalities, more and more of us are *purchasing organizations* who will in turn broker our labour outputs to the wider marketplace. Increasingly empowered by the tools of the Digital Age, many people may now view themselves as *customers* in the world of work as well as suppliers. And this, at least for those with the ability to fly rather than to fall as they are turfed from the nest of traditional employment practices, changes everything. There are no longer slaves and masters; nor employees and employers. Instead, there is just a marketplace in which all are trying desperately to survive. Communicating and living this new labour reality undoubtedly presents a great challenge indeed. However, as the following chapters will demonstrate, it is a challenge that is inevitable given current transitions in our knowledge media, expanding geographic horizons, and the new, organic productive forms of the Future Organization.

Part III
Knowledge Media

8
Escapes from the
Here & Now

A SIGN OUTSIDE A church on a road into Nottingham reads 'Shared values last longer than valued shares'. This clever play on words is obviously intended to make passers-by think about the value of communal beliefs. For most people, whilst physical possessions and the virtual electronic property of money are important, some degree of social and cultural wealth also prove vital for happiness and stable mental health. Indeed, even within many business organizations, fostering a holistic range of strong cultural values is now regarded as critical for sustained success.[181]

As was noted towards the end of the last chapter, one of the reasons that drives people to seek an organizational affiliation is their desire to become part of a unified whole. In order to maintain (if not to thrive upon) our very humanity, we constantly need to made aware of practices and beliefs that deliver us a clear sense of identity amid life's unsettling sea of change.

The following three chapters chart the evolution of the *knowledge media* used to transmit ideas and values across the times and distances that separate human minds. Quite clearly, methods for the communication and recording of human experience have changed radically across the ages. Whilst cave-dwellers painted on walls and the great civilizations of antiquity carved symbols into stone, some of our more recent ancestors developed paper and the printing press. Then, within the Present Age, photography, radio and television—not to mention the telephone, gramophone records, compact discs and video cassettes—rose to play a widespread role as carriers of information and entertainment. And today, as we look ahead, there is the promise of a ubiquitous and unbounded global information 'superhighway' destined to bring together the many previously distinct media of computing, education, and audio-visual entertainment. As so many pundits have recently claimed, we are now witness to the dawn of the 'Information Age'.

Whilst all of the above may well be the case, it is not simply advances in technologies for shifting information around the planet that will be charted herein. Rather, analysing the changing *knowledge media* of humanity presents us with a more subtle yet distinctly different pathway for investigation. What's more, the progression we will explore involves a journey which most futurists have either ignored or entirely missed.

DEFINING TERMS

To understand exactly what I am referring to by 'knowledge media' we need to return to some of the ideas presented earlier within this book. Looking back to **chapter 1**, we may recall that the unit of cultural transmission is now referred to as the 'meme'.[182] To remind ourselves further, memes may range from simple catch-phrases or clothes fashions, through to the most complex of scientific ideas or social conventions. Popular memes will be those which propagate and replicate most quickly from brain to brain, and which in doing so render fresh patterns of uniformity, progress, and group identity.

If memes are the railroad wagons which carry fresh ideas, practices or understandings, then *knowledge media* comprise the tracks along which memes travel. Knowledge media are meme carriers. In addition, knowledge media also provide a means of *replicating* the meme wagons which travel over them. In totality, I am defining a knowledge media herein as the aggregation of all of those conventions and technologies used for the storage, replication and transmission of memes at any one particular point in time.

Across the ages, differing knowledge media have been associated with an evolution of technologies for information storage and communication. In common with many other analysts, Mark Poster of the University of California has proposed that every age has employed different 'modes' of information exchange.[183] In particular, Poster contends that three 'modes of information' may be isolated up until the present day. The first of these involved face-to-face, orally-mediated exchanges. Information mode two then comprised written exchanges mediated by print. Finally, Poster states that today's mode of information is based around electronically-mediated communications.[184]

Poster's analysis of the mode of *information* is simplistically attractive. Indeed it is also of some value in many sociological contexts. However, I do not believe that we may use such a simple technological progression to detail the advancement of *knowledge* media across time. For a start, forms of writing have been used consistently as a means of recording and transmitting ideas for over 5000 years. The use of the spoken word for passing knowledge between generations also goes back even further in our history.

New forms of communication—new modes of information—may have altered the means used to store, to replicate, and to transmit memes. However, they have not substantially altered the use of speech nor of text as knowledge-transmissive carriers. Rather, new communications forms have permitted *additional media channels* to be used to carry memes. It is therefore the increasingly-multiple use of new communications channels *in aggregation* which I believe to truly delineate different categories of knowledge media past, present and future.

Table 8.1 illustrates my chosen knowledge media progression. In past times, only *single channels* of oral communication or symbolic representation were available. These were in the form of either spoken language or the written word. Across the Present Age all of this has changed, as *multiple channels* of sounds, pictures, text, and moving images, have all become available. Finally in future, with the technologies and conventions which may link people together continuing to converge, an interactive, *metachannel* knowledge media will emerge. Metamedia communications forms are already identifiable within rudimentary forms of computer-generated virtual reality. A visit to a Disney-style theme park in some ways also provides an all-embracing metachannel experience. In the future a metachannel knowledge media is destined to provide cross-sensory patterns of stimuli integrated to such a level that the separation of more traditional channels of information delivery from within its sphere will prove nigh-on impossible.

Timeframe	Knowledge Media	Examples
Past	Single channel	Spoken language *or* the written word *or* pictures.
Present	Multi-channel	Text *and* sounds *and* still pictures *and* moving images.
Future	Metachannel	Computer-generated VR *and/or* controlled-reality environments

Table 8.1 Broadening Knowledge Media

Clearly the greater the number of channels available for idea replication and communication, the broader the knowledge media they so constitute, and the faster fresh memes may take hold across such media. Indeed, it is almost certainly due to our expansionary evolution of knowledge media that we have become witness to a near-exponential influx of new innovations, technologies and ideologies within the Present Age.

INFORMATION & KNOWLEDGE

Finally before delving back in time (and with an awareness that I am perhaps opening this chapter with too many definitions), I feel I ought at this point briefly clarify the difference between 'information' and 'knowledge'. Although used interchangeably—even in learned circles— these two terms refer to quite distinct phenomenon. On the one hand, information is the product of filtering and then processing raw data into a *potentially useful* form. On the other hand, knowledge stems from the analysis of information within an expert frame of reference so that it becomes attributed with actual *meaning*. **Figure 8.1** illustrates this progression diagrammatically.

Figure 8.1 Data, Information & Knowledge

To provide an example, barcode-scanning supermarket checkouts may now provide a store manager with a continuous stream of sales *data*. However, in order to prove potentially useful, raw sales figures will need to be aggregated and formatted into sales *information*. Such filtering is usually taken care of automatically by a computerized management information system (MIS). This is likely to provide sales figures by checkout, product line, store area, or whatever. However, the information contained within an MIS report will only take on significant *meaning* when reviewed by the store manager in order to determine the status of business operations. It may well be that only one or two key figures from each MIS report will impact significantly upon the manager's *knowledge* of his or her store's continuing performance. It is also likely that only a manager with experience of supermarket operations will be able to spot which figures these may be. The extraction of information from data may now easily be automated by a computerized system. However, the translation of information into meaningful knowledge still requires human *expertise*.

The distinction between information and knowledge is subtle and context sensitive. However, it is a distinction of ever-increasing significance in a world in which potential data and information sources continue to accumulate. The distinction between information and knowledge also provides another reason why I am choosing to concentrate herein upon aggregate media for the communication, storage and replication of knowledge, rather than of component data or information.

EARLY LANGUAGE DEVELOPMENTS

As several geneticists have now gleefully reported, the DNA codings which distinguish human beings from chimpanzees only differ by around two per cent. However, one vital difference between ourselves and our nearest primate relatives concerns our ability to distinguish the present from the past and from the future. Monkeys, poor souls, are simply 'trapped in the present'—within the here and now—with no true comprehension or awareness of time.[185]

Almost certainly, the evolution of early forms of spoken language and pictorial representation played a major role in permitting our distant ancestors to evolve the awareness of time which stamped them as human.[186] By speaking to each other, or by making marks on natural surfaces, early human beings[187] developed the ability to focus upon events from which they themselves were separated. Exactly how spoken languages developed will inevitably remain a mystery. One hypothesis is that very primitive human beings probably used hunting and other calls similar to those still exhibited by most animals. Later groups of humans with good memory skills may have then begun to break up such calls into particular sounds capable of rearrangement. By using commonly accepted sounds in different combinations, our distant ancestors could have learnt to communicate with an increasingly wide range of vocal messages. As more and more distinct sounds and combinations thereof came into play, primitive forms of grammar could thereby have emerged.[188]

As language evolved to permit the labelling of physical items and events within the present, so it also became possible to communicate ideas across time and distance. Through stories passed down generations (or from community to community), early humans became capable of communicating with others whom they did not (and often could not) directly know. Before literacy developed, the primary means of keeping cultures and traditions alive had to be by word of mouth. Exactly how effective this may have proved is difficult to judge, with the distorting effect of 'Chinese whispers' immediately springing to mind. This said, the use of lengthy oral genealogies to sanction rights of conquest, discovery, and ownership, across scores of generations has been noted by ethnologists who have studied preliterate peoples of the contemporary world.[189]

In addition to evolving spoken languages, early human communities also left legacies in the form of paintings, carvings, and other artifacts bearing symbolic representation. Cave paintings depicting hunts, battles, rituals, and sexual exploitations, date back tens of thousands of years to

Palaeolithic times.[190] Animal bones bearing engravings have also been unearthed from the period of the last Ice Age.[191] Whether the markings upon such artifacts were created in order to pass on knowledge, for aesthetic purposes, or perhaps as a means of denoting ownership, is open to debate. However, we may reasonably surmise that it was refinements in early forms of pictorial representation which led to the evolution of the first written languages.

THE BIRTH OF LITERACY

There is, of course, a great deal of difference between being able to talk or to create an image, and being able to function as a literate human being. Therefore whilst the use of spoken language and pictorial symbolic communication date back tens of thousands of years, we should not be surprised to learn that written language is a far more recent innovation.

The first forms of writing were developed around 5000 years ago, from which point in time onwards our chronicles of history tend (fairly obviously) to be far more complete. Indeed, one of the first uses for the tool of literacy was to record the past. Such records could prove useful as a validation of the structures (such as royal lines) of value or of potential dispute within the present. As literacy developed, written records thereby came to play a role in society comparable with the myths and ancestral memories of preliterate days.[192]

Literacy and written record keeping were almost certainly first invented in Mesopotamia, where the very earliest form of writing was developed by the Sumerians not long after 3300 BC. This first written media used pictorial symbols—known as pictograms—that were made by either scribing with a reed, or by pressing with a seal,[193] upon soft clay tablets. The clay was then baked to preserve its markings. Around 3000 BC, pictographic writing slowly developed into a script known as 'cuneiform'. This was comprised of characters formed with differing arrangements of one basic shape. In fostering systems for memorizing and copying cuneiform characters, Sumerian priests became the first custodians of an organized system of education.

Although famous for their hieroglyphic script, the ancient Egyptians almost certainly 'imported' the concept of calligraphy from Mesopotamia.[194] Whilst some primitive hieroglyphics date back before 3000 BC, written records using the pictorial characters did not appear until a couple of centuries later. However, whilst the Egyptians did probably not invent writing, their strong territorial stability, coupled with the persistence of their religious hierarchy, did allow their early written language to maintain a more notable continuity than that of any other early civilization.[195]

The Egyptians carved and/or painted hieroglyphics recording great battles, mythologies, religious ceremonies, and lines of royal ascent, upon many of their temples, tombs, palaces and artifacts. They also made religious, administrative and economic records upon stone tablets and papyrus scrolls. Over time, hieroglyphics were increasingly also used for magical and artistic purposes. Unfortunately, this started to limit their flexibility for general communication. Indeed, over 6000 hieroglyph symbols were eventually developed—some representing entire words or names, some being phonetic, some being alphabetic, and some being 'determinatives' used to denote the classes or action types of other words.[196] The ability to read and write was considered a mark of great respect amongst the ancient Egyptians. As such, the knowledge involved was kept a closely-guarded professional secret by the priesthood. Scribes were better off and even more valued than Egyptian soldiers. Many Egyptian princes and viziers therefore chose to be depicted in sculptures holding a reed pen and a papyrus scroll.[197]

Writing was almost certainly one of the tools which helped to cement together the many dynasties of ancient Egypt for so many thousands of years. It also served many organizational functions, such as permitting the production of scrolls of early tax lists. Meanwhile at Uruk in Mesopotamia, Sumerian priests were recording their expenditures upon clay tablets, thousands of which remain intact as the first accounts ledgers in history.[198] As in the early Egyptian kingdoms, writing had become a means not only of easing the administration of complex agricultural processes, but also of strengthening the powers of government and organized religion.[199]

SPREADING THE WORD

For many centuries, the only way to duplicate a book or any other work of literature was to painstakingly copy it out by hand. This labour of love was usually undertaken by monks, who could rarely complete more than one volume per year.[200] Written works were therefore in very short supply. As a result, literacy remained the rare privilege of the church and a limited number of scholars and academics. It was therefore to take the invention of printing to allow written language to evolve into a mass media.

The early empires of the Orient developed paper and then printing long before the West. As early as the 2nd century AD the Chinese were printing with wooden blocks. By the 10th century they had even begun to publish large numbers of books by this method.[201] A century later, and the Chinese had also invented movable type. However, this method of printing (wherein existing blocks of characters are rearranged as required in order to form written texts) was soon abandoned as impracticable due to the vast number of characters which exist within the Chinese language. Some three centuries later the Koreans also experimented with movable type (using characters formed from moulds), although they too found this method less practical than earlier wooden block technologies.

The insularity of early Eastern cultures, coupled with their rapid abandonment of movable type, greatly reduced the potential impact of the processes which they pioneered. It was therefore not until 1450—when German diamond polisher Johannes Gutenberg invented the first European printing press—that books started to become widely available outside of the East.

Gutenberg's innovation owed nothing to the Eastern influences—save perhaps indirectly due to the invention of paper by the Chinese around 105 AD.[202] Rather, Gutenberg and his associates brought together in one process 12th century principles for marking images onto textiles, a form of wooden press developed for wine making, new oil-based inks, and most importantly the first application of cast-metal movable type. It was the use of the latter which proved to be the biggest innovation, and which allowed Gutenberg to set the text for his famous Bible. This first true printed book was published around 1456, and led to Gutenberg's ennoblement by the Archbishop of Mainz. By 1500, some thirty-five thousand separate book editions had been published—probably equating to around fifteen to twenty million volumes in print.[203] In contrast, before Gutenberg's press there had only been around thirty-thousand books upon the entire continent of Europe.[204] The diamond polisher of Mainz had indeed sparked a media revolution.

As books became more widely available and literacy spread, so changes in the structure of society were inevitable. Most notable was the impact of the printed word upon the church. Before books could be printed in large numbers (and hence before widespread literacy) most people had to rely upon priests to read a church copy of the Bible to them. Citizens therefore had to trust their religious superior's interpretation of the gospels. However, when mass printed volumes became available during the Renaissance, ordinary individuals were afforded the opportunity to read the Bible for themselves. They were therefore free to make up their own minds about its teachings. The authority of the church thereby started to crumble—often leading to violence, wars, and long periods of social unrest.[205]

THE FIRST MASS MEDIA

Ten times as many books were printed in the 16th as in the 15th century.[206] As the number of volumes in circulation continued to increase, so the geographic scope and intellectual diversity of humankind also expanded. Boundaries to knowledge sharing rapidly fell. Information and knowledge—science, politics, propaganda and fiction—could for the first time be spread with ease across hundreds of thousands of minds. Within the 16th and 17th centuries, texts were published and distributed detailing a vast range of subjects. A previously unthinkable volume of human communication therefore started to take place at both the individual and the corporate level.[207]

The wooden presses of the 15th to 18th centuries were capable of making around 250 page impressions an hour. However, by the early 19th century, much larger iron machines had become capable of running-off many thousands of pages in the same time period.[208] Steam power was also soon applied to work printing mechanisms in the place of manual labour.[209] Printers using curved drums (rather than flat plates) were then introduced in the mid- to late-19th century. Of particular importance were those capable of printing from rolls rather than single sheets, as these greatly eased the production of newspapers. By the mid-1800s, printing machines devised by the American inventor Richard March Hoe were producing 20,000 impressions an hour.[210]

Books and then newspapers were the world's first mass-produced products. They were therefore responsible for the first mass markets in a world lusting for information. To some extent printed works even enforced the nation state boundaries of the geographic areas across which they came to be distributed.[211] By reading the same books and newspapers, literate citizens could partake in an increasingly wide geographic identity. No longer were people limited to keeping up with events and ideas from their own hamlet or village by word of mouth. Rather, the mass reproduction and distribution of the printed word allowed citizens to learn of happenings across entire countries or regions.

PROGRESSIONS IN TIME

To create and then master spoken language probably took early human beings several tens of thousands of years. In stark contrast, written languages were developed from scratch in around five millennia. Even more remarkably, commonly available technologies for spreading the printed word evolved towards ubiquity in little more than four centuries. An increasing rate of metamorphosis in the channels available for meme storage, replication and transmission also continues to this day.

Towards the end of the 19th century, human beings could only accurately share their thoughts and knowledge via the spoken word or written language.[212] In the period of time which has followed, not only have a great many more meme channels become available. Perhaps far more significantly, the *coupling together* of many emergent channels of information storage, replication, and transmission, has also progressed to become the norm.

The popular press began to talk of the 'multimedia revolution' in the late-1980s. However, as we shall witness in the next chapter, multi-channel knowledge media actually began to develop almost one hundred years before this time. Despite what computer journalists and advertising copyrighters claim, multimedia is not the future. Rather, it is a means of meme replication which arrived many years ago, and whose wane is already on the near horizon.

9
Cyberia:
First Steps

Imagine what it would be like if TV were good. It would be the end of everything we know . . . .

Marvin Minsky[213]

CYBERSPACE—THE CONSENSUAL HALLUCINATION experienced daily by billions. Cyberspace—the shared, computer-mediated electronic realm of information and communications. Cyberspace—the data jungle of computer connectivity. Cyberspace—where your money is stored and where your telephone calls are. Cyberspace—the next business frontier. Cyberspace—an artificial, 3-D graphical environment. Cyberspace—the sanitized emotional vacuum occupied by computer geeks and couch potatoes who really ought to go outside and get a life.[214]

As Michael Benedikt muses in the introduction to his classic *Cyberspace: First Steps*, cyberspace, for the most part, does not exist.[215] Or as the first six of the above definitions may have inferred, cyberspace is merely a mental abstraction which may help us to better cope with certain applications of new technology.

The word 'cyberspace' was first used by science fiction author William Gibson in 1984.[216] Since that time, the 'cyberspace concept' has matured to provide a lexical home for many researchers and technoevangelists keen to advance, or to preach the coming of, the Digital Age. Whether the average computer user chooses to believe that a little piece of cyberspace exists within the box on their desk really does not matter. What does is how various electronic media have transformed the storage and transmission of memes across the Present Age.

Douglas Rushkoff, amongst others, uses the word 'Cyberia' to refer to the place where people go when communicating across territories with no physical bounds.[217] Whilst including the electronic world of cyberspace within its sphere, Cyberia is a far wider concept embracing all manner of 'out of body experiences'. Since the beginnings of collective humanity, the mystical teachings of every religion have alluded towards the existence of a post-terrestrial plane. However, it is only since the dawn of the Present Age that electronic innovations have coalesced to allow us to 'touch' Cyberia in the form of its cyberspace manifestation.

Every time we communicate by phone or via a computer link we engage in meetings of minds that leave the flesh encasements of our bodies behind. Every time we watch a film, a video, or a television programme, we may come to empathize with people whom we can see and hear, yet who are not really with us at all. Cyberia is undoubtedly the dominant meme carrier of the Present Age. In contrast to knowledge media of past times, Cyberia is also multi-channel. And in allowing us to gather information from multiple sensory sources, Cyberia is effectively multimedia. In a few pages we will begin to explore this concept—and its implications—more fully. However, before we begin, let us be reminded of those innovations which permitted our knowledge media to broaden from the single to the multi-channel in the first place.

NEW MEDIA FORMS

As we have already witnessed in other chapters, from around the mid-19th century onwards mass technology began to radially transform the western world. The printed word was already in widespread distribution, with books, journals and newspapers uniting nations and scholars across previously precarious geographic divides. Several other important single-channel meme carriers were also soon to rise to prominence. First was to be the electric telegraph—invented in 1836—which allowed people to communicate over great distances via an interconnecting wire. By 1851 London and Paris were linked by a cable under the English Channel, whilst by 1866 the first transoceanic cable was permitting instantaneous telecommunications across the Atlantic.[218]

As telegraph links were accruing across the world, the potential for electrical wires to carry voices as well Morse code messages[219] was also being investigated. Alexander Grahame Bell is credited for inventing the telephone in 1876. However Elisha Gray applied for a patent for the same innovation only hours later. It also took the invention of electromagnetic microphones by D.E. Hughes in 1888 in order to permit the creation of telephones capable of carrying voices and other sounds over long distances.

Technologies for recording the human voice were also emerging at this time. The first gramophone (or 'phonograph') was invented by Thomas Alva Edison in 1877. It also soon proved popular with the general public. Surprisingly, techniques for recording sound upon magnetic media were also developed not long after.[220] However, it was not until the introduction of audio cassettes in 1966 that magnetic tape became a popular mass media.[221]

In addition to telephony and sound recording, a third emergent media of the mid- to late-19th century was photography. A French physicist named Joseph Niepce had used photosensitive chemicals to produce recognizable images as early as 1826. In 1841 the Englishman Fox Talbot had then patented the first process to use negatives from which photographic prints were subsequently made. However, it was to take the introduction of the Kodak camera by the American George Eastman in 1888 to open up photography for the masses.

Unlike its predecessors, the Kodak camera was compact, relatively cheap, and fairly easy to use. It was also loaded with reels of celluloid film which could be returned to a Kodak lab after pictures had been taken. Photographers were therefore no longer required to possess a background in chemistry in order to obtain negatives and prints from their labours.

Catalysed into the public imagination by Eastman's innovation, photography quickly spread across the world. For the first time pictures of actual events could be captured without the need for their interpretation into drawings, paintings, or text-based media. New printing technologies soon also permitted photographs to be included alongside text within some publications. As early as the January of 1890, the first extensively illustrated newspaper—*The Daily Graphic*—was launched in Great Britain.

MAGICAL CREATIONS

Even before still photography had become a common process, there had been several experiments with machines designed to create the illusion of moving images.[222] These led to the invention of a movie camera by Étienne-Jules Marey in 1882. This recorded sequences of images on strips of photographic paper. By 1894, sprocketed 35 mm celluloid film had replaced its more delicate paper counterpart in the coin-operated 'Kinetoscope' movie machines pioneered by Thomas Edison and William Dickson.

Kinetoscopes quickly became a popular amusement in New York, London, Berlin and Paris. The French capital was also to host the first paying film show when, in 1895, brothers Louis and Auguste Lumière projected ten short films in a Parisian cafe.[223] As one man who saw their presentation later remarked, its 'marvelling' and 'extraordinary' sights had to imply that 'the world had changed'.[224]

Over the ensuing three decades silent movies spread across the world. Pathé's newsreel gazettes also began the pictorial transmission of world events internationally from 1909. However, the cinema did more than open eyes to other ways of life across distant horizons. In addition, it gave people a chance to escape from the bleakness of reality into a world of stars and glamour and pure fantasy. Whilst Neil Armstrong did not set foot upon our barren satellite until 1969, George Mèliës *Trip to the Moon* captured the public imagination in 1902.

As cinema was becoming a more and more popular pastime, so another apparently 'magical' communications media was also in its infancy. Its name was radio, and, unlike its telegraph and telephone forebears, it actually permitted signals to be transmitted *without wires*.

Scientists James Maxwell and Heinrich Hertz had first explored the feasibility of sending messages through the ether in the 1870s and 1880s. However, it took the Italian Guglielmo Marconi to developed 'wireless telegraphy' into a practical and commercial reality. In the December of 1901, Marconi sent the first wireless signal across the Atlantic. Only two years later radio news services began transmission in London and New York.[225]

By the 1920s wireless sets were being produced in relatively large numbers. Entertainment programmes were also in regular transmission.

Radio therefore started to catch up with cinema as the great popular mass media.

MULTI-CHANNEL KNOWLEDGE MEDIA

As we have already noted, some of the media innovations of the late-19th and early-20th centuries were the result of many years of painstaking scientific development. However, in the public eye, the innovatory single channel media of the telephone, sound recording, photography, silent movies, and radio, all arrived for general consumption within barely two decades. In doing so these five media also transformed the world. During the lifetime of a generation, the means available for the communication and the replication of information, knowledge and entertainment had multiplied several fold.

At first it may not be obvious why the above list of technological developments may be upheld as heralding the birth of multi-channel knowledge media. After all, with the exception of those publications offering readers both text *and pictures*, most media forms of the late-19th and early-20th centuries only utilized one communications conduit (in the form of pictures *or* sounds *or* text). However, such single channel information media were inevitably utilized in amalgamation from their very beginnings.

Take the spread of news as an example. In the mid-19th century, distant events of public significance were only likely to become known via newspaper reports. Happenings within families were also only likely to be rapidly shared across any distance by letter.[226] However, once new media forms emerged, knowledge and information came to acquire several additional carriers over which to travel. By the early-20th century, details of important events and new fashions were being communicated via newspapers *and* cinema *and* radio. In a similar vein, the tragedies and tribulations of families and friends were starting to be communicated by telephone *as well as* by the handwritten word.

Photography also permitted happenings from wars to marriages to holidays to be immortalized not just by text or word of mouth, but *in addition* with an accompanying picture. For the first time children could learn of distant or deceased relatives from photographs as well as recounted memories. Through the ages humans beings have evolved to seek knowledge and verification of events via a variety of senses in combination. And, since the turn of the century, the existence of multiple media forms has enabled us to do just that. Hence, although not multimedia within themselves, the emergence of the telephone, sound recording, photography, silent movies, and of radio, did for the first time permit memes to travel between human minds via a combination of multiple pathways. As a result, due to these aggregate multi-channel mass media, the *quality* of people's interactions substantially increased.[227]

MASS PROPAGANDA—& ALL THAT JAZZ

Even before the world had ceased to reel from the influx of so many new forms of information capture, communication and entertainment, the first true multi-sensory media also emerged. In 1927 audiences across the globe wowed as Al Johnson spoke down from the movie screen to inform them that they 'ain't heard nothing yet!'.[228] In many venues the sound of *The Jazz Singer*'s subsequent song-and-dance act was drowned out amid cheers and gasps of astonishment. Over the next couple of decades movies with synchronized sound—'talkies'—became the norm. Colour films also increasingly replaced those shot in black and white. The impact of cinema upon the public consciousness and imagination just grew and grew.

As cinema attendance became habitual for large numbers of people, so it was inevitable that movies became the first media of mass propaganda. Unlike radio, cinema was a meme conduit which did not require citizens to purchase their own reception technology. The fact that movies were watched in large groups—and that beyond the 1930s most used the multimedia combination of moving pictures and sound—also made films far more effective propaganda weapons than radio broadcasts. In particular, in its early days the cinema was used to spread fascism in Italy, the message of Nazi 'superiority' in Germany, and communism in the Soviet Union. During WWII the allies also used propaganda movies to manipulate their populations to great effect. By having propaganda shorts screened before every feature film presentation, all manner of regimes guaranteed that the majority of the population got their message.

CITIZENS OF CYBERIA

Cinema screens and wireless sets were the most common tools used to link and program human minds in the first half of the 20th century. However, since the 1950s, television has taken their place as an even more powerful mass multimedia. If Cyberia exists anywhere today, then it does so within the confines of the TV sets which occupy so many homes around the globe. The 'information superhighway', its present Internet incarnation, or even interactive CD-ROMs,[229] may turn out to be the multimedia of the future. However, in comparison to television, these pubescent Cyberian meme channels still have a lot of growing up to endure before they really mature.

It was the Scottish inventor John Logie Baird who, in 1926, first demonstrated a system for transmitting pictures electronically. His ideas were further developed by the Marconi Company in the United States, whose black and white transmission system was adopted across Europe and America in the 1930s.[230] This said, whilst a television service was available in this decade (the BBC, for example, began transmissions in 1936), television did not really start to take off until after WWII.

By the time the 1950s began to boom, no other media could match television's hold over the hearts and minds of those with access to a set boasting even the smallest of screens. The film industry gallantly attempted to fight back with widescreen formats and gimmicks such as movies watched through 3-D glasses or in 'Smell-O-Vision'. However, regular audiences continued to abandon cinema queues in their droves. Most inhabitants of the new suburbia preferred a box in the corner of their living room to a group pilgrimage to the box office. By the time that colour television started to become widely available in the 1970s, television's multimedia dominance was unstoppable.[231] As Ithiel de Sola Pool reported in his *Technologies of Freedom*, as early as 1977 less than one in five words in America were being delivered by print media.[232]

Whilst it may have curtailed many group and community activities in the flesh, television has undoubtedly brought people together mentally as citizens of national and global Cyberia. For example, *Eurovision* events (such as the annual song contest which commenced in 1955) have been consciously arranged to foster a sense of European identity across nations.[233] Television has also enabled a large proportion of the global population to share in the experience of momentous world events. As we noted in **chapter 3**, around half a billion people watched the US moonlandings.[234]

As television has spread as the dominant media for popular entertainment, so the small screen has also become a key tool for mass influence. From wars to washing powders, pretzels to presidents, television has been successfully used to manipulate the minds, habits and actions of entire populations. John F. Kennedy was arguably the first US President to be elected following a successful television campaign. Indeed, Vladimir Zworykin, one of the pioneers of US television, was once introduced to him as 'the man who got you elected'. Initially shocked at the suggestion, Kennedy went on to praise Zworykin for his terrific and important achievement. To this Zworykin simply commented, 'Have you seen television recently?'.[235]

Debates concerning the influence of television (and in particular of televisual sex and violence upon young children) continue to rage. Indeed, 'v-chip' censorship technology is soon to be introduced into new television sets in the United States, and possibly also in the UK. However, whether one chooses to consider the influence of television upon society as either positive or negative, the extent of such influence cannot realistically be ignored. In terms of time spent, within most industrialized societies, for most people watching television is second only to work and sleep.[236]

Given the above, it is hardly surprising that television programmes have evolved into social events which have come to ritualistically dominate our lives. Many people will go to great lengths to avoid missing their favourite show. After all, being 'unaware' of an episode may not only mean missing out on the enjoyment of an unravelling story. In addition, those who have not seen a programme will be unable to contribute to any discussion of its content with workmates, family members, and friends. Watching television—like regular weekly cinema attendance before it—remains a herd activity. This said, with the spread of new audio-visual technologies in recent years, the cosy sanctity of externally programmed televisual behaviour is increasingly coming to be challenged.

THE INTERACTIVE GENERATION

It took but one innovation—that of the inexpensive domestic video recorder—to break the hold of television programme schedulers upon the habits of entire nations. Sony introduced its Betamax home video machines in 1975. However, home video did not really take off until the VHS format became the de facto market standard in the mid-1980s.[237] With video recorders came the freedom to timeshift television output to suit the schedules of individuals rather than broadcasters. Such a capability put the meme channel of television on a par with that of text or audio-based media, which had both been available for consumption at an individual's leisure since their emergence as mass communications forms. Video recorders in the home finally allowed television programmes to be stored as well as watched. More than any other technological development, video recorders therefore put the public (and their business organizations) in control of the knowledge conduit of their age.

Since the introduction of home video, increasing user control has been a feature of most new media innovations. Also in the 1980s, audio compact disc (CD) technology gave consumers digital *random access* to prerecorded material. For the first time, individuals were permitted to *program* stereo systems to play selected tracks in any order they desired. In the late-1990s, Digital Video Disk (DVD)[238] systems now also permit video to be accessed in a similar non-linear manner. And this is just the beginning.

Multimedia servers upon the forthcoming 'information superhighway' will shortly allow far more widespread random-access 'video on demand' links into the home or office. Don't like the TV schedule? Then simply program your own. As Nicholas Negroponte suggests, the practice of blanket broadcasting to a mass audience will in future be replaced by flexible 'narrowcasting' to many audiences of one. Interactively customized to order, television will in future be a 'boutique' service scheduled by its viewers.[239] What's more, as the computers that will process the information streams of the Digital Age get more powerful, distinctions between many media will disappear. As will be detailed in the next chapter, metachannel media are already starting to emerge. Future 'datacasters' may be able to transmit a model of weather data, or of uncut news events, to be turned into a video report, a radio announcement, a magazine article, or whatever, according to the desires of the consumer and the capabilities of their computerized data receiving system.[240]

As the above paragraph clearly reminds us, driving the development of new random access, programmable media has been humankind's recent friend or foe the computer. Co-inhabitants of our shrinking planet since the ENIAC was created in 1945,[241] computers and their networks will undoubtedly provide the infrastructural backbone for future knowledge media. As we began to explore in **chapter 4**, the world is rapidly becoming a single wired computing machine—a single 'global hardware platform' across which all Future Organizations will function.

Such an evolution is at present being spearheaded by the increasing use of the Internet (the 'international network', or simply 'the Net'), to which individual users and organizations may connect via a personal computer. By 1996 there were approaching fifty million Internet users worldwide. Some forecasters were even predicting a user base of over one billion by the turn of the century.[242]

Whilst many business sceptics consider the Internet to be a fad—as Don Tapscott, author of *The Digital Economy*, puts it, 'Right now there appear to be more prophets than profits on the Net'[243]—its great computer anarchy is already an amazingly powerful meme conduit.[244] News and views that would be censored, or simply not voiced, over traditional media are increasingly finding their own communications channels in cyberspace. As so many have claimed, a connection to the Internet gives everyone the power of a press. It is, perhaps, therefore hardly surprising that more words are published on the Internet in a week than in all of the books published in the US in a year.[245] As author Howard Rheingold demonstrates to such great effect in *The Virtual Community*,[246] the Internet already empowers individuals, and groups thereof, in the face of physical, mental and political adversity. And as several Governments have already found, trying to censor the Net is like trying to hold water in a sieve.

HIGHWAYS AHEAD

As even its most ardent advocates have to admit, the Internet of the late-1990s can be terribly slow and unreliable. In many ways this is due to the Internet's success (the more traffic, the slower the system), and in particular the popularity of the world-wide web (WWW) graphical interface which tens of millions now use to 'surf' or 'browse' seas of on-line information. The more people who want to view photographs, video clips, and even virtual reality models,[247] upon their desktops, the slower the current Internet will become. Help, however, is soon predicted to be at hand. Whilst any timescale for completion is still debated, it is now commonly agreed that a high speed 'information superhighway' will sooner or later emerge. Known more shortly in some quarters as simply 'the highway'[248] or 'the I-Way'[249], this forthcoming meme-transmission superchannel will either evolve out of, or entirely replace, the current Internet. It will also be like nothing humankind has ever witnessed before.

The physical infrastructure of the information superhighway is likely to consist of a complex interweaving of fibre-optic cables, satellite links, digital wireless communications, and probably some copper wiring. It is unlikely in the extreme than just one communications technology will dominate. This will, however, enable the reach and capacity of the superhighway to be as broad as possible, so permitting multimedia in all previously known formats to be transmitted interactively and instantaneously at a global level. Communications will finally know no bounds, and (in theory at least), *everyone* will have the capability to become a broadcaster.

Within his own future-gazing book *The Road Ahead*, Microsoft founder Bill Gates states that the birth of the information superhighway will represent a far more significant media shift than that witnessed with the rise of television in the 1950s. As Gates contends, whilst television has become a major influence upon our lives, in effect it 'was just a replacement for commercial radio, which had been bringing electronic entertainment into homes for twenty years'. In comparison, no broadcast medium is comparable to what the information superhighway will be like.[250] And will people actually *want* the information superhighway? Will they ever! Already personal computers are outselling televisions by

far, with seventy per cent of computers going into the home.[251] The
fresh market opportunities, let alone the knowledge transmission
potential, of future computing-based communications media (and in effect
this means almost *all* future communications media), will be enormous.
They may even spark new business value to such a level that the globe
will briefly heave itself out of recession. Unfortunately, as always, social
dilemmas are also poised to spring. As Don Tapscott reminds us:

> Despite its unhealthy impact upon people, television at least brought
> families together around an electronic hearth. But in my family today, it's
> not unusual for the four of us to be clicking away on our keyboards in
> separate rooms. Further, some families will have better access to the new
> media than others.[252]

THOUSANDS & THOUSANDS OF LIES

They used to say that a picture was worth a thousand words. In the future
a picture, let alone a video clip, is more likely to be worth a thousand
lies. With around half of our brains devoted to visual processing, most
people still tend to trust what they see. Whether or not a camera can lie
is a matter for philosophical interpretation. However, whether many of
the images which now bombard us contain untruths is not open to
question. Lies—even if they are created in the name of entertainment and
possibly education—are the media industry's stock-in-trade.

With the ubiquitous digital technologies on the near horizon, every lie
conceivable will be able to be made 'real'. The ancient Egyptians may
have built the Great Pyramid at Giza. However, it was *Time Magazine*
who successfully shifted it sideways a bit in order to make it more
aesthetically fit on their February 1982 front cover.[253] Or as Mark
Slouka, one of the most fluid articulators of the 'dark side' of the digital
revolution suspects, Sylvester Stallone was not really photographed with
Churchill, Roosevelt and Stalin in 1945, contrary to what a picture above
his desk appears to demonstrate.[254]

The paradox of mass media development is that the more powerful
most forms of human communication become, the less reliable they may
be. In the 1950s and 1960s actual television pictures could be trusted, as

recording technologies were primitive, and moving-image manipulation was nigh-on impossible.[255] Voices over the telephone were also never synthesized by computers, and pictures in newspapers could generally be relied upon to be representations of the 'truth'. However, in the 21st century, all such realities will change. Most single channel media will have to be treated with some scepticism—as worth no more than the binary patterns from which they are formed. Even the multimedia of television programmes, video recordings, and (especially) interactive computer data sources, will have to be relied upon with a proverbial pinch of salt.

As we will explore within the final chapter of Part III, the need for, and the implications of, the next step-evolution in our knowledge media will be enormous. Most important will be questions of validity rather than technology. For Future Organizations attempting to build value upon imagination, upon knowledge, and upon information content, the convergence of single and multi-channel knowledge media into future metachannel forms may therefore constitute the most worrying dilemma which they will have to face.

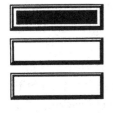

10
Shared Nightmares, Shared Dreams

A FEW YEARS AGO I became one of the first members of my department to be supplied with a personal computer boasting a CD-ROM drive.[256] A copy of Microsoft's *Encarta* multimedia encyclopedia was also included along with my new desktop hardware. Once this fact became known down the corridor, several of my colleagues dropped by to 'investigate' this particular CD-ROM application. Some were soon marvelling at the video playback of a venus flytrap consuming its latest insect victim. Others were more impressed by the dulcet musical tones which my office PC was now also capable of producing.

Interested in potential academic application, one of my colleagues asked me to conduct an *Encarta* search based upon a single keyword related to his subject area. A list of relevant articles was soon displayed upon my monitor screen. Starting to browse the contents of these entries, my colleague commented how he would have to read all of them at some time 'in order to check that he had been getting it right all of these years'. A shiver ran down my spine. Here was a noted academic in a top university stating (if perhaps in jest) that the computer was more likely to be right than he was. A better example of the oft-misplaced trust which people tend to vest in information technology would be hard to find.

New computer-based media are not necessarily more definitive than their more 'humble' paper-based relatives. Emerging 'cybermedia' may present information in a wide range of highly interesting and entertaining formats. Unfortunately, such delivery 'advancements' are rarely also matched with increases in the quality and/or the accuracy of the message being conveyed. In fact, the reverse often proves to be the case. As any surfer of the world-wide web will tell you, the Internet currently contains a great deal of garbage. There are also a large number of web information sources of dubious integrity. Indeed, as was noted at the end of the last chapter, digital technologies are now making it increasingly easy for the 'truth' to be distorted whether by accident or design.

The prequel to this book was entitled *Cyber Business: Mindsets for a Wired Age*. Unfortunately, the US Library of Congress keyed the subtitle *Mindsets for a Wired Aged* into its cataloging-in-publication (CIP) database. In days gone by this error would only have affected the information stored in one or a few library systems. However, in today's world of mass computer connectivity, the error has run on and on. Almost all libraries now source new title details directly from the CIP archive. Every library system which I have checked therefore infers that my previous book concerns an electrically-augmented geriatric.

It sometimes appears that the more advanced our media forms become, the less likely they are to report accurate information. If perhaps a little cynical, this view should certainly be kept in mind as we begin our investigation of likely future media developments. For as a common saying now goes, 'whilst to err is to be human, to really muck it up takes a computer'.

METAMEDIA EMERGE

This chapter details the transition ahead as a 'metachannel' form of knowledge media emerges to replace the multi-channel knowledge media of the present. As defined herein, a metachannel knowledge media involves the combination of many previously distinct media forms into one synergistic whole. A metachannel knowledge media may thereby enable the transmission of memes via the replication, storage and communication of synthetic human *experiences*. In contrast, previous knowledge media only proved effective in processing and communicating knowledge, data or information.[257]

The last chapter noted how a multi-channel knowledge media emerged as people were bombarded with information from many distinct yet complementary single channels. In a similar fashion, an amalgamated metachannel knowledge media is emerging around us today as many multi-channel media come to be utilized in synergistic combination. For example, when multi-channel media first emerged, people may have relied upon newspapers, radio reports, and silent movie newsreels, to verify new knowledge and information. However, today we may be influenced by television, CD-ROM encyclopedias, and the Internet, as three distinct multi-channel media used in metachannel combination. And, of course, previous single channel media will also still impact upon our perceptions.

Our increasing parallel utilization of many multi-channel media may signal the dawn of the 'metachannel media revolution'. However, just as it took television to really kick-start the multimedia age, so it will take the development of revolutionary new *metamedia* to trigger the next truly evolutionary step in knowledge media progression. Such metamedia will package the storage, replication and communication of complete synthetic experiences into one delivery format. Metamedia will therefore need to integrate an extremely wide variety of previously single or multi-channel modes of communication into one cohesive whole. Today television, cinema, or paper-based multi-channel media, only excite our senses (with either sound and vision *or* text and still images) when we happen to be looking in the right direction. In contrast, future metamedia will blanket a far broader sensory and perceptual range to a level which may in some instances approach ubiquity.

MULTIMEDIA CONVERGE

Several variants of metamedia are starting to be conceived in the late-20th century as the previously distinct industries of telecommunications, computing, and audio-visual entertainment, digitally converge.[258] The most obvious emerging metamedia is computer generated virtual reality. Other metamedia developments include the increasingly metachannel medium of the Internet's world-wide web,[259] and arguably even interactive television. The predicted-to-increase application of computer technology within our lives, our homes, and our organizations is therefore likely to go hand-in-hand with many metamedia advancements.

Fully-immersive remote virtual reality connections will sooner or later replace many of the video links which are even now starting to supplant conventional telephones. Eventually we will be able to feel, smell and taste remote digital environments—and each other—in addition to experiencing 'virtual' synthetic sound and vision. Far sooner many couch potatoes may be transformed into interactive surfers, shoppers, and virtual community members, living part-digital lives upon a blossoming information superhighway. Like it or not, the age of mass electronic interconnection has only just begun.

In contrast, some forms of non-digital metamedia have already been with us for many years. These metamedia deliver all-encompassing synthetic experiences within artificially manipulated physical spaces. They will therefore be referred to herein as *controlled reality environments* (or 'CREs'). The most obvious examples of CREs today include theme parks, theme restaurants and hotels, and holiday complexes hidden away under vast artificial domes. CRE attractions are continuing to grow in popularity in many leisure sectors. However, it is possible that in future CREs could also prove highly effective human resource management tools. In particular, 'corporate CREs' may one day provide a focus for fostering organizational meme propagation and portfolio-worker loyalty. The potential development of CREs for such purposes is discussed later in this chapter.

As metachannel knowledge media become more and more dominant, so education and social patterns, in addition to business communications and personal entertainment, look certain to be radically transformed. By a wide variety of methods, future metamedia will soak us in an ocean of integrated, interactively-controlled perceptual stimuli. The limits of knowledge transmission will therefore move way beyond those of today's most influential multi-channel media of mass-broadcast television. Any significant investigation of metamedia development therefore has to include some discussion of the potential use and/or abuse of any new knowledge media for distorting our perceptions of reality. As the opening gambit to this chapter should have clearly intimated, we are already far too eager to place a deep trust in the religion of microelectronics. And this is before true metamedia have begun to significantly impact upon our lives.

In the relatively near future, human *experiences* will be able to be replicated and conveyed to others with a previously undreamt of totality. By controlling and manipulating metamedia forms, both individuals and organizations will be able to lie—to each other or to themselves—as never before. The remainder of this chapter will therefore not only explore the potential development and application of virtual reality graphics worlds and physical controlled reality environments; in addition, it will also seek to investigate how the boundaries between what is 'real' and what is 'imaginary' may in future come to be blurred.

OUR INTERPERSONAL FRIEND

Digital convergence has already been noted as one of the key forces driving the metamedia revolution. Whether it will be telecoms giants, mass entertainment corporations, or software publishers, who will dominate the final industries which will emerge from such convergence remains far from clear. However, what is certain is that the dominant technology of digital convergence is the computer.

Pick up an introductory textbook from only a few years ago and you will find computers described as 'information processing tools'.[260] Yet today computers are used for far more than processing and storing information. In addition, computers are now rapidly becoming the primary technology used to link people together. It will not be long before *all* of humanity's most influential memes are routed between our minds via microprocessor. Or as Timothy Leary so nicely put it in his thought-provoking *Chaos and Cyberculture*, we have already entered an age of 'interpersonal computing' wherein 'relatively inexpensive gadgets place the power to create platonic, electronic realities in the hands of interacting individuals'.[261] Rather than talking of the 'PC' on our desktop, we should therefore now refer to our communication-enabling 'IPC' or *interpersonal computer*.

As the most popular replicators and communicators of contemporary let alone future humanity, computers and their lifeblood networks are already approaching ubiquitous application. Computers and networks are around us. Everywhere. I was recently somewhat surprised to learn that one of my undergraduates has set up a network to interlink the four PCs in his student house. What's more, he didn't even consider this to be unusual. Today, it is the computer not regularly connected to any other which is increasingly rare.

In homes, as well as in offices, computers are finally being used for information and knowledge sharing rather than hoarding. As the infrastructure of the information superhighway continues to emerge, the increasing perception of computers as digital communicators rather than digital cupboards will—and should—only continue to gather pace. Already, to try to build an empire by controlling information is not only a foolish activity, but one sooner or later fated to fail.

THE ELECTRONIC EXPERIENCE

Artificial reality guru Myron Krueger contends that we are no longer creatures of just five senses. Instead, digital technologies now provide us with literally hundreds of means of environmental perception.[262] We can see in the dark via infrared vision, look inside our bodies with x-rays, ultrasonics or magnetic imaging, gaze at molecules or atoms beneath electron microscopes, and bear witness to weather patterns or distant galaxies swirling before the receptors of satellites far out in space. We can also gauge the age and composition of ancient materials and artifacts via spectral analysis, and may compress, expand, or even halt time, with advanced recording and playback techniques. Augmented by the digital, our primary, 'real-time' environmental scanners of sight, hearing, touch, taste and smell have been opened up to a teeming plethora of new secondary means of perceiving both natural and artificial creation.

The ultimate technology-empowered metamedia will one day be fully immersive computer generated virtual reality (VR). Linked either directly or indirectly to our bodies by various means, future VR systems will become capable of blanketing us with as few or as many sources of sensory input as we wish to experience.

The most basic forms of VR will simply try to fool our eyes. The most advanced will stimulate all of our 'traditional' senses *and more*. A surgeon operating in virtual reality will be capable of switching between 'normal', 'x-ray' and 'macro' vision. She will also be able to hear the beat of her patient's heart in addition to the banter of her colleagues. Architects walking through virtual buildings will not only be able to view walls, floors and ceilings. At the same time they will also see how the structure will be stressed under the weight of its construction, as well as how air will circulate around passages and how sounds will resonate. Engineers will be able to spot fractures inside an aircraft turbine whilst feeling the exterior surface of its blades. In short, immersive VR systems will augment our current perceptions of the world in order to enable us to complete many tasks more effectively. They will also allow us to learn and communicate in new ways.

Cyber Business contained an extensive review of present and future technologies for computer-generated VR. Many other books have also offered comprehensive VR hardware guides.[263] A drawn-out discussion of specific current hardwares from head-mounted displays (HMDs) to datagloves therefore hardly seems warranted herein. Suffice it to say that most present technologies for immersing human beings in electronic virtual worlds are rapidly advancing but still somewhat primitive.

The majority of current VR systems position two low-resolution colour screens before the eyes. A 3-D wand, 'flying mouse', dataglove, or other gesture device, is then placed in or on one hand.[264] Head movement is also tracked. The user can therefore see in 3-D in a computer generated world. They may also navigate and manipulate their virtual surroundings by hand and finger movement. More elaborate VR systems additionally provide stereo audio via a headset, as well as tracking a greater range of body motions with a wider array of gesture devices. Some current systems even provide limited sensations of surface tactility and/or force feedback.[265] However it is likely that the true metamedia VR systems of the early-21st century will be far more advanced.

PHASES OF DEVELOPMENT

The hardware required to immerse human beings in computer generated virtual worlds will almost certainly evolve in two distinct phases. Phase one will involve the refinement of head mounted displays, motion sensors, and systems for synthetic force-feedback.[266] As a result, entire VR bodysuits (or other clothing/jewellery combinations) will come to be created. These will be capable of permitting their wearer to inhabit a virtual manikin crafted in computer graphics. All of the actions of the user will be mirrored in VR by this manikin. In parallel, all of the sensations 'experienced' in a virtual world by this software body will be fed back to the wearer of the suit via the senses of sight, sound and touch.

When hardwares capable of permitting the above level of VR immersion finally become cheap and reliable, our inhabitation of computer-generated graphics worlds will skyrocket. However, whilst future body suits will allow for the highly effective transportation of human beings into virtual environments, they are unlikely ever to permit a level of VR experience indistinguishable from reality. Regardless of how much sophisticated clothing a future VR participant is willing to have sealed tight to their body, it seems improbable in the extreme that 'bolt on' VR peripherals will ever fool anybody into believing that they are actually eating a sandwich, kissing a lover, smelling a flower, or feeling wet grass beneath computer-generated feet.

Strapping peripherals to our bodies to in turn stimulate our natural sense receptors will always remain a second-best solution for VR immersion. The second phase of VR technology development will therefore have to involve the refinement of techniques and technologies for *directly interfacing* human beings with computer systems. As Timothy Leary muses, our brains are mere 'info-wired organs' connected to the sensory arrays of our bodies.[267] All physical sensations may therefore be considered 'crude fabrications' of our little grey cells.[268] By sufficiently refining technologies for directly feeding electric signals into our nervous systems, 'real' sensations may therefore one day be induced into our consciousness without any direct stimulation of our eyes, ears, tongues, noses and skin. A complete, multi-sense immersion of human beings into metamedia VR environments will thereby be permitted.

Some may be surprised that I talk of interface technology 'refinements' in the previous paragraph. However, experiments involving the rudimentary artificial stimulation of the retina, the optic and auditory nerves, and other parts of the brain, have already begun to progress with some success.[269] As developments in microelectronics and genetic engineering converge into a combined science of human–computer interface nanotechnology, so possibilities for highly advanced direct data connections between human beings and computer systems are certain to spawn. Granted, the day when the option to have a skull jack fitted to permit direct VR immersion *may* be twenty or even fifty years ahead. Yet, despite the childish and total dismissal of such future interface developments by many so-termed 'experts', it is a day whose dawn will certainly rise.[270]

FLIGHTS OF FANTASY

Even when they remain limited by the inadequacies of a head-mounted display and a bodysuit, cost-effective forms of VR are still likely to find widespread application. Not only will the VR systems of the next decade enable people to design, learn and play in safe synthetic environments (as is already fairly common even today). In addition, as the computing engines which generate VR environments increasingly come to be networked, so multi-participant *distributed VR* will become a common communications form.

Via distributed VR, human beings from a range of physically remote locations will be able to be teletransported into the same virtual world. Rather than holding a telephone conversation, people will be able to meet (and touch) in VR. Electronic global communications may therefore become far more subtle. Surgeons in hospitals around the planet will be able to operate as a team on a single and/or a remote patient.[271] Office work will also be able to take place in cyberspace as VR users 'virtucommute' into computer generated 'corporate virtual workspaces' (CVWs).[272] Already joint industry–academia research projects such as *Virtuosi* are pioneering the creation of the VR office and the VR factory.[273]

Many forms of leisure are also likely to be transformed by the new metamedia. School children will be able to take VR fields trips not only to the zoo, but in addition beneath the sea, to the Moon, or back in time to witness famous historical events. 'Come as you aren't' VR parties—with attendees wearing a 'fancy-dress' VR body—have also been proposed.[274] The possible use of VR bodysuits to allow remote individuals to meet in cyberspace for virtual sex—'cybersex' or 'teledildonics'—has in addition raised some hearty debate.[275] Just as television developed into the dominant media form of the 20th century, so VR holds much promise for personal and business application in the 21st century and beyond.

Think a human colonization of cyberspace won't happen? Think again. Fifty years ago television was a fad of the few—a technological one-day-wonder which many did not expect to last and most had not experienced. After all, as television's early sceptics argued, how many people would be prepared to spend large proportions of their time gazing at a tiny, fuzzy, black-and-white screen? Similarly today, VR sceptics look at the most basic of VR systems and wonder why anybody would want to spend hours wearing a heavy, clammy helmet in order to float 'unrealistically' in a world of blocky, jerky computer graphics. However, just as tiny, fuzzy, black-and-white screens were not to be the future of television, so VR systems will also substantially evolve towards a level of immersive quality adequate for mass acceptance.

Today a great many people spend more time watching television than engaged in any other flesh-material reality.[276] In future, so will it be with the currently infant medium of VR. We have already witnessed many, many times across history how a new media has radically altered human perceptions and social patterns. However, for some reason, many still believe that any such new-media-driven cultural revolution can and will not happen again. Yet already there are many varieties of PC VR headsets retailing for but a few hundred dollars.

We should also not forget that, unlike television, VR will be an interactive medium for individual as well as mass communication. Distributed VR will hence be a competitor to the telephone (and the videophone) as well as to the goggle-box in the corner of the living room. So hold tight humanity. Just as previous generations discovered writing, printing, movies or television in *their* adolescence, so the inhabitants of the early-21st century will experience the joys of adulthood as their understanding of the pleasures and powers of VR are similarly awakened.

KINGDOMS OF MAGIC

As long recognized by the Walt Disney Company, tailoring full-scale, physical imaginary worlds (into which people are then placed) can prove a highly effective means of blanketing the human sensorium with synthetic input. Controlled reality environments (CREs) from Disneyland to themed Las Vegas hotels and 'living' museums, are continuing to grow in popularity as safe escapes from the Kingdom of the Real. Often crafted to identical specification around the globe, CREs can prove extremely effective in meme propagation or reinforcement. Immersion in a CRE is therefore likely to become an increasingly significant method for enabling human experiences to be shared.

Some may question my interpretation of controlled reality environments as media forms, let alone as forms of emerging metamedia. However, there can be no denying the power of synthetic creations like Disneyland to manipulate the contents and frameworks of our minds. Whether 'real' or 'artificial', our environment influences who we are and how we behave. At a broader level, CREs clearly also 'contaminate' the cultures into which they are implanted. As philosopher Umberto Eco once commented, the most internationally familiar landmark in the United States is not the White House, but rather Mickey's Magic Kingdom.[277] It is therefore hardly surprising that France, together with various other xenophobically-inclined nations, has in part resisted the encroachment of CREs such as McDonalds or Disneyland into its territory lest its own sense of cultural identity be consumed.

As well as proving popular leisure escapes and educational resources, CREs may soon also be developed as critical human resource management tools. At present around sixty per cent of the employed Western population spend the majority of their working lives in a communal office to which they travel. However, as digital technologies and portfolio lives come to dominate our working patterns, less and less is commuting to a shared office likely to remain the norm. Teleworking, and eventually virtucommuting, look certain to become more and more popular. The practice of hotelling—wherein workers have to 'book' space in their own office as and when required—is also already proving highly successful within pioneering organizations such as Ernst & Young.[278] As discussed in several other chapters, digital technologies are increasingly allowing workers to be remotely distributed into more cost-effective virtual teams.

As the above trend gathers pace, there may in future be few (if any) task-related reasons requiring many co-workers to meet in a common physical location. Flesh-socialization may therefore be drastically reduced. As a result, organizations may find it more and more difficult to instil a sense of loyalty and unifying cultural identity across their membership. One answer to this problem may be the use of 'corporate CREs' as 'organizational playgrounds' within which distributed teams will be required to occasionally gather in order to share quality, group-enhancing experiences.

CRE DEVELOPMENTS

Two categories of CREs are likely to emerge to serve the business world. The first will be organization-specific training establishments. These will have the limited objective of ensuring that all company workers have the same skills and are aware of common standards and cultural codes. However, the second and more interesting CRE variant will be far less directed. Within, teams of individuals who rarely encounter each other in the flesh will meet to undertake a range of physical and mental tasks in order to foster their group skills and inter-member knowledge. Whether teams meet to pilot a starship, to defend a Wild West outpost, to explore a shipwreck, or simply to solve abstract puzzles, will not matter. What will is how, in overcoming challenges as a team, they will develop a greater sense of unity as a single work unit. 'Missions' conducted by a group in a CRE may also trigger the conception of fresh ideas of value to their organization.

The group accomplishment of 'artificial' tasks as an aid in human resource development is, of course, nothing new. For many years outward-bound training has been used to heighten professional and managerial skills. However, such courses usually cost hundreds if not thousands of dollars per participant. They are also often not practical for some individuals due to strength and fitness requirements. Organizations are also starting to become alarmed by the serious injuries which some of their people have suffered during outward-bound forays. Broken collar bones *et al* are experiences which any worker can afford to do without! For this variety of reasons, *controlled* reality environments—charged with ubiquitous metamedia stimulations and yet also the cosy safety and the price tag of Disneyland—would appear to offer far more sensible options for fostering group skills and group identity amongst large numbers of employees. Under controlled environmental conditions, it is also possible to ensure that different teams on differing occasions will all benefit from the 'same' experience.

The design of CREs will prove a critical factor in their failure or success. Running and stage managing CRE activities is also likely to become big business. One highly innovative example of a CRE which existed for several years was *The Crystal Maze*. This artificial reality was designed and constructed by Artem for Chatsworth Television in the UK.

Known to millions of viewers, *The Crystal Maze* was approximately the size of a football pitch and consisted of four 'zones' broken down into a total of twenty-four game cells. Teams of six players progressed through the maze on a mission to collect vital crystals. These could be gained following the successful completion of a range of physical and/or mental challenges. Whilst each challenge had to be completed by a single player, team mates looked on and could offer verbal assistance and encouragement. Players could become 'locked in' if they failed to solve the challenge of a particular game cell. Their comrades then had to decide whether it was in the team's best interests to 'buy them out' with a hard-won crystal. At the end of their journey remaining team members exchanged their crystals for time spent in the 'crystal dome'. Within they had to collect enough golden tokens to win a group prize. Although constructed for television, *The Crystal Maze* complex was on occasions hired out for corporate use

Someone once said that the most complementary technology to the Internet was the Jumbo Jet. Journalist Howard Rheingold similarly argues that any virtual team or virtual community will only really prove effective if it is based around a core of people who regularly interact in the physical world.[279] As has been discussed, whilst Future Organizations may use digital media to disperse their workers either at home or out in the field, so they may also find it effective to periodically bring their people together in controlled reality environments in order to foster a sense of team spirit upon which their future success may depend. CREs may therefore become the key complementary media to empower the widespread and successful application of many distributed, computer-enabled new working practices.

PROPAGANDA TOOLS?

This chapter is entitled *Shared Nightmares, Shared Dreams* to serve as a reminder that future media developments carry with them both positive and negative implications. All future metamedia will be capable of creating and supporting what have been termed 'simulacra'—or, in other words, perfect copies of realities which don't, can't, and never did exist.[280] All forms of metamedia will therefore have at least the *potential* to be perverted into highly effective propaganda tools. As possible weapons to empower an abstract and highly clinical 'hyper-reality',[281] metamedia of all genres will provide their masters with the keys to vast stage sets within whose bounds they may practise the precise and deliberate manipulation of human minds.

At least most current mass media purport to mirror happenings in the real, physical world. In contrast, many metamedia will not even try. Rather, they will stimulate us with something 'better', so allowing us to share feelings and experiences unbounded by eon-old constraints. Whilst exciting and incredibly stimulating, there is therefore the danger that emerging metamedia will remove us once and for all from reality: that they will permanently provide passage for millions to enter into plastic-and-microelectronic synthetic lives.

On the other hand, there is also the possibility that further metamedia development will lead to us turning-back from an oft-feared digital retreat. Indeed, the use of future metamedia may bring the human race full circle in terms of knowledge media progression. As experience sharing across cyberspace becomes increasingly multi- and then meta-channel, so in turn people may once again come to truly appreciate the value and the joy of conducting business in the flesh. Or, to put it another way, the closer to reality our digital encounters become, the more we may yearn for more of the real thing.

We no longer live in a world in which information primarily conserves itself in textual objects called 'books'.[282] Rather, today information is on-line all around us. Increasingly available to anyone, any time, information has become a dead resource. Indeed, like air, information is fast becoming a 'hygiene factor' within our lives—something we only notice the value of in its absence. In the near future, as everyone and everything becomes 'wired', information will no longer add value. Rather, it will simply be a transparent prerequisite for value creation.

Ten or twenty years ago, a PhD student could review all key literature sources in their area. Maddeningly for many, no longer is this the case. Tens or hundreds of new and interlinked sources of fresh information are posted across computer networks every day. Searching for a 'definitive' list of references upon any topic has therefore become impossible.

All that access to networked information now tells you is how much there is that you can't possibly ever know. As a consequence, hunch and intuition—gut instinct, creativity, knowledge, expertise and imagination—are of increasing and valued importance. New knowledge media, if they are to be effective, therefore have to allow for the sharing of *experiences*, whether in environments virtual or real.

As our reliance upon the metamedia of cyberspace continues to grow, so in parallel our need for the warm reassurance of real physical encounters is also likely to expand. Today many businessmen want to handshake with a modem. In contrast, the most effective future managers may once again strive to start meetings with a clasp of living flesh.

* * *

EVEN IN THE DARK YOU DON'T BELIEVE ME . . .

A few years ago I gave a lecture on the rise of 'virtual organizations' to an audience of around 100 senior communications managers. Whilst I espoused the benefits of e-mail and other groupware applications[283] for empowering virtual teams, the audience scribbled copiously. However, as soon as I shifted to descriptions of future corporate virtual reality workspaces, pens clicked shut and arms were folded. An acceptance barrier had been crossed in many minds. The guy from the Ivory Tower had suddenly veered off into science fiction.

Sensing the change of mood I immediately challenged, 'I can see that you don't believe me'. A moment later, having briefly forgotten that the area before the stage was only dimly lit, I changed my pronouncement to 'Even in the dark I can see that you don't believe me'. And it was true. Whilst there was no way in which I could make out the expressions on the faces of any audience members, I could somehow *see* that many were harbouring doubts.

Human communication is a strange, subtle, and oft unconscious beast. Today we are only just beginning to develop metamedia, such as immersive VR, which will in time enable us to 'see' human feelings in the dark over great distances. Yet such new metamedia are destined to become as important in our lives as the new media of the television and the telephone in the 20th century.

Successful organizations need at least to understand, if not to control, the knowledge media—the meme carriers—of their age. The digital tools of the computer and the emerging information superhighway therefore ought not to be ignored. Clearly there is a danger that computer-based digital media may erode many presently concrete information sources into a worthless debris cloud. However, this danger ought not to imply that new media forms be either feared or resisted. Rather, it should give us an even greater impetus to develop fresh metamedia, and hence to begin to rely upon as many parallel media channels as technology makes it possible for us to assimilate.

Only if we place too much trust in the potential tools of the hyper-real will we be at risk of having our minds and our businesses separated from reality. Treated with caution and respect, the metamedia of cyberspace ought only to augment, rather than degrade, our present experience range. As metamedia emerge, ever more stimulating and inspiring perceptions of both the real and the virtual ought to result. Indeed, as Timothy Leary so beautifully once wrote:

> Intimacy at the digital level programs and enriches exchanges in the warm levels. You do not lessen the richness of your murmur-touch-contact with your lover because you can also communicate by phone, fax, and hand-scrawled notes. Warm-breath interactions with your touch-friends will be more elegant and pleasant with the digital-reality option added.[284]

Ultimately, although potentially tinged with danger, future metamedia should prove incredibly powerful *human* technologies allowing for the ultimate sharing of all of our dreams. For as *Paradigm Shift* guru Don Tapscott reminds us:

Past technological paradigms—the broadcast media and the old model of the computer—were hierarchical, immutable, and centralized. As such, they carried the values of their powerful owners. The new media are interactive, malleable, and distributed in control. As such, they cherish an awesome neutrality. Ultimately they will be what we want them to be. They will do what we command.[285]

PART IV
GEOGRAPHIC SPAN

11
Within these Walls

GEOGRAPHY DOMINATES OUR LIVES. National geographic boundaries determine which languages we speak, which cultures we inherit, which gods we worship, and to whom we pay taxes. Local geographic bounds additionally influence our immediate social relationships, where we spend our work and leisure hours, and even our choice of supermarket. The emerging tools of the Digital Age may in many ways enable us to make geographic distances *appear* transparent. However, for a very long time to come, physical remoteness will remain a significant constraint upon many human strategies and actions.

The following three chapters concern the ever widening *geographic span* across which individuals, nations, and organizations, have come to command influence. In Part III we explored developments in knowledge media which opened up incredible communications pathways. However, the influence of differing communications forms upon the geographic span of any society, economy or organization is far from absolute. In parallel, just as significant in determining physical boundaries are the transportation systems employed to move people, goods, and natural resources, from one location to another.

As was noted in **chapter 4**, whilst human beings remain biological entities, so the production and transportation of physical produce must continue to occur. In the near future a very large number of business transactions are likely to take place across the single computing infrastructure of the information superhighway. However, business in cyberspace will still have to relate back to the fashioning and trade of tangible goods in the 'real' world. Granted, computer technology will alter the way in which many Future Organizations interface with and administrate their physical resources and transportation machines. Yet, until the matter transporters of *Star Trek* fame themselves materialize, information technologies will fail to remove many of the most significant barriers of geography from our lives.

BATTLING CHAOS & DECAY

Throughout history curiosity alone has been enough to drive individuals to travel in order to broaden their minds. In contrast, collective human societies have almost always sought to widen their geographic reach solely for economic or political gain. Indeed, as detailed in **chapter 3**, to this day humanity's greatest geographic expedition remains a moon-landings programme intended to demonstrate the national superiority of the United States during the Cold War.

Across time, broadening geographic spans have provided human beings with access to a widening spectrum of resources, markets, climates, cultures and knowledge. As a result, by increasing their geographic spans human societies have become more resilient to internal decline and stagnation. Geographic expansion has thereby proved a critical prerequisite for the survival of human civilization. Yet to fully understand why we first need a brief lesson in the physics of matter itself.

One of the most basic physical principles is the Second Law of Thermodynamics. This states that all energy in the universe degrades irreversibly. As a consequence of the Second Law, all isolated systems are therefore doomed to decay. As time progresses, unless some positive external influence is brought to bear, the fate of any isolated system can only be to succumb to the degenerative forces of chaos. This occurs as the levels of incumbent energy or information attributable to any isolated entity degrade. As physicists put it, in isolated systems the level of chaos or 'entropy' will always increase.[286] Or, as more common experience and language inform us, disorder prevails if things are simply left to themselves.[287] In our lives as in energy theory, chaos is always more probable than order.

In thermodynamic terms any discretely bounded collection of physical matter represents an isolated system—be it a drink, a skyscraper, or a single human being. Left on the counter a cup of tea will cool to room temperature rather than remaining hot or even warming up by extracting heat from its environment. Similarly, over time buildings have a tendency to fall down rather than remaining to stand. The process of human ageing towards death also serves as an example of the inevitable degeneration of any finite physical body over time.

It is my contention herein that human communities from early tribal settlements to entire towns, regions, cities, or even nations, are most sensibly treated as isolated thermodynamic systems. All human communities are therefore inevitably subject to the Second Law of Thermodynamics. As such they will always tend towards decay and stagnation unless fresh physical resources are delivered into their closed boundaries in order to render new and continuing life energies. Consequently, any group of humans who continue to live within a fixed geographic region will face extinction unless they make progress in widening their geographic horizons.

By constantly moving around, early nomadic communities avoided the curse of living within an isolated environment with a limited resource base. However, as civilizations advanced to construct larger and larger settlements, continual relocation became impractical. Across history, the geographic spans of most successful human collectives have therefore been constantly expanded across lands and oceans in order to commandeer fresh raw material supplies. Just as importantly, patterns of trade between different regions have also arisen in response to the limitations of isolated economic geographies. By opening up trade between two or more isolated communities, each becomes permitted to concentrate upon those productive activities in which it enjoys comparative advantage. The overall effectiveness of resource utilization by many regions in economic amalgamation thereby comes to be improved.[288]

BROADENING HORIZONS

Since the days of early civilization there has been a continual widening in humanity's geographic dominance from the *constrained* to the *relaxed* and beyond. For thousands of years, small, geographically isolated kingdoms witnessed little resource depletion. Reliant upon only minimal external trade, these early human groupings had little reason to advance their extremely constrained geographic horizons. Significant pressures for the development of advanced transportation and communications systems therefore did not exist. Indeed, many people lived out their entire lives in a single small village or local region.

From the mid-17th century population expansion began to shake the world.[289] This was accompanied (and in part driven) in the late-18th and 19th centuries by rapid industrialization. As a result, isolated regional economies became less and less economically sufficient. Mechanical engines were subsequently developed as the need to relax the geographic constraints upon the movement of people and traded resources became more and more pressing. Over the three ensuing centuries, citizens, economies, and organizations, came to be bounded by the geography of a nation rather than a local region. Levels of economic prosperity also continued to rise. For a while at least, the relaxed geographic spans of national rather than regional trade kept the degenerative demons of any isolated system at bay.

Unfortunately, in latter half of the 20th century, even the largely artificial geographic boundaries of trading nation states have become too limiting for the continuance of economic prosperity in comparative geographic isolation. Nations and their organizations have therefore been forced to open themselves up extremely broadly to the world at large. So critical is this need today that 'globalization' in all manner of forms has been argued to have become the key concept—the dominant meme—of the 1990s.[290]

Early in the 21st century problems of population expansion, resource depletion, and environmental catastrophe, are likely to become more and more critical for the single, closed economic and social system which we call the planet Earth. Every responsible government or other Future Organization therefore needs to consider itself an active player within a joint global ensemble battling the forces of decay. Like it or not, science if not common sense inform us that within a closed system like the world entropy is bound to increase. And no such system may be everlasting. Or, as a favourite timelord of mine once surmised, in a closed system, 'the more you put things together, the more they keep falling apart'.[291]

In his book *Globalization*, sociologist Malcolm Waters argues that it is material exchanges (of physical goods) which localize, whilst political exchanges internationalize, and symbolic (communications) exchanges globalize.[292] However, as I hope to have at least begun to demonstrate, this inviting treatise does not take into account the need for human societies to command influence over increasing and/or more widely-integrated geographic spans simply in order to survive and progress. Globalization has to be seen as more than a function of a perceived global *awareness* enabled via modern knowledge media. Instead, and far more significantly, globalization needs to be appreciated as the manifestation of the latest phase in humankind's battle to hold the forces of chaos at bay.

In some minds the above statement may—and indeed should—strike alarm. However, just at present, perhaps we ought not be too concerned. For humanity at least, all is still far from being lost. Thankfully, globalization remains a fairly recent phenomenon. Possibilities for opening up our isolated systems of civilization beyond their presently relaxed geographic boundaries also continue to abound. However, before such future options are detailed, let us once again take a brief foray back into the past—to a time of uncharted territories, and of vast frontiers yet even to be named.

EARLY EMPIRES

Archaeologists believe that human beings first started to settle in geographically fixed communities after the last Ice Age some 10,000 years ago. Our early ancestors then slowly evolved from savage hunters into farmers who domesticated animals and cultivated the land. As early as 6150 BC one of the world's first cities was flourishing at Çatal Hüyük in central Turkey.[293] Some three thousand years later, and the most famous of the early Near Eastern civilizations had begun to carve out increasingly geographically-wide empires comprised of several clans and agricultural communities in alliance. The early kingdoms of ancient Egypt were united under the single rule of Narmer with the unification of Upper and Lower Egypt between 3100 and 2700 BC.[294] Further south around this period, the smaller, multi-city kingdoms of Sumer and Akkadia were also emerging in the lower Mesopotamian valley.

Both the early and later kingdoms of the Near East were dependent upon great rivers. In Egypt the Nile proved perfect for trading. Its currents could take boats down river, whilst southerly winds were always available to bring them back up.[295] As well as providing easy passage for reed or log rafts and other sailing craft, the Nile and its tributaries in Egypt (and the Tigris and the Euphrates in Mesopotamia) also watered farming lands and fertilized them with minerals. A wide variety of animals, plants, and mineral reserves, were also to be found in the Near East some 5000 years ago. Indeed, it was almost certainly an agriculturally-friendly climate, the availability of waterways for transportation and communication, and this abundance of natural resources, that permitted the first great human empires to spawn and flourish in this region.[296]

Like most early cities, those of the Near East were based around one or two main crafts and technologies, such as the making of pottery or glassware.[297] Trade both between cities and outside of their wider kingdoms was therefore inevitable. Raw materials had to be imported, whilst trading links were also vital for the export of finished products.

Until around 2000 BC horses were not tamed. For a thousand years oxen were therefore the main source of locomotive power used to drag carts or wagons loaded with heavy goods. As early yokes were inefficient, land transportation only proved viable for moving goods over relatively short distances. Imports and exports into and out of Egypt or Mesopotamia therefore depended upon water-based transportation. As a result, the pathway of natural waterways significantly limited the geographic reach of the Near Eastern empires—especially as most early Egyptian or Mesopotamian boats were only suited for river rather than sea-going travel.

Although initially blessed with a multitude of resources, the early Near Eastern empires soon found it essential to broaden their geographic spans in search of more raw materials. During the ages of pyramid construction the Egyptians dispatched regular convoys of armed miners into neighbouring Sinai. Expeditions also took place up the Nile in search of gold, silver, ivory and timber. As its kingdoms unified under the Akkadian ruler Sargon the First around 2300 BC, Mesopotamia also expanded its territory in search of resources such as tin, which had become vital in forging bronze. Wars with neighbouring territories also forced the Mesopotamians to venture across the Eastern Mediterranean in search of vital minerals. Trading relations with Cyprus, Crete, and the islands of the Aegean, thereby came to be stimulated.

By 2500 BC Egyptian merchants were starting to fare the seas in order to raid resources from the East Coast of Africa. Like those of the Mesopotamians, Egyptian ships had open decks and were equipped for propulsion by either oar or sail. By around 1500 BC the Egyptians were stitching together wooden vessels up to 70 feet in length. These carried perhaps twenty oarsmen, and were used to transport cargoes including elephant tusks, trees, copper ingots, and monkeys.[298]

GREEKS, ROMANS & ROADS

With travel on foot or under animal power remaining somewhat restrictive, subsequent empires of both the East and the West were also heavily dependent upon seafaring merchant trade.[299] By around 800 BC the Greeks virtually dominated shipping in the Mediterranean with their high-sterned, oar-and-sail vessels. By 600 BC 'triremes' featuring three tiers of oars were being rowed by up to 200 men. They could therefore be used to transport large cargoes when not functioning as vehicles of war.[300]

Whilst it largely copied its shipping designs from those of the Greeks and other races, the Empire of Rome did advance transportation with the construction of its infamous roads. This said, the first system of roads maintained by a central authority was actually developed by the Persians around 500 BC.[301] Roman roads, however, were generally more substantial than those constructed by other empires. Indeed, so 'over-engineered' were many Roman roadways that some authors have cruelly described them as 'walls buried in the ground'.[302]

The Roman road infrastructure was also far more extensive than that of any other empire. As such it proved an extremely effective organizational tool. Indeed, despite the reliance of Rome upon grain, oil and wine brought by sea from distant lands, the coherence and expansion of its Empire mainly depended upon road planning and construction. With its vast, pan-European road network, Rome could rapidly move legions

of soldiers to quell local disturbances. Messengers carrying vital news
were also permitted to travel at speeds of fifty or more miles per day.[303]

THE IMMOBILE MAJORITY

During the thirteen centuries which followed the fall of the Roman
Empire, a lack of resources and political will led to its roads falling into
a sorry state of neglect.[304] The geographic span of most of the world's
population also remained highly constrained during this period. Granted,
European civilization did expand across large portions of the globe.
Merchants and armies also obtained a fair degree of national and
international mobility from around 1500 onwards. However, whilst
patterns of trade between both regions and nations multiplied several fold,
increases in the speed and capacity of sailing vessels and horse-drawn
carriages did not really broaden most of humanity's geographic reach.

Inland transportation links did not begin to significantly improve until
the construction of canals in the 17th and 18th centuries.[305] Many road
building projects were also undertaken in the 18th and then 19th century.
However, without transport—let alone powered transport—canals and
roads remained trading pathways between largely isolated geographic
regions, rather than key arteries linking the towns and cities of cohesive
nations. Hence, for most citizens, travel over any distance remained
arduous, time-consuming, sometimes dangerous, and often prohibitively
expensive. Indeed, it remains difficult to imagine the immobility of most
people before the advent of modern transportation. In part this may be
due to the fact that most historical accounts focus upon the activities of
merchants, soldiers, adventurers, and their ilk, most of whom did enjoy
comparative geographic freedom.[306]

BEASTS OF FIRE

The age of modern transportation was spawned in the early-19th century
when steam was harnessed as a new means of propulsion.[307] Richard
Trevithick demonstrated the first practical steam locomotive at

Penydarren in South Wales in 1804. Twenty-five years later George
Stephenson had overcome many of the problems experienced by
Trevithick when his *Rocket* won the famous Rainhill Trials.[308] Step-
henson's locomotive design was consequently adopted for use upon the
Liverpool and Manchester Railway. Opened in 1830, this offered the first
timetabled rail service for both passengers and freight.[309]

By the middle of the 19th century the construction of mainline railways
in Britain was almost complete. British engineers were also in great
demand to construct railways around the world. The decline of canal
transportation was rapid once railways became established. However,
canal building had allowed engineers to become expert in skills—such as
cutting, tunnelling and embanking—which were to prove vital in railway
construction.

The impact of the early railway networks cannot be underestimated.
Before steam trains arrived, inland transportation under animal power had
rarely been able to exceed ten miles per hour. In contrast, even
Stephenson's *Rocket* was capable of speeds in excess of 25 mph. Railways
also provided an extraordinary freedom for personal travel to citizens of
Europe, India, Asia, and the Americas. Urbanization thereby went hand-
in-hand with railway development in many countries. Capital markets
were also transformed, as, for the first time, private investors were
persuaded to sink their wealth into large-scale construction and engineering initiatives. Whole professions were also instituted in a need to foster
skilled workers capable of maintaining tracks and locomotives in good
condition.[310] A supportive infrastructure of stations, signal boxes,
buffets, and even magazines, also accompanied the growth of the rail
network. Indeed as historian R.A. Buchanan claims, by the end of the
19th century railways had probably entered into the imaginative experience of more people in the world more quickly than any other technological innovation.[311]

Whilst railways were opening up inland transportation links—and in
the process were allowing local regions to more closely trade as cohesive
nations—steam powered ships were also improving transportation by river
and ocean. Steam powered boats were pioneered in the late-18th
century,[312] whilst by 1807 the first paddle-wheeled steam boat—the
Clermont—was making its maiden trip from New York to Albany down
the Hudson. By 1819, the *Savannah* had become the first ship to employ

steam propulsion in an Atlantic crossing. Thirty years later, even the sleekest sailing clippers[313] could no longer compete with their faster and larger steam counterparts. Steam power thereby came to dominate oceanic as well as inland transportation. Oil-driven motor transport was also soon to arrive. As a new century loomed closer, the world was already starting to be perceived as a smaller and smaller place.

FROM REGIONS TO NATIONS

Archaeologists report that early tribes of Neanderthal man subsisted upon materials drawn from within a twelve mile radius.[314] However, over many millennia, a complex evolution of new resource needs, wars, and political battles, led to a multitude of technological developments which empowered much wider human settlements. These towns, cities and kingdoms subsequently coalesced into even less geographically-constrained nations. Indeed, by the late-19th century, the geographic spans of humanity had widened to such a degree that the movement of people and goods between local regions within nations was not only commonplace but essential. Trade between nations was also increasingly fluid.

Within the next chapter we shall explore how constraints upon the functioning of nations themselves have lessened as the geographic span of humanity has broadened from the constrained to the relaxed during the Present Age. As globalization dawns no longer are human beings significantly bounded by the land of their nationality. In many ways this empowers individuals and organizations by permitting them to operate frictionlessly across previously disruptive geographic divides. However, in many other ways, globalization threatens humanity with a crisis of identity. For today comfort and refuge may no longer be found quite so easily within the traditions and meme sets of a parent nation.

Developments in transportation and communications up until the late-19th century clearly permitted nation states to evolve into well-defined, black box economies. However today, further technological advances are instead allowing both businesses and individuals to rip apart nation states under a new regime of global mass individualism. In Part II we noted how people and organizations are now having to redefine their working relationships. As many traditional geographic boundaries continue to relax, so in parallel nations and organizations are also having to re-engineer in the face of global economies, global media, global citizenship, and looming environmental problems which will simply not recognize petty national delineations.

12
The Rise & Demise
of Nations

CROWD: (CHANTING)   Yes, we are all individuals!
                             Yes, we are all different!

LONE VOICE: (DISSENTING)   I'm not!

Monty Python's Life of Brian[315]

ACROSS THE PRESENT AGE nationalism rose to xenophobic heights. In the first half of the 20th century two world wars pitted nation against nation. For several decades afterwards the Cold War then cemented geographic divisions between the East and West. After WWII the rise of the welfare state in many countries also acted as a powerful force for cohesive nationalism. Hence, despite great advances in global transportation and communications, up until the 1980s most citizens and many organizations remained rooted in geographically-constrained national identities.

Then, almost of a sudden, a 'new world order' began to emerge. The Cold War ended whilst the green issues of global environmentalism rose to prominence in the public imagination. The capabilities of nations to support their post-war commitments to the socialist ideology of a totally free welfare state additionally started to falter.

Over the past two decades all barriers to traditional international telecommunications have fallen. The Internet has also been enthusiastically adopted by tens of millions as the first many-to-many global channel for uncensored news and information. And often quietly unnoticed amid cycles of political upheaval and economic turbulence, many organizations have now finally committed to fully global mindsets as well as operations.

Consequently, as the 20th century draws to a close, the intense national boundaries which characterized its youth and middle-age have come to be replaced by a complex new hybrid of both globalism *and* individualism.

As my opening citation from *Monty Python* hopefully suggests, it is only possible to become an individual within a wider unified whole. There has to be a crowd with a common identity against which one can stand out. And such a crowd is increasingly global.

Today communications and causes sweeping the planet are starting to permit the people of the world to share in a single, global identity. Already perceptions of global citizenship are starting to eat away at the stubborn psychological and political barriers which have for so long characterized national divides. Global citizenship can only be good for business and world peace. However, in choosing to become a part of the New World Order, citizens do have to cast aside some of their ties to the societal structures and regimes which once fostered community spirit and patriotism. Paradoxically, therefore, whilst global citizens may be increasingly unified in totality, in a local context they are also likely to feel increasingly alone. Just as workers are fast losing the certainty of long-term organizational membership, so in future people are also destined to become less and less enshrined within the culture and values of a parent nation. The cost of global unity unfortunately has to be a degree of national disaffiliation.

BROADENING GEOGRAPHIC SPANS

This chapter concerns the broadening geographic span of humanity across the Present Age. In particular much of the content focuses upon the rise and demise of the nation state over the breadth of the 20th century. The past one hundred or so years has been witness to the greatest potential increases in geographic freedom ever on offer to individual and collective humanity. Unfortunately, for many decades, it has also had to contend with some of the strongest nationalistic forces ever to have held back widening horizons. Opposing cultures, politics, and economic systems, have constrained geographic expansion since the dawn of human civilization. However, never as in the 20th century have they so curtailed human aspirations in the face of such incredible opportunities.

Most citizens of many nations have only even had the *potential* for widespread geographic mobility since the mid- to late-1800s. It is therefore a shame that it is only now, around a century later, that the bipolar geopolitical world has disintegrated to leave us with a new and dynamic global environment boasting few economic walls, knowledge that knows no national or regional boundaries, and increasingly-wide areas of free, international trade.[316]

FREEDOM & FLIGHT

Knowledge media developments, in addition to political and social action, have played a major role in shaping the geographic spans of most citizens and organizations across the Present Age. However, towards the end of the 19th century, it was almost certainly the application of the internal combustion engine which had the greatest impact upon the broadening of geographic horizons. Just as the 19th century came to be dominated by rail travel, so the 20th has come to be ruled over by the automobile and the aeroplane.

Internal combustion engines—that is engines which explode a fuel to provide a means of locomotive output—had been hypothesized for many years before fuels suitable for powering them became available.[317] In 1859 French engineer Étienne Lenior constructed a single-stroke engine which used coal gas to power a flywheel. In 1876 a German by the name of Otto then devised the first smooth-running four-stroke internal combustion engine. 'Otto-cycle' engines proved viable alternatives to their steam counterparts in the late-19th century. However, it was not until oil-based fuels like petroleum were exploited that mobile internal combustion engines could be manufactured and transportation was transformed.

Gottlieb Daimler produced the first petrol driven vehicle—a motorbike—in 1885. In the same year fellow German Karl Benz produced the first genuine petrol-driven motor car or 'horseless carriage'. Automobiles soon caught on across Western Europe and North America. Henry Ford built his first automobile in 1896, and by 1903 had established his soon-to-flourish Ford Motor Company. As already detailed in **chapter 6**, mass production techniques led to millions of Model 'T' Fords and many other makes of car being produced over the ensuing decades.

Petrol-driven internal combustion engines proved popular in the late-19th and early-20th centuries as they began to permit ordinary citizens the freedom of personal transport. Around this time engines which ignited their fuel by compression rather than with an ignition spark were also being developed. Rudolf Diesel produced the first such engine in 1892. Two decades of development later, and Diesel engines had become widely adopted for heavy-duty usage in tractors, ships, and lorries, as they remain to this day.

Mobile and lightweight petrol and then gas-turbine engines was also put to good use by those innovators who had always dreamt of travel above the ground. In the December of 1903 Wilbur and Orville Wright made the first successful controlled powered flight. Again interest around the world was soon rampant. By 1909 Louis Blériot had flown across the English Channel, whilst by the late-1930s the first experimental gas-turbine or 'jet' aircraft had flown in the United States.

The first civil airlines were also established in the late-1930s. These soon proved especially popular for moving goods or passengers between widely separated urban areas.[318] However, the impact of both a previous and a looming world war upon developments in humanity's geographic span around this period cannot be ignored. We may be thankful indeed that the 20th century has been the first of mass production, mass communications, and mass participation. Unfortunately, we are somewhat less blessed that in the wake of new technologies it also became the first century of truly mass killing.

THE MADNESS OF WAR

At the beginning of the 20th century six European empires dominated most of the world. A fragile peace existed, although tensions between nations were rife.[319] In Sarajevo on the 28th of June 1914, Bosnian Serb extremists assassinated Archduke Franz Ferdinand, the heir to the Austro-Hungarian throne. Unfortunately this single event served as a trigger for four years of bloodshed.[320] On the 28th of July Austria declared war on Serbia. Russia then came to Serbia's defence. Germany subsequently allied itself with Austria against Russia, invaded Luxembourg and Belgium, and declared war on France. Having promised to guarantee Belgian sovereignty, Britain also entered the war against Germany.

The 'Great War' as it became known was unprecedented both technologically and psychologically. It also signalled the beginning of the end of Europe's international supremacy. Few believed that 'modern' wars would last very long or could take millions of lives. Yet the Great War was to be protracted, futile and bloody.

For the first time high explosives, poison gas, machine guns, tanks, submarines, and aircraft, were used in mass battle. Trench warfare dominated the land campaigns, with millions of men doomed to live and die in misery amid the cold, mud, lice and fear of the killing fields. Conditions for conscripts mobilized amid a naïve patriotic fervour were unthinkable. Slaughter occurred on such a scale that corpses often had to be left rotting where they fell. As a veteran of Verdun describes, 'rats would start eating their faces. First they'd gnaw at their lips and noses, then get into their coats and start eating the rest'.[321]

Just as the duration, intensity and horror of the war outran all expectations, so too did its geographic extent.[322] Japan, Turkey, Italy, Greece, Portugal, Montenegro, Romania, and the United States, all came to be involved before hostilities were finally ended in the November of 1918. Sixty-five million men were called-up from over twenty countries and nearly nine million were killed. Economies as well as the lives of many survivors were left in tatters. Across Europe people starved. National hatreds were also left deeply engrained, whilst many of those nations who had been 'victorious' would take years to recover.

The Great War was supposed to be the international conflict to end all others. Indeed, a League of Nations was established in 1920 to foster international peace and cooperation. Unfortunately its power was illusionary. The United States never joined, and it quickly became apparent that there were no sanctions against nations who did not wish to conform to its ideals.

The severe reparations burdened upon Germany after WWI almost certainly fuelled the rise of the Nazis several years later. As soon as Hitler came to power in 1933 he took Germany out of the League of

Nations. An industrially-prospering and territorially-aggressive Japan also left in the same year, following a commission report condemning its 1931 invasion of Manchuria in China. Italy also left the League after invading Ethiopia.

Whilst most of the world was suffering the ravages of the 1930s depression, Germany ignored the Versailles Treaty which had formally ended WWI and began to rearm. Other nations followed. Pacifism flourished in many countries, yet in vain. A civil war in Spain brought gunfire back to Europe in 1936. In 1938 Hitler reunited Austria and Germany, and, in the March of 1939, marched his troops across Czechoslovakia. The Nazi invasion of Poland followed. Two days later Britain and France declared war on Germany.

It is a sad indictment indeed that the Second World War was to be the first truly global event. Almost every continent was drawn into the fighting. Civilians became targets and their homes the battlefield. Bombs had been used by the Japanese on Shanghai in 1937, and by the Germans in the Spanish Civil War, but never on such a scale. Cities across Europe lived in fear of and suffered nightly air-raids for years.

Japan bombed Pearl Harbor in the December of 1941. Its attack killed 1500 people, destroyed hundreds of aircraft and ships, and drew the United States into the fray. However, some of the bombing undertaken by the Allies was even more horrific. Raids upon Dresden and Tokyo in 1945 killed tens of thousands and left utter destruction in their wake. The ultimate atrocity of the two atom bombs dropped upon Hiroshima and Nagasaki in the August of 1945 killed nearly 120,000 outright. Thousands more were left with horrific burns and life-long sickness. The power to trade intercontinentally in mass death as well as across mass markets had been won by our race. A war which had claimed fifty million lives had been brought to a close by the detonation of two nuclear devices. However, barriers between nations would still take decades to crumble.

SUBURBIA & THE WELFARE STATE

The two world wars demonstrated the global geographic spans across which nations and their citizens could function with modern transportation and communications systems. The conflicts also revealed the incredible manufacturing muscle and organizational might of rising industrial societies. Whilst the citizens of most nations had soon wearied of lengthy conflict, a capacity had continued to be demonstrated to conscript, equip and transport soldiers into battle. Across the world it had been shown that industrial production could be ratcheted up and up and up. Indeed, in the United States during WWII, some 'liberty ships' and aeroplanes had been completed from prefabricated parts in days rather than as previously in months or years.[323]

Rising industrial prosperity in the United States after WWII quickly led to the emergence of a new, suburban citizenship. In purchasing 'dream homes' remote from industrial locations, suburbans bought a new lifestyle as well as a residence. Private cars, together with improved public transport, for the first time enabled people to commute considerable distances to their place of work. For an increasing torrent of car owners the barriers of local geography became transparent. Into the 1950s and 1960s air travel also became commonplace. In particular, many Americans began to think nothing of taking a plane across a state or continent. Huge discount stores and supermarkets also began to appear to support the new out-of-town lifestyles of a car-owning population. Consumer credit also became a popular means of affording a wide range of new domestic appliances—including televisions—in an age of boom and undreamt of prosperity.

Unlike the Americans, the Europeans (along with the Japanese) were left with a momentous task of industrial reconstruction after WWII. Whereas food was not even rationed in the United States after 1945, many continental Europeans were living hand-to-mouth and thousands were dependent upon soup kitchens.[324] Many nations were bankrupt, whilst their populations were desperate and impatient for recovery having suffered for so long.

After the harsh winter of 1946–1947 the Americans offered a huge programme of aid to Europe known as the Economic Recovery Plan, or more commonly the Marshall Plan. The aim was to make Europe prosperous again, and in the process to boost export markets for the United States and to prevent the spread of communism. Whilst many Europeans were suspicious, sixteen Western European nations accepted aid totalling nearly $13bn.[325] The Soviet Union and its satellite neighbours refused. Agriculture, coal and steel, power generation, shipbuilding, and heavy manufacturing, all benefited as European economic recovery got under way. Soon Europe would be booming just like America; its citizens also enjoying previously unknown levels of prosperity and geographic freedom.

Many post-war governments aspired towards a new social as well as economic national prosperity. In Britain the newly elected Labour Party launched a welfare state to in part incorporate a new form of social citizenship.[326] A free national health service and benefits including state pensions were the bedrock of a system intended to foster a just society. The idea was that incomes would be relatively equitably distributed across the nation. To this end, all of those in work contributed to the welfare state via their taxes and specific National Insurance payments.

Welfare states also sprung up in many other nations to a greater or lesser extent. The social cohesion which they attempted to create—and to a degree managed to attain—inevitably bred a national dependence (and hence national affiliation) into many individuals. Many industries were also nationalized post-war, again fostering nationalistic capital and identity. Across communist Eastern Europe and China planned economies also came to totally dominate the lives of citizens who largely became the pawns of their nation.

EAST & WEST DIVIDED

Despite rapidly increasing international trade during the post-war boom years, nationalism continued to remain a dominant and restrictive force of global delineation into the 1980s. During WWII political differences between East and West had been buried in order to defeat fascism. However, only months after the war had ended, goodwill between the American and Russian superpowers evaporated. Having suffered such heavy casualties during the war, the Soviets rapidly extended communism to their neighbouring countries of Eastern Europe in order to prevent any future threat from Germany.[327] Germany itself was divided, along with its capital city of Berlin.

By as early as the Autumn of 1945 the Soviets and the Americans were openly speaking of each other as enemies more than allies. The next year ex-British Prime Minister Winston Churchill made a speech calling upon all English-speaking peoples to ally in resistance to Soviet ambitions. By the spring of 1947 the majority of the world was divided on East/West lines. The Berlin blockade and airlift,[328] the Vietnam and Korean wars, and the 1962 Cuban missile crisis, were just some of the events which then came to characterize the abysmal state of East/West relations for more than three decades.[329]

During the Cold War the inhabitants of Russia and most other communist countries were totally cut off from the rest of the world. Foreign travel, let alone foreign media and communications, were banned beyond the limits of the so-termed 'iron curtain'. Propaganda spread on both sides breeding fears across the world of an unknown and unseen enemy. That the technologies for truly global communications and transportation existed was therefore largely irrelevant.

With American forces vastly outnumbered by those of the Soviets (who were spending around sixty per cent of their gross domestic product on defence), the United States relied upon the supremacy of its nuclear deterrent. However, by 1949 the Russians had developed their own nuclear weapons programme, and the nuclear arms race began. At its height literally tens of thousands of warheads were targeted intercontinentally between nations, with the capacity poised to destroy all of human civilization many, many times over. Just as WWII was the first global conflict, so WWIII could easily have been the first to make use of truly global weapons. We are therefore fortunate that the threat of global armageddon was one of the key forces for change soon to be championed by ordinary citizens around the planet.

A NEW WORLD ORDER

During the 1980s it became increasingly apparent that nation states no longer provided the most effective means of geographic let alone economic governance. Nuclear wars or reactor failures, global warming, the AIDS epidemic, decreasing biodiversity, and the pollution of our ecosystem, were just some of the threats to humanity which rose to prominence within this decade. Clearly none of the hazards associated with the aforementioned problems could be controlled within the artificially isolated geographies of a single nation. It is therefore hardly a surprise that responses began to emerge on a global scale.

International non-governmental organizations became powerful pressure groups in the 1980s. Notable examples included the Campaign for Nuclear Disarmament (CND), the Friends of the Earth, Greenpeace, and the World Wildlife Fund. International welfare and human rights organizations, such as the Red Cross, Oxfam, Live Aid, and Amnesty International, additionally exhibited a worldwide scale and scope of operations in the wake of a rising global public conscience. In response to the fears and pressures of their populations, the vast majority of governments also saw fit to reduce the sovereignty of their states in accordance with international agreements.[330] Most significantly these included nuclear non-proliferation and test-ban treaties, together with international conventions for limiting atmospheric pollution and the destruction of the environment.[331] More recently the United Nations has also attempted to play an increasing role in the quest for world peace, if with dubious success.

Mass political reforms have also played an important role in transforming patterns of human unity in the final decades of the 20th century. As economic stagnation swept the Eastern bloc so political unrest increased and its citizens demanded change. In Poland in 1981 Lech Walesa, the leader of the illegal trade union *Solidarity*, led a crusade for a free society in the face of overwhelming communist resistance and the imposition of martial law. By 1985 the political tone was also changing in the USSR under Mikhail Gorbachev's radical agenda of 'glasnost' (openness) and 'perestroika' (restructuring).

Poland led Eastern Europe to freedom in 1989 after Solidarity's right to exist as a political party was acknowledged. Towards the end of the year, and during a visit by Mikhail Gorbachev, anti-government demonstrations in West Germany also led to the demolition of the wall which had divided Berlin for so long. With the fall of this single greatest icon of the post-war East/West divide, demands for change only continued to accelerate. In 1990 Lech Walesa was elected Polish President. Bulgaria, Hungary, and Czechoslovakia, also held free elections, the latter of two of which returned non-communists to power. Germany also reunited in 1990.

By the December of 1991 a new Commonwealth of Independent States was even replacing the once-mighty international empire of the Soviet Union. With regional conflicts rife across Europe world peace still remained a distant hope. However, the Cold War was most definitely over, with the associated threat of nuclear armageddon significantly reduced.

Popular and global concerns for freedom, peace, unity, and ecologically-friendly practices, could not have swept the world without the availability of international knowledge media. During the Cold War communist governments had the power to restrict the free flow of information across their borders. Human rights atrocities and acts of mass pollution or environmental destruction could also usually be committed well away from the public gaze. However, the revolution of the microchip was to tip the balance of power away from totalitarian states and faceless, brick-walled organizations.

In the 1980s camcorders and personal computers for the first time empowered activists across the planet to become effective global reporters. Satellite broadcasting also started to deny any nation state total control over the broadcast messages received by its population. In addition, by the early-1990s the Internet had begun to thrive as a many-to-many global media almost immune from censorship. Accurate information upon international happenings could therefore be passed around the world in an instant.

With such advanced electronic media at their fingertips, successful activists found that they had the power to turn local events into stylized, global soundbites. Happenings from oil spills to the student demonstrations in Tiananmen Square subsequently became a focus for world change. For the first time populations came to be rapidly united by a common ethic rather than through a common regional or national identity.

In recent decades the cultures as well as the politics of previously insular nations have also come to be exported via global electronic media. As communications theorist Marshal McLuhan boldly contested over thirty years ago, virtually-instantaneous electronic communications have the capacity to drag events together and hence to render them interdependent.[332] As we have witnessed across the Present Age—and in particular across the past two decades—the world has begun to implode into a 'global village' witness to a increasingly homogeneous culture, polity, geography and economy. Globalization has indeed become the dominant meme of the late-20th century. It will therefore impinge with great effect upon the functioning of the Future Organization.

THE GLOBAL BUSINESS

Over the last two decades a whirlwind of social, political, cultural and environmental forces have gone a long way towards unifying, if not *integrating*, previously discrete nations.[333] However, above and beyond such transitions, arguably the most significant forces for globalization have been and remain economic. As Kenichi Ohmae of McKinsey & Company in Tokyo argues, economics, not politics, define the landscape against which all else must operate.[334] As the political, cultural—and often religious—constraints upon global geographic operations have fallen in recent decades, so an effectively borderless economy has emerged. Against this backdrop the nation state structure so clearly cemented in the first three-quarters of the 20th century has not only begun to crumble. Even more significantly, nation state 'boundaries' have become almost *irrelevant* in many business contexts.

The revving engine of economic globalism may most clearly be monitored by looking at developments in international trade.[335] Between 1870 and 1913 world trade tripled,[336] whilst between 1965 and 1985 it increased nearly tenfold.[337] The range of countries involved in international trade has also rapidly expanded in recent years. In part this has been due to rising international investment in the developing world, which has in itself contributed to the globalization of many markets.

Around the turn of the century Britain, France, Germany, and the United States, dominated the bulk of world trade. However, today the entire European Union, together with the United States, account for less than fifty per cent of world trade volumes. Trade barriers in the form of tariffs have also fallen significantly in the past fifty years. For example, whilst in 1934 the United States levied an average sixty per cent tariff on imported goods, by 1987 this figure had fallen to just over four per cent.[338] In the late-1990s GATT negotiations are also continuing in an attempt to reduce international trade barriers further still.[339]

As a near-borderless world economy has emerged, so many businesses have come to operate upon a global level. Increasingly, many multinational organizations are operating across global infrastructures without the spatial reference points of a home parent nation. Global financial markets are already totally fluid, and, as more and more products and services come to be traded in digital or 'virtual' forms, so many other industries will follow in their wake. As we shall explore further in **chapter 16**, by adopting the new groupware tools of the Digital Age, truly global Future Organizations will not have to exist anywhere or any time.

As home markets stagnate, so the only possibilities for generating new income streams are increasingly to be found outside of national home territories. In the 1990s companies such as McDonald's, Benetton, Ford, Coca-Cola, Microsoft, IBM, Nike, and Reebok, are not only operating globally, but are proving increasingly successful in the marketing of homogeneous, global products.

By manipulating the mass media and emerging metamedia, global organizations may now foster a global awareness of tastes amongst their customers. A convergence in global consumer wants may thereby be fostered.[340] Alarmingly to some, an increasing number of branded global products now transcend many previous cultural barriers within wider and wider geographic frames of reference. Indeed, the most successful global corporations are now seeking as much to export a 'new' native culture which will then demand their products, as they are to overcome the problems inherent in transcultural marketing.

As George Ritzer contends, the globe is fast becoming 'McDonaldized'—or even 'McDisneyized'—as mighty transnational organizations 'reorder' consumption as well as production on a planetary scale. As McDonald's, Disney, the Holiday Inn *et al* seek such reordering, not only do the operational efficiency, calculability, predictability and control of their products and service provision improve and converge worldwide. In addition, a greater conformity of tastes continues to geographically spread until every mall or high street looks identical and offers the same variety of global products and services.[341] Is it therefore hardly surprising that some conclude that cultural regionalities of opinion, product, taste and character risk extinction.[342]

In opposition to the above bleak tale, one may also contend that economic globalization will at least ensure that as many consumers as possible have access to the best product ranges the world has on offer. We may all increasingly consume the same foods, drinks, clothes, cars and entertainment. However, at least all of these goods and services should prove to be of an optimal quality. In addition, the emergence of a global product range should permit each and every geographic region to specialize in just those areas of production in which it enjoys comparative advantage. Indeed, one constant theme emerging from most studies of globalization concerns the polarization of effective economic activity between global and regional levels.

THE RISE OF THE REGION STATE

In a borderless world it is simply no longer efficient to control economic activity at the intermediate level of the nation. The problem is that national geographic areas are usually too big to be regionally cohesive, whilst remaining too small to provide an alternative to global operations. As Ohmae explains:

> Nation states are no longer meaningful units in which to think about economic activity. In a borderless world they combine things at the wrong level of aggregation. What sense does it make, for example, to think of Italy as a coherent economic entity within the European Union? There is no "average" Italy. There is no meaningful social or economic group precisely at the midpoint. There is an industrial north and a rural south, which are vastly different in their ability to contribute and their need to receive. For the public official or private-sector manager, treating Italy as if it were fairly represented by an average is to mortgage usable insight in return for an economic relic—and a destructive one at that.[343]

The sentiment expressed above for Italy may be applied equally to almost any late-20th century nation. Hence, rather than using nations as the staging posts of the global economy, business is now better suited to treat regions—or what Ohmae terms 'region states'—as the dominant economic units of the globe. Such regions must be large enough to muster some global economic leverage, yet small enough to be shaped by the contours of the global economy. They must also welcome free trade both into and out of their sphere of influence—thereby avoiding the nation-state hang-up of desiring foreign investment whilst simultaneously trying to protect local producers from foreign competition.[344] The city state of Singapore provides just one example of a thriving locally-cohesive yet nationally-competitive economic territory today. Other regional giants and nimble local entrepreneurial communities also look set to take centre stage as nation states with too diverse a macroeconomic policy fade into the background of history.[345]

UNCERTAIN TIMES AHEAD

Across the 19th century nation states enjoyed the first of two key phases of progressive evolution. In Russia and continental Europe the powers of the feudal nobility became centralized in the hands of absolute monarchs. In contrast in Britain, Holland, and the United States, more liberal demo-cratic states emerged. In either case the roles of 19th century nations were minimal. Externally states were charged with using military force and diplomacy to secure raw materials and trading links. Internally state provision was largely restricted to the maintenance of a basic tax regime and the enforcement of common law.[346]

As the 20th century dawned, so nation states entered a second and more organized phase of development. As we have witnessed across this chapter, the world wars, the emergence of the welfare state, and communist revolutions, all led to the emergence of nations with a far wider range of interventionary and administrative functions. Both the internal and external roles of nations increased considerably around the middle of the 20th century. Such expanded role sets reflected new concerns and strategies for industrial development, economic and fiscal management, and international political, military and trade alliances. However, as the 20th century draws to a close, the internal and external activities which once secured national boundaries and identities have become so broad as to prove unsustainable. New mass media are permitting fresh planet-wide memes to sweep the world. International trade conducted between an increasingly large number of global corporations is also making the segregation of the planet into discrete national territories no longer economically acceptable.

In aggregation the above changes suggest that nation states no longer constitute the most effective building blocks for political or economic prosperity. Like it or not, constrained or even relaxed geographic spans will therefore no longer prove broad enough territories for the optimal operation of most Future Organizations. Granted, as and if nation states decline in their significance, so citizenship, welfare rights, and perhaps even liberal democracy, may be threatened. Indeed, to cope with the geographic spans of the global, new forms of social security, political expression, and niche culture, will almost certainly need to emerge.[347] Quite how is admittedly still far from clear.

As we shall explore in the final chapter of Part IV, optimizing the utilization of global resources represents a critical challenge for the very future of humanity. Whether nation states will have a significant role to play is uncertain. However, large Future Organizations will most definitely have to become very heavily involved.

Quite possibly the 21st century may come to be dominated by a clan of global business organizations whose economic might will give them the muscle to dictate patterns of citizenship and to program tastes and cultures to their whim. More positively—and perhaps in tandem—another possibility is that a 'highly differentiated yet relatively consensual family of nations' will emerge. Such a family may pursue a shared global agenda whilst punishing the deviant and protecting the defenceless.[348] Indeed, for all of our sakes, and in the name of so many victims of 20th century armed conflicts, we can all but hope that the latter proves to be the case.

13
Our Island Earth

Earth is the cradle of the mind, but one cannot live in the cradle forever.

Konstantin E. Tsiolkovsky[349]

IN 1785 JAMES HUTTON proposed that the world constituted a single superorganism.[350] By this he meant that it was possible to consider all of the lifeforms which comprise our ecosystem as the component cells of a single, wider entity. If such a view is taken, then to understand life and its evolution scientists ought not to study human beings or other animals and plants in isolation. Rather, they should investigate how all of the fauna and flora of the Earth *interact* as a single lifeform in amalgamation. The idea of viewing the world as a single superorganism is therefore not just philosophically novel. The implications are also extremely wide ranging for a great many traditional disciplines.

Although not popular in his day, Hutton's ideas have been afforded some scientific popularity and public exposure in more recent times due to James Lovelock's so-called *Gaia Hypothesis*. According to Lovelock, Gaia—named after the Greek goddess of the Earth—is the living entity which spans the Earth's surface, and which regulates the environment of the planet. Gaia is therefore 'the superorganism composed of all life tightly coupled with the air, the oceans, and the surface rocks'.[351]

By means as yet unclear, Gaia keeps our planet habitable by controlling the mix of gases in the atmosphere. In doing so she also manages to filter out harmful solar radiation and to maintain a safe surface temperature. Lovelock argues that for the mix of gases in the atmosphere to remain constant something must be regulating them.[352] As he goes on to explain, the natural chemical equilibrium of the atmosphere would be 98 per cent carbon dioxide, with little nitrogen and no oxygen. This is in stark contrast to the 78 per cent nitrogen, 21 per cent oxygen, and 0.03 per cent carbon dioxide, found in actuality, and without which life could not exist.[353] Lovelock has a similar fascination with the fact that the climate of the Earth has remained stable for life for around 3.5 aeons.[354] This is again surprising since the heat output of our sun has increased by 30 per cent over the same period.[355]

Fortunately for our purposes, theories of metasystem superorganisms are no longer limited to the purely biological. In 1993 Gregory Stock heightened the debate when he defined the superorganism of *Metaman* as constituting the next observable phase in the evolution of human civilization. As the dust jacket to his breathtaking work bids us consider:

> Imagine looking down from the moon at the night side of the Earth, pitch dark and invisible except for a brightly lit network of human constructions—luminous cities, highways, canals, telephone and power lines. A faint, speckled web of light would seem to float in space. Some regions of this lacework would form intricate geometric patterns, others would seem random and disconnected. Far from inert, this distant pattern of light would change and grow over the decades as you kept watch, shimmering fibres forming, extending, and joining in an almost vegetative fashion.

> This resemblance to life is not mere happenstance; the thin planetary patina of humanity and its creations is actually a living entity. It is a "superorganism", that is, a community of organisms so fully tied together as to be a single living being itself. Instead of referring to this entity using a term already filled with associations, let's start fresh and simply call it "Metaman".[356]

Stock's vision of the emerging superorganism of Metaman differs significantly from that of Hutton or Lovelock. For a start Hutton and Lovelock effectively view nature itself as a living entity. In contrast, Stock describes a superorganism comprised of the lone species of humankind in combination with the vast, artificial infrastructure of his own civilization. Hutton and Lovelock also describe a metasystem which has existed for millions upon millions of years. However for Stock, Metaman as a global lifeform is only just being born as all of the previously geographically and technologically isolated economies and societies of humanity coherently intermesh. Metaman is therefore the embodiment of humankind's now unlimited planetary geographic span.

Metaman's body is also only part biological. All of the super-organism's vital organs may be living beings. However, the arteries and nerves which connect them are the hardwares and softwares which comprise the meme carriers and transportation systems of the late-20th century. Metaman is therefore the first natural cyborg to emerge on our planet—a gigantic, evolving creature part flesh, and part metal, silicon, concrete, tarmac and glass.

AVOIDING THE INVISIBLE FOREST

I mention the complementary theories of Hutton, Lovelock, and Stock, as they provide us with a distinctly alternative perspective upon globalization to that presented within most business, scientific and social literatures. In the last chapter we began to examine how the individual economies, cultures and societies of the world are melding together into what we may accurately term single 'metaeconomies', 'metacultures' and 'metasocieties'. Such new social and economic creations require radically new means of analysis at the metasystem level. No longer may we take sensible x-rays of our condition from the sidewalks of a city on the ground. Rather, we need a holistic approach where we step back—or rise up—for the bigger, global picture.

For far too long top-down metascience or 'helicopter' perspectives have been shunned in a world hell-bent upon the bottom-up science and social science of single problems and isolated case histories. Granted, in most day-to-day circumstances there is a great deal of value to be gained from 'reductionist' approaches which seek to explore and modify the detail of particular technologies, companies, or problem sets. This said, the narrow-but-deep reductionism of our current systems of business and education end up breeding a blinkered race who rarely ever even want to see the forest. Instead most people and organizations are quite content to examine the lines on the bark of one of its many trees.

Another problem associated with splitting science or social science into narrow disciplines with narrower still foci is that everyone tends to assume that somebody else is asking the big questions.[357] Unfortunately, with very few Huttons, Lovelocks or Stocks roaming the planet, this passing-the-buck proposition rarely proves to be the case.

In this final chapter before we put the construction of organizations themselves under the microscope, we will take a little time out to try and identify some of the really big agendas which lie ahead for humanity as a collective, global species. This chapter will therefore unashamedly push the bounds right out; and it will push them very hard indeed.

Attempting to look too far ahead, especially in a global context, is something for which futurists and their works are frequently heavily criticized. This said, the trick in achieving future success surely has to be in embarking upon the right journey. It is therefore surprising that many seem to forget that you first need to have some appreciation of where you are to travel in order to select an appropriate highway. As Henry Kissinger once noted, 'if you don't know where you are going almost any road will get you there'.[358] However, for the Future Organization which wishes to prosper and survive long-term, just picking any road simply will not do. So please, over the next few pages, open your mind as wide as possible to futures and possibilities decades or even centuries hence. It is a shame indeed that most managers today look further ahead when planning their own careers than they do when plotting strategies for the future trajectory of their organizations.[359]

A GLOBAL MINDSET

It never fails to surprise me when people debate global issues within national mindsets. As just one example, in the July of 1996 the British Member of Parliament Jack Straw appeared on the BBC's *Newsnight* and stated that Britain operates in a global economy. Wrong. What he should have said is that Britain *constitutes part of* the global economy. The difference? Only that if every nation *operated in* a global economy—rather than being *part of* one—then the global economy would not actually exist. Indeed, the single most important element of adopting a global mindset has to be an abandonment of the notion that there is an 'us' and a wider 'them' with which we may or may not choose to play. In contradiction to the popular slogan, we are now all both part of the solution *and* part of the problem.

The bedrock of adopting a global mindset is simply accepting that we are all in the same boat. In *Cyber Business* I suggested that, when acquiring a computer, individuals or organizations should no longer consider themselves to be purchasing an isolated box of electronics. Rather, they ought to imagine that they are obtaining a stake in the expanding 'global hardware platform' of all computers worldwide. My reasoning was that a great deal of the value to be reaped from a computer now derives from its use in combination with others when linked across a local or wide-area network.[360] The benefits to be gained in buying a computer are therefore inevitably part-synergistic beyond the immediate advantage of the purchasing individual or organization.

For example, suppose that four friends spread across a broad geography all have home computers with an Internet connection which allows them to exchange electronic mail messages. If a fifth friend obtains such a computer then not only will she find it easier, cheaper and faster to communicate with her friends. In addition, the four other friends will also find it easier, cheaper and faster to communicate with her. Companies who want to sell services to this 'wired' group will also benefit from each of their individual computer purchases, as a new electronic highway will become available into their homes. Indeed, we could even argue that every person who establishes an Internet connection potentially adds value to the lives and activities of every one of the fifty million plus other users around the globe. Of course to take the point this far is extreme. However, there can be no denying that the more interconnected the peoples, economies, and organizations of the world become, the greater the potential benefits to be enjoyed by all concerned.

In terms of value added the networking which characterizes globalism technologically, culturally, and politically, cannot fail to become a two way street. Globalizing trends therefore ought always to lead towards a win-win social and economic scenario. Yet many people do not appreciate this outcome or simply refuse to accept it. Instead they cling to the mentality of the techie who purchases *their* computer from a mysterious *them* for *themselves*. An attitude therefore prevails of countries or organizations working *in* global markets—or gaining access *to* them—in opposition to a belief that all nations and organizations are now most sensibly viewed as an economic metasystem in amalgamation. If we are to make the most of living and working together globally then such an attitude quickly needs to be eradicated. Indeed, if the human race is to prosper long-term, then a broad base of cooperation for the common good will soon become absolutely critical.

DWINDLING RESOURCES

Like most large creatures the superorganism of Metaman has an enormous appetite. Without food in the form of natural resources it will cease to survive and evolve. Indeed, as Metaman grows it is becoming more and more hungry. It is therefore rather unfortunate that at present its feeding habits are constrained to the larder of a motherworld whose cupboard is starting to run bare.

We have all at times heard scenarios reporting an increased scarcity of natural resources. To cite just one, if by 2050 a world population of 11.5 billion had managed to obtain a standard of living comparable with that achieved in the United States in 1988, then world petroleum reserves would all be used up in seven years, aluminium deposits in eighteen years, copper in four years, zinc in three, and so on.[361] No doubt many economists and scientists would wish to revise the figures contained within this hybrid of conjecture. However, it is not the exact figures —even to within hundreds of years—which are important. More significant is the obvious message. Either decades or centuries into our third millennium the world will be depleted of many of the material deposits upon which human civilization depends.

In response to the above some will leap from pew to pulpit with ideas for new and sustainable sources of energy and raw materials. Such individuals—and they are both multitudinous and powerful—will preach that solar power and windmills; organic plastics and derivatives thereof; will provide prosperity for future humanity. And yet, unfortunately, such individuals simply have their heads stuck in the sands. A submarine crew trapped at the bottom of the ocean would not expect its supplies to last out indefinitely. So why is it that humankind still believes that its first planet will provide it with eternal food, shelter, and other resources?

In **chapter 11** I noted how the Second Law of Thermodynamics condemns all geographically isolated communities to stagnate and eventually decay unless they actively seek to expand their horizons to access fresh material supplies. The development of human civilization in accordance with this line of reasoning has been clearly demonstrated since the empires of antiquity sought wider and wider patterns of trade and geographic governance. As we have explored within recent chapters, across history cities have amalgamated into kingdoms; kingdoms and regions into nations; and nations into today's emerging global meta-system. Time and time again the laboratory of past events has demonstrated that closed human geographies are simply not sustainable long-term. Yet at present a great many citizens of the planet have somehow come to believe that through enlightened environmental management we may overcome the resource limitations of Mother Earth.

THE (UN)SUSTAINABLE ETHIC

Comedian Ben Elton once delivered a superb routine in which he described how he spent most of his undergraduate student days 'eking'. By this he meant that financial impoverishment forced him to stretch out everything as far as possible. Teabags had to be reused and all manner of rubbish recycled for other purposes. One drink had to last all evening, whilst in the winter he was forced to huddle in as many layers of clothing as possible before a single-bar electric fire in order to minimize fuel bills. Although a well-observed piece of comedy, Elton's routine also provided a powerful illustration of the underfunding of higher education in the United Kingdom. The wider ethic it demonstrated was equally serious.

The notion of making things last as long as possible has been passed down from generation to generation and serves as an reminder of hard times both past and present. Indeed, there is absolutely nothing wrong in an economically-prudent ethic of eking things out *per se*. To the contrary, in today's often over-disposable society, the eking ethic ought to be applauded. However, when eking does become dangerous is when it constitutes an entire race's sole survival strategy.

I happen to be one of those individuals who stops to turn out the light in an unoccupied room and who retrieves waste paper for scrap. However, despite a reasonably ecologically-friendly mentality, I still have great difficulty in understanding the popular green concept of 'sustainable development'. The World Commission on Environment and Development defines such development as that which 'meets the needs of the present generation without compromising the ability of future generations to meet their own needs'.[362] Or as environmental strategist Richard Welford explains, sustainable development implies that 'at a minimum, all human activity must refrain from causing any degree of permanent damage through its consumption of environmental resources'.[363]

If the issue under discussion were not so serious we ought to laugh out loud at such definitions. It is *impossible* to live today without degrading *some* resources which could be used tomorrow. Remember the Second Law of Thermodynamics? It reminds our common sense that *all* isolated systems—even those as big as the Earth—are doomed to decay. So either the laws of physics are about to be rewritten, or 'sustainable development' sadly has to be a myth.

As I hope to have made clear above, this is not to say that I wish to knock green issues and the environmental movement. Minimizing waste and safeguarding the beauty of our planet is a responsibility in which I strongly believe we all must share. This said, as even James Lovelock, the champion of the Gaia hypothesis, freely admits, pollution is not a product of moral turpitude. Rather, it is an inevitable consequence of life itself.[364] It is therefore as daft to try and obliterate pollution as it is to legislate against dung from cows.[365]

Some degree of pollution has to be accepted as a natural consequence of human existence. It is therefore totally unrealistic to assume that there is any environmental policy which constitutes more than an eking ethic. Sooner or later the Earth is doomed to decay and stagnate *regardless* of the actions of humankind. Granted, like a student superorganism sitting sipping diluted tea before a single bar fire, we may be able to make our natural resources last out a few centuries more. Yet, such a far-from-pretty future of increasing squabbles is all that is on offer unless, like our ancestors, we decide to explore resource possibilities outside of our immediate home terrain.

FRONTIERS FOR THE 21ST CENTURY

The majority of our ancestors looked up to the heavens and failed even to recognize space as a frontier to be conquered. Today, of course, most people know that there are planets, moons, and a wider universe of other galaxies, way beyond the limits of the Earth's atmosphere. Yet few people still fully comprehend the true potential of space.[366] In part this is due to the fact that our early forays outwards from the Earth—whilst magnificent in their ingenuity—were driven by politics rather than economics. As Eric Drexler, author of *Engines of Creation*, explains:

> Some of the [early] pioneers had seen what to do: build a space station and a reusable spaceship, then reach out to the Moon or asteroids for resources. But the noise of the flustered politicians promptly drowned out their suggestions, and the US politicians clamoured for a big, easy-to-understand goal. Thus was born project Apollo, the race to land a US citizen on the nearest place to plant a flag. Project Apollo bypassed building a space station and a space shuttle, instead building giant missiles able to reach the Moon in one great leap. The project was glorious, it gave scientists more information, and it brought great returns through advances in technology—but at the core, it was a hollow stunt.[367]

Just as space programmes expanded as the hostilities of the Cold War escalated, so they have diminished in the less politically polarized climate of the past two decades. In these more recent times the nations of the world have largely closed their eyes to the possibilities of space. Instead public attention has become more and more focused upon noble if short-termist environmentalism. However, as the natural resources of our closed globe continue to dwindle, it is high time once again to look up towards the stars.

The resource potential of even just our own solar system is enormous. In addition to the Moon and other planets there are a great many asteroids whose resources may be reaped for human advantage. Indeed, in the medium-term, mining the asteroids is likely to prove far easier than attempting to extract and transport usable materials from planetary bodies.

Whilst some asteroids contain ordinary rock, others boast water, oil shale, and even meteoritic metal alloys. One of the numerous kilometre-wide 'chunks' of the latter form of space debris could supply literally trillions of dollars worth of currently precious metals.[368] A few asteroids are even large enough to be able to bury the Earth's continents half a mile deep with raw materials.[369] And resources to be extracted long-term from the planets and their many moons are potentially many orders of magnitude greater.

As the number of human beings in simultaneous existence continues to increase, settlements upon Mars or the moons of our own or other planets may prove more and more attractive. Alternatively, gigantic space stations could be built from extraterrestrial materials for mass human occupation. With internal CRE amusements or VR suites, such stations could be made quite habitable and a real 'home from home'. Indeed, there is simply no technological or economic reason to believe that the current generation of humanity has to be the first to face finite and hence critical geographic boundaries. As the astronauts and cosmonauts of the early space programmes so clearly demonstrated, all terrestrial boundaries are now artificial, potentially invisible, and ultimately meaningless.[370] All it will take to drive human beings and their organizations outwards for long-term survival is some hope, a great deal of vision, and an open imagination.

SHIPS FOR THE THIRD MILLENNIUM

Since Yuri Gagarin first crept into orbit, space travel has been extremely expensive. All of the craft used to transport men to the Moon and back were based upon multi-stage, non-reusable rockets which jettisoned spent sections during flight. However, since its Apollo programme, NASA has developed the space transportation system (STS) more commonly known as the space shuttle. This launches a reliable, reusable winged space plane astride a fuel tank side-strapped with solid rocket boosters.

The STS programme has significantly reduced the cost of space missions as both shuttles and boosters may be reused. As a result, space travel has been able to become far more frequent within the fifteen years in which the space shuttle has been flying. Indeed NASA's current fleet of four shuttles has already carried a combined total of over 220 astronauts into space.[371]

Unfortunately, even with the advances of the shuttle, the cost of travelling beyond the Earth still remains high. For a start it takes many months and man hours to overhaul a shuttle after each mission. Just as significantly, spaceport overheads remain spread over very few launches per year. For space travel to become cost effective, future craft need to be capable of launching and returning to Earth in one piece without the need for extensive refurbishment. A great many space flights will also need to be taking place in order to spread fixed infrastructure and development costs over as many flights as possible. Just imagine the cost of flying from Heathrow to New York if the running costs of these airports had to be divided between only a handful of flights per year!

Having noted the above, it is heartening to discover that private as well as public sector organizations are now playing an active role in the development of low-cost, high-volume space transportation systems. Indeed, NASA does not even intend to build and operate future reusable space craft. Instead it will purchase launch services from industrial contractors.

By as early as 1990 studies by the Boeing Aerospace Company were estimating that reusable shuttles flown like airliners could cut launch costs by a factor of fifty if sufficient economies of scale were to be applied.[372] More recently, NASA has instigated a reusable launch vehicle (RLV) programme. Through various research initiatives it now also has several industrial partners.

Due to advancements in structures, materials, electronics, and propulsion technologies, over the past quarter of a century, space vehicles which take-off and land in one piece have finally become a technical possibility. Prototypes of various 'single-state to orbit' (SSTO) RLVs are also well into development. However, without the glitz of Cold War politics, the progress of such programmes rarely receives significant media attention. It's as if electricity, automobiles, television, or personal computers, were being invented from scratch in a dark closet.

One of the most advanced RLV prototypes is the DC-XA or 'Delta Clipper' being developed by NASA and McDonnell Douglas Aerospace. This forty-three foot experimental vertical take-off and landing SSTO rocket ship is intended to demonstrate a range of new space technologies and materials in action. Several successful test flights of the DC-XA have already taken place. A pad crew of just fifteen people has also managed to refurbish a rocket so quickly that two flights of the same craft have taken place within twenty-six hours.

Another SSTO RVL technology demonstrator is the X-33. Unlike the DC-XA, this SSTO space plane is designed to take-off vertically but to glide into land horizontally like existing space shuttles. In July 1996 a cooperative agreement was issued by NASA for Lockheed Martin to build and fly the half-scale X-33 prototype by the March of 1999. Although around $1bn is being invested by NASA, Lockheed-Martin is also to contribute over $200 million. The shared goal is to demonstrate the technologies necessary to construct the next generation of full-size SSTO RVLs which will provide low-cost access to space.

At the time of writing NASA had also just released a research announcement for a fast-track RVL technology demonstrator vehicle known as the X-34. Due to begin flight testing in mid-1998, the X-34 is hoped to be able to launch for less than $500,000 per flight. A long-term high payoff (LT/HP) main propulsion system (MPS) programme is also running to advance the state-of-the-art chemical rocket technologies needed to support the full range of NASA's RVL initiatives.

CONQUESTS NO LONGER IMPOSSIBLE

The reusable SSTO space planes and rocket ships of the early-21st century ought to empower the next great geographic expansion of human-kind. No longer will our geographic span be limited to planet Earth. No longer will we have to remain isolated within the solar system. Instead, a multitudinous range of new mineral reserves will be at our fingertips.

Solar power stations will also be able to be constructed in orbit. Whilst it may be possible to build solar power stations here on Earth, they will prove far easier to construct in zero gravity where they will also not occupy vast areas of valuable land. Solar cells in space will additionally prove far more efficient as they will be able to capture the sun's rays free from the filtering of the atmosphere. Indeed it has been estimated that one single space solar cell will be able to gather over one billion watts of free sunlight night and day.[373]

In addition to providing homes, future space stations will also serve as factories for the production of complex crystals and pharmaceuticals in zero gravity. Raw materials will also one day be processed by self-replicating and self-maintaining robots either out in space or upon the Moon.[374] As the frontier of space opens further, solar 'lightsails' will probably also be developed. Rigged with several square kilometres of thin, reflective sail, these future clippers will tug millions of tons of raw materials between planets and space stations under the gentle force of the solar wind. Ion and/or proton engines may also be developed to increase possibilities for widespread interplanetary travel without the need for bulky liquid rocket fuels.

Many more centuries into the future humans may even 'terraform' the red planet of Mars into a vegetated green world with an atmosphere suitable for human habitation without space suits. In creating such a 'New Eden' or 'Mars II' the surface temperature of the planet will need to be raised by around 50°C. This may be able to be achieved with vast solar mirrors and/or by applying a heat-absorbent black coating. As the temperature rises both water and frozen carbon dioxide will be released from the polar caps, hence assisting in the process of thickening the atmosphere, and providing a potential source of oxygen.[375]

To the business-hearted the speculations of the previous few paragraphs may sound like pure fantasy. Yet so were powered flight, talking pictures, wireless communications, and computers, at the dawn of the Present Age. It is perhaps also worth noting that just as IBM once saw no future in personal computers, so in 1956 Britain's Astronomer Royal described the whole idea of space travel as 'utter bilge'. Indeed, if we are to learn only one lesson from our history, it has to be that humankind has almost always managed to rapidly develop 'impossible' technologies in relatively short frames of time.

* * *

GLOBAL HORIZONS

My first port of call for information upon NASA's reusable launch vehicle programme was the personal computer upon my desk. Barely five minutes after launching an Internet web browser I was marvelling at full-colour pictures and schematics of the space agency's incredible prototype reusable craft. In only a few minutes more I could have also downloaded videoclips of test flight footage, computer simulations, and significant speeches made by advocates of the programme.[376]

That I could so rapidly access such a rich variety of multimedia information from an unknown computer somewhere half way around the world provides just one demonstration of globalization in action. Today such a browse of the public knowledge of networked humanity is literally child's play.[377] Ten years ago for most people it would have been unthinkable. A decade hence and *only* being able to access 2-D graphics, rather than an interactive, 3-D virtual reality simulation, will be a major let down.

It is perhaps not pure coincidence that global metacultures, meta-economies, and metasocieties, started to emerge in the same decades in which geographers really started to use satellite imaging to 'get at all those still uncharted little pockets of our planet'.[378] Geographic expansion and developments in transportation and communications have always gone hand in hand. Or as Freud once noted, whilst technology allows far away people to speak on the phone, it also permits them to be far away in the first place.[379]

The challenge of the geographic frontier of the solar system is great indeed. Yet it is neither insurmountable nor its conquest a fantasy. The solar system is only vast today in the sense that the Earth and its skies were vast to our recent ancestors. Distance has never been a barrier to humankind. Rather, we have only ever been limited by our evolution of suitable forms of transportation and communication. Hence, just as technological progress enabled our forebears to reach outwards to survive and shrink the planet, so the embryonic technologies and theories of space engineering may enable another major geographic expansion. It is perhaps unlikely that many readers of this book will ever live off-planet. However, many people alive as you read these words are almost certain to benefit from products, raw materials, and energy sources, exported down onto planet Earth. Likely, that is, providing that enough Future Organizations recognize the enormous profit opportunities now needed to catalyse our race into any positive survival action.

In the following and final Part of *Challenging Reality*, we will crash back to Earth to explore the productive forms of organizations past, present and future. However before we do so, there is perhaps one final issue upon which this star-gazing aside ought to briefly touch. Many environmentalists today feel that nature is something with which human-kind ought not to further interfere. Even if a conquest of space becomes both technologically possible and a survival necessity, some therefore contend that it is not necessarily a choice of action we ought to pursue. We have, after all, already abused and polluted our first home planet. Do we therefore have the right to rape and scar the solar system beyond Mother Earth?

To this understandable argument I can offer but two answers. The first is that concepts such as 'nature' and 'technology' and 'civilization' are totally artificial linguistic constructions in which we currently choose to believe. In practice humankind—and its technologies, civilizations and pollutions—are all a part of the 'natural' environment. A human progression outwards to the stars is therefore no more and no less natural than the evolution of life itself.

My second argument in defence of the human 'exploitation' of the solar system is far less academically contrived. The known planets, moons, and voids of space, may be serene, unspoilt, and as natural as any creator intended. Yet they are also barren, hungry and cold. Therefore, far from polluting the tranquil beauty of space, future humanity will instead bless it with the richness and variety of life.

PART V
PRODUCTIVE FORM

14
Tools of the Overlord

SOME READERS COULD BE forgiven for thinking that this book has lost its way. After all, over the past few chapters, we have explored virtual reality and metamedia, political and cultural globalization, not to mention environmental dilemmas and the conquest of space. So what, some may reasonably ask, has all of this to do with the characteristics of the Future Organization? The answer is that, in exploring the progression of the reality facets of achievement focus, member status, knowledge media, and geographic span, over the past twelve chapters, we have cemented a shared technological, economic, social and cultural context within which to analyse our final, organization-specific reality facet of *productive form*.

The development of organizations may not sensibly be studied in isolation from wider social, cultural and technological change. The following three chapters therefore investigate how productive systems have evolved across history amid a shifting achievement focus, an evolving work–command relationship, the development of multi and metachannel media forms, and an ever-widening geographic span. Specifically, the history of organizations will be detailed from *feudal/craft* to *bureaucratic* to *organic* modes of productive activity.

Once each of the above broad phases of organizational evolution has been outlined, **chapter 17** will draw together some general themes from across ***Challenging Reality*** as aids for the Future Manager. In particular, a 'Future Mindset' for forward-looking management practice will be presented in the final chapter.

AN EVOLUTION OF FORMS

Any attempt to divide the evolution of the means used to produce goods and services into a simple past–present–future progression is certain to prove contentious. It is therefore with a degree of apprehension that I stick my head above the parapet to present my three-phase sequence. As already noted, my proposal is that productive structures were largely *feudal/craft* based in the past, have exhibited a *bureaucratic* nature across the Present Age, and are now starting to evolve the extremely *organic* forms which will prove characteristic of most Future Organizations. **Table 14.1** places some more flesh upon the bones of this framework. A more detailed explanation also follows to place organizational evolution in a slightly richer context.

It is almost impossible to pick one strict label to adequately classify all of those systems of production which existed from antiquity up until the mid- to late-19th century. Indeed, in choosing to categorize the dominant productive form of this vast span of history as 'feudal/craft', I have in a sense admitted defeat and accepted that no single label may sensibly apply.

Most early formal organizations arose as the autocratic tools of the few and drew upon the physical labours and/or craft skills of the many. Those citizens cajoled into mass collective action by monarchs, lords, priests, and slave masters, built mighty structures like the Pyramids. They also kept many an ancient empire rich and prosperous, and fought numerous military campaigns.

The above noted, it also needs to be appreciated that seldom were most people in past times involved in major collective mass efforts. Instead, families or small communities—rather than larger, formal organizations—provided the primary focus for productive activity and patterns of daily routine. Indeed, most people laboured as farmers or craftsmen in the production of the food and other products essential for their very survival. For example, it is now widely believed that the majority of the workforce who built the Pyramids of Egypt were peasant farmers who toiled on the land for most of the year. They could therefore have only been mobilized into mass collective action as the dictates of the seasons allowed.[380]

Timeframe	Productive Form	Description
Past	Feudal/Craft	Most productive forms autocratic, and/or involving the practice of individual craft skills.
Present	Bureaucratic	Most productive forms based upon the metaphor of organizations as machines—wherein employees specialize within role frameworks as productive components.
Future	Organic	An increasing number of productive forms focused upon flexible process operations involving dynamic networks of capital and human resources.

Table 14.1 The Progression of Productive Forms

Granted, as managed individuals, most citizens of past times were effectively controlled, owned, or enslaved by their poverty. Most people did therefore in theory form part of a wider autocratic structure or organizational regime. However, kings, lords, and masters, were rarely in the possession of the technologies or management principles required to break down the efforts of their citizens into a range of specialist activities which could have empowered sophisticated, large-scale organizational mechanisms. Indeed, up until the period of the mid- to late-industrial revolution, the majority of products and services were produced by individuals and/or families on a craft basis, rather than by larger integrated teams of workers labouring as one. Despite the vast autocratic spans potentially capable of mobilizing mass human resources, it therefore remains reasonable to classify the productive form of past times as mostly feudal and/or craft-based.

Far easier to place within a single classification are the organizations of the Present Age. As productive plant concentrated in towns and cities in the late-19th and early-20th centuries,[381] so it became common for factories to employ hundreds or even thousands of workers. The rising paradigm of mass production was also starting to permeate industrial logic at this time. Rather than exercising a range of craft skills, individual workers were increasingly employed to perform only a few narrow procedures. Impersonal yet efficient bureaucratic productive forms thereby emerged to dominate organizational construction. Subsequently the mechanisms of organizations became more important than individual labour skills. And as this shift occurred, the majority of worker actions came to be dictated by precise and 'scientific' rules and operational procedures.

Until the latter decades of the 20th century, bureaucratic organizations proved the most effective means of production for the maintenance of industrial societies. However, since this time a flexibility of operations incompatible with the rigid confines of bureaucracy has arisen. In response we have seen hierarchies flatten, a greater use of outsourcing, and far more flexible worker–organization relationships as discussed in **chapters 6** and **7**.

Within the organic organizations of the late-20th century and beyond, a bare minimum of capital is likely to be dedicated to a specific task base. Instead, most resources will be allocated either internally or from the marketplace only as and when appropriate. As discussed in **chapter 16**, in place of the feudal/craft or bureaucratic organizations of the past and present, we are now witness to a new logic of productive form which champions flexibility, continual learning, and constant evolution. Indeed it is extremely unlikely that many Future Organizations will seek to establish rigid structures and practices expected to endure as optimal for significant periods of time. Rather, continual adaptation in the face of constant change is already becoming the order of the day.

IN SEARCH OF A BEGINNING

Most histories of organization kick-off around the dawn of the 20th century with the work of the management writer/practitioners known collectively as the 'Task School'. Chief amongst such gurus were Frederick Winslow Taylor and Henri Fayol.[382] As discussed in **chapter 6**, Taylor championed a paradigm known as 'scientific management'. This involved improving worker efforts via the rigid application of rules for effective specialization. Taking a slightly more macro perspective, Fayol proposed fourteen principles of management. These included the division of work and the creation of lines of authority, as well as the idea that organizations must strive for a 'unity of command' and a 'unity of direction' in order to achieve success. Fayol also pointed out that organizations were predicated on the subordination of the individual interest to the general interest. Finally he noted that order, equity and fairness (or *esprit de corps*) were vital for effective organizational functioning.[383]

Whilst influential to this day, we do not need a great knowledge of history to realize that Taylor, Fayol *et al* were hardly the first to 'discover' organizations and their management. As earlier chapters have already demonstrated, the ancient Egyptians, the Mesopotamians, the Greeks, the Romans, and many other early empires, all engaged in great organizational undertakings. It may even be argued that the division of labour upon which all productive structures are predicated dates back to the earliest of stone age times. Indeed, anthropologists suggest that one of the simplest ways of improving an early family unit's chances of survival was by assigning specialist roles to different individuals in order to improve collective group performance.[384]

The Chinese, Mesopotamians, Egyptians, Greeks, and Romans, were all making records of their organizational activities many thousands of years ago. It is therefore a little unfortunate that we are unable to glean any significant body of knowledge from their surviving writings.[385] This said, it does remain clear that early organizations were dominated by the same concepts of tasks, goals, aims, and objectives, which remain fundamental to this day. Indeed, as noted way back in **chapter 1**, organizations have always been collective mechanisms of human beings brought into existence for the accomplishment of tasks beyond the reach of lone individuals. We also know that the earliest known formal organizations—such as those which build the greatest monuments and empires of past times—were just as mechanistic as those to follow right up until the Present Age.[386]

ANCIENT ORGANIZATION IN CONTEXT

Ancient records aside, we may also gather some insights into early productive structures by considering their wider technological and social background. To this end, **table 14.2** provides a listing of our previous four reality facets in days long gone by. Drawing from this contextual framework we may be fairly certain that many of the larger organizations of past times were focused upon the construction of a single, physical creation—be it a tomb, temple, castle, cathedral, wall, canal, or other such edifice. We may also reasonably state that the people who laboured within the largest productive structures of past times did so with little free will. This is regardless of whether they were technically classified as serfs or slaves. Means of communicating ideas between those involved in past, awe-inspiring undertakings were also limited, as were their reaches of geographic span. In fact, given the above, one could start to wonder quite how any of the great projects of ancient and olden times ever came to be completed.

One answer could be that whilst large in scale, many of the great organizational undertakings of antiquity involved very clear physical goals. Those responsible for great pyramids, walls and canals could therefore have presented their workforce with an extremely transparent set of objectives towards which to aim. Complex modes of communication, monitoring and administration would therefore have proved unnecessary. In contrast, most of today's organizational goals—to gain a twenty per cent market share, for example—are complex, abstract, and hence open to wide-ranging interpretation.

The perceived rewards to be reaped from the successful completion of many ancient and olden time building projects were probably also very great indeed. Walls around cities or between territories provided defences which literally protected lives. Ancient waterways such as the Grand Canal of China also provided transportation for food to stop populations starving. Labouring upon a tomb or temple could probably have even bestowed safe and favoured passage into the afterlife.

In the modern world in which so many of us no longer have to fight for our physical well being, the relative perceived rewards of great organization projects are almost certainly smaller than those to be reaped by our ancestors. We may therefore labour less intently in our throwaway

Reality Facet	Typical Nature
Achievement focus	Awe (at physical/spiritual might)
Member status	Serfdom or slavery (owned individuals)
Knowledge media	Single channel (word of mouth or writing)
Geographic span	Constrained (regional with national/ international trade)

Table 14.2 The Organizational Context of Past Times

society of constant distraction. As living standards and expectations have risen well beyond survival, more comprehensive systems of organizational administration, monitoring, and control, may therefore have become necessary.

MILITARY MACHINES

Aside from large construction projects, the other great organizations of past times were those of great armies. The Romans in particular proved highly effective in orchestrating the actions of legions of troops across their Empire. In part this was due to a strict regimental structure and the maintenance of a sound system of communications. Many centuries later the army of Frederick the Great of Prussia also became a valuable icon for the construction of any effective, mechanistic organization.

Ruling between 1740 and 1786, Frederick had inherited an army largely composed of criminals, paupers, unwilling conscripts, and foreign mercenaries. In his quest to reform such an unruly mob into a reliable and efficient organizational instrument, he quickly introduced ranks and uniforms, extended and standardized regulations, and increased task specialization. Frederick also introduced standardized equipment, created a command language, and introduced a systematic training which included an army drill. As Gareth Morgan takes up the tale:

> To ensure that his miliary machine operated on command, Frederick fostered the principle that the men must be taught to fear the officers more than the enemy. And to ensure that the miliary machine was used as wisely as possible, he developed the distinction between advisory and command functions, freeing specialist advisers (staff) from the line of command to plan activities. In time, further refinements were introduced, including the idea of decentralizing controls to create greater autonomy of parts in different combat situations.[387]

INDUSTRIAL UPHEAVAL

Not long after the reign of Frederick the Great, the development of early factories, mills, mines, and transportation infrastructures, heralded what came to be known as the 'industrial revolution'. In the mid- to late-18th century death rates were falling, with population levels correspondingly starting to rise. Major scientific innovations were also accruing, whilst international trade was of increasing importance.

Resultant pressures upon the supply of resources and finished goods meant that a rural, agriculturally-based economy was no longer sufficient. Driven by economics and technological progress, more and more people had to move off the land to be transformed into factory hands.[388] The late-18th century therefore signalled the beginning of the end for modes of production centred around individual- or family-based craft activity. This said, it should be remembered that the transformation of productive structures took many, many decades. Indeed, up until the early- to mid-19th century there were still many people—even in industrialized nations—untouched by the science and ingenuity of factories, foundries, and mines.[389] Therefore, whilst the industrial revolution certainly heralded a change of organizational paradigm, it was not one which became widespread until the dawn of the Present Age.

As larger and larger organizations charged with undertaking more and more complex tasks became widespread, so Frederick the Great's vision of a 'mechanized army' gradually became a reality in the factory and the office.[390] In 1776 Adam Smith applied principles of specialization to factory workers. In the process he transformed individual craftsmen and women into organizational components.[391] In common with Frederick the Great's soldiers, people at work became bound by an increasing number of standardized techniques and rigorous discipline. In 1801 Eli Whitney demonstrated mass production techniques for the most effective assembly of guns from interchangeable parts. Thirty-one years later computer pioneer Charles Babbage published his own paper advocating labour specialization and strict organizational planning.[392] However, it was the work of German sociologist Max Weber which proved the most comprehensive in detailing the rising requirement for 'bureaucratic' productive forms.

THE MOST SUPERIOR FORM

Today the word 'bureaucracy' is usually associated with an unwieldy organization stifled with red tape. However, Weber saw bureaucracies as technically capable of attaining the highest degree of organizational efficiency. He described bureaucratic administration as 'fundamentally the exercise of control on the basis of knowledge'.[393] In doing so he perceived a bureaucratic structure as 'superior to any other form in precision, in stability, in the stringency of its discipline, and in its reliability'.[394]

Key to Weber's analysis was a study of three types of authority. Initially he noted that many organizations rested upon a 'traditional' authority form. Within such structures a belief in the sanctity of tradition prevailed. As a consequence, those in charge ruled without question solely due to their status as a king, emperor, master, or other variant of overlord. Throughout the majority of past times it seems likely that most organizations operated under such a strict and domineering regime. However, Weber viewed such organizational forms as sub-optimal, as the authority of their leaders was not legitimized on any rational basis.

Weber also questioned authority built upon 'charismatic' foundations. Within organizations utilizing charismatic forms of control, authority rests upon devotion to the sanctity, heroism or character of a specific individual person or order. Again it is unlikely that such authority will be rationally founded. This is especially the case when followers come to be swept along almost against their will by powerfully charismatic leaders such as religious fanatics or military dictators.

Weber's final category of authority was the 'rational' form of a bureaucracy. Rational authority rests upon the common acceptance of the 'legality' of impersonal roles and normative rules. It also depends upon workers accepting the right of those higher up in a hierarchy to issue commands.

ROLES & REGULATIONS

According to Weber, one of the great strengths of a bureaucratic organization lies in its ability to be totally impersonal. This is because bureaucratic structures are comprised of roles—what Charles Handy has termed 'empty raincoats'[395]—rather than specific individuals. Within a bureaucracy, nobody therefore ought to feel owned or manipulated. Rather, everyone should find themselves treated with equity. Indeed, the same set of rules ought to apply to every organizational member, subject only to the rational boundaries of their specific role.

Weber studied successful bureaucracies emerging in many private clinics, hospitals, and religious orders. In particular he noted the major role played by bureaucracy within the Catholic Church. In common with Frederick the Great, he also analysed modern armies as pure bureaucratic forms 'administered by that peculiar type of military functionary known as the officer'.

Perhaps the most significant organizational development associated with bureaucratic organizations was the emergence of a new breed of administrative worker. When organizations had been feudalistic and based around craft skills, there had been no need to elect or appoint impartial work coordinators. However, as workplace specialization increased, the creation of a new administrative managerial class became both inevitable and essential. Industrial society could simply not survive without bureaucratic structures to coordinate an ever-more complex range of productive activities. The only alternative would have been a return to an agricultural society living at a basic level of subsistence.

With freely contracted employees working for hard coinage, bureau-cratic organizations were also essential in fuelling the rise of capitalism. Without a population with money in its pockets, no fiscally-based economy could hope to prosper. Widening geographic spans and improved communications also both required and empowered bureaucratic organizational forms across the late-18th and 19th centuries. Ingenious new innovations additionally required radical new forms of organization to ensure their realization and widespread availability. Hence, just as feudal/craft productive structures were inexorably intertwined with an achievement focus of awe, a member status of servants and slavery, a single channel knowledge media, and a constrained geographic span, so the progression of these reality facets into the Present Age also demanded its own, new mode of organization.

ADMINISTERING THE MASSES

What is perhaps most remarkable about the vast organizational endeav-ours of past times is how regimes with no real mass-productive technol-ogies or advanced communications media managed to amalgamate the individual labours of so many. Whether workers gave of their efforts freely is not really the issue. Even if enslaved, the builders of pyramids, temples, great walls, and great cities, needed to be effectively adminis-tered. They must have also required a highly effective support infrastruc-ture. Indeed the construction of the pyramids of ancient Egypt was not just remarkable in terms of the scale of the labourforce involved. Just as significant has to be the organizational mechanism which supplied bread to continually feed tens of thousands in the desert.

Humankind has always sought to develop more and more effective modes of organization in order to most comfortably survive and progress. In the next chapter we shall investigate the myriad of organizational structures which have served the industrial and highly technological age of the 20th century. In many respects the productive forms of recent times have been far in advance of those of the ancients in terms of their sheer size and administrative sophistication. However, in other ways, organiz-ational mechanisms have changed little through the ages. Great organiz-ational problems have been and remain those of planning for uncertain times ahead, and of coping with complexity and the human irrationality of both workers and the competition. The role of an effective manager may therefore be one which in essence has changed very little since the dawn of civilization.

15
Monoliths
of Stone

PEOPLE ENJOY THE CERTAINTY of a concrete organizational home. In fact, as the traditional social institutions of Western society increasingly corrode, for many individuals large organizations offer their last bastion of stability. It is therefore hardly surprising that organizations seeking more flexible structures often encounter considerable worker resistance. Granted, economic circumstances in many industries may be crying out for change. However, this often does not stop the 'monuments of stone' which have characterized the organizations of the Present Age being defended to the hilt. Of course, simultaneously in more 'enlightened' market sectors, lumbering concrete monoliths are also being demolished from within.

Regardless of whether they are currently loved or loathed, there can be little doubt that large-scale, mechanistic productive structures have served industrialized societies admirably throughout the majority of the Present Age. Within the following chapter we will therefore chart the proud rise and dawdling demise of the bureaucracies of mass production. This history will then serve as a background to the evolution of future productive forms in **chapter 16**.

For many people, rules, hierarchies, and jobs based upon hours and roles rather than processes and value added, continue to represent the world of work. One of the objectives of this chapter is to investigate why such a perception still so powerfully lingers. Further, we shall explore why the hostile business environments of the late-20th century do not bode well for the survival of inflexible, organizational giants. Bureaucratic structures may still provide concrete homes for around half of the working Western population. Yet they are homes which, due to their increasingly poor state of repair, remain doomed—sooner or later—to crumble into the yellowing pages of history.

Table 15.1 lists the Present Age categorization of the reality facets of achievement focus, member status, knowledge media, and geographic span. In doing so it reminds us of the wider context within which most of the organizations of the 20th century have operated. From the table we can see that the productive forms of the Present Age have focused upon reaping value from acts of ingenuity. Towards such ends they have engaged a largely full-time, dedicated workforce. Present Age organizations have also been able to utilize a fairly sophisticated multi-channel knowledge media. Additionally, their operations have been strewn over a far more relaxed geographic span than their business counterparts of past times. **Table 15.1** thereby nicely highlights the conditions commonly associated with the rise of the large-scale, bureaucratic productive structures of the late-19th and early-20th centuries.

THE RISE OF BUREAUCRATIC ENTERPRISE

Up until the middle of the 19th century, almost all business organizations traded in single lines of product or service. Most also only operated within a local geographic region. Such 'single-unit' enterprises therefore had no need for rigid, bureaucratic productive forms. However, with the arrival of the railways and telegraph communications, 'multi-unit' organizations began to emerge. These boasted a number of operating units to cope with a greater scale and/or range of activities. As a result they could no longer be managed successfully by a single owner/manager. The implementation of bureaucratic hierarchical structures was therefore inevitable. As noted in the last chapter, a new breed of worker—the 'middle manager'—also emerged at this time to staff the growing number of administrative bureaucratic positions.

Initially bureaucratic hierarchies were most prominent within railway companies themselves. Indeed, as these organizations began to operate more and more miles of track, geographic segmentation was essential. Typically offices were created to administer between fifty and one-hundred miles of railroad.[396] Then, as improved transportation and communications links became more widely available, the organizations

Reality Facet	Typical Nature
Achievement focus	Acts of ingenuity (the realization of techno-logical wonders)
Member status	Employees (workers paid for their time in fulfilling organizational roles)
Knowledge media	Multi-channel (word of mouth, writing, and audio-visual electronic forms)
Geographic span	Relaxed (national with international trade)

Table 15.1 The Organizational Context of the Present Age

who were the customers of the railways also began to develop bureaucratic hierarchies to enable them to similarly operate over wider geographic spans.

SCALE & STANDARDIZATION

By the late-19th century large-batch and continuous process mass-production had been perfected.[397] The technique of fabricating items of machinery from interchangeable, standardized parts was also emerging. The development of all three of these forms of mass production subsequently provided an impetus for the construction of large organizations capable of reaping considerable economies of scale.

In the 1880s and 1890s several pioneering enterprises had begun to integrate mass production with mass distribution. Notable examples in the United States included American Tobacco, Diamond Match, Quaker Oats, Heinz, Proctor & Gamble, and Eastman Kodak.[398] Mergers between firms who had previously operated loose cartels were also commonplace from the 1880s onwards.[399] Combined, all of these forces led to the establishment of very large business enterprises within an increasing number of operating units. In turn, these organizations required more and more complex systems of administrative control. By the early-20th century, centralized, hierarchical bureaucracies had therefore become the dominant productive form.

As discussed in **chapter 6**, mass-production techniques progressed even further in the early-20th century when Henry Ford revolutionized automobile manufacture with the moving assembly line. As Ford so admirably demonstrated, at this time the only way to produce cost-effective, complex products which consumers could afford was by making homogeneous items upon a grand scale. To achieve this, dedicated capital, labour specialization, and effective managerial control, were all essential. Indeed, the entire philosophy of 'Fordism' has been defined as the 'progressive development of specialized machinery operated by closely supervised, deskilled labour to mass produce a standardized product'.[400]

To administer its vast works, the Ford Motor Company implemented an extremely detailed bureaucracy. Strict and narrow functional responsibilities were allocated to all levels of worker within a sprawling, rule-bound hierarchy. Product and process innovation were also deliberately sacrificed in favour of mass-productive efficiency.

As the practices of 'Fordism' spread, a whole host of consumer wares, in addition to cars and agricultural machinery, came to be mass produced in vast, dedicated works consisting of multiple factory units. Like the armies of Frederick the Great, these centralized, bureaucratic monoliths ran like smooth, organizational machines. Decision making may have been inflexibly top-down, the range of outputs extremely narrow, and workers no more than semi-skilled, interchangeable components. Yet such organizations remained the most successful arrangement of productive form for several decades. A simplified example of a bureaucratic, hierarchical structure for a typical manufacturing organization is illustrated in **figure 15.1**.

VERTICAL INTEGRATION & MULTIDIVISIONAL FORMS

By 1917, over 86 per cent of the largest 278 organizations in the United States had vertically integrated production with distribution.[401] In the

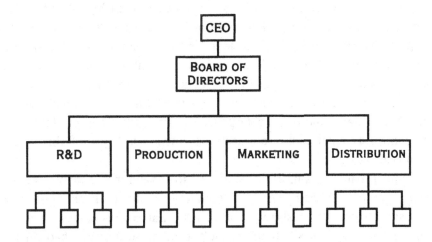

Figure 15.1 A Hierarchical Bureaucracy

years to come many companies were also to take the vertical integration of all possible phases of manufacturing to the extreme. For example, the Ford Motor Company built its own steel mill and glass plant. It even founded plantations in Brazil to source latex for tyres, and bought the railroad which serviced its works at River Rouge. All of these operating units were amalgamated into the company's mighty, static bureaucracy. Ford's logic—like that of its contemporaries and indeed most organizations up until the 1980s—was simply to internalize (and hence to control) as many stages of value creation as possible.

Even service industries like movie making adopted a vertically-integrated, logic-of-scale mentality. For example, during the heyday of the studio system, Universal, Metro Goldwin Meyer, 20th Century Fox *et al* all acquired vast backlots and all of the pre- and post-production facilities they could conceivably require. In-house regiments of stars and key creative personnel were also contracted to the studios for long periods. They were then required to make films on a production line basis. Disney and other animation houses also applied a production line approach to the creation of cartoons. As a result, movies, like cars and other consumer goods, came to be churned out at lowest cost week after week.

From around the 1920s industrial companies with highly vertically-integrated operations found it more and more difficult to continue to expand. They therefore began to adopt an explicit strategy of diversifying into areas of business well beyond their traditional market sectors. Conglomeration was subsequently launched as the next trend in organizational construction. By 1947 in the United States a relatively small number of 'large industrial enterprises' had integrated and amalgamated to control 47.2 per cent of all manufacturing assets. By 1968 this figure had risen to 60.9 per cent.[402]

Whilst many organizations continued to expand in the early- to mid-20th century, increasing vertical integration and diversification gave rise to significant administrative problems. Large businesses—and in particular large diversified and/or multi-product businesses—had simply become too large and too complex to be governed by one central management. In response, decentralized, 'multidivisional' forms of organization emerged. These granted divisional management teams autonomy over the day-to-day running of their part of the business. Top management at the centre then took on a strategic rather than operational role.

Multidivisional, decentralized hierarchies soon proved to be a most effective productive form for very-large-scale industrial enterprises. Indeed many organizations still exhibit such structures today. An illustration of a decentralized multidivisional organization is provided in **figure 15.2**. Some readers may wish to compare this illustration with the previous centralized hierarchy as shown in **figure 15.1**.

UNWIELDY MONSTERS

Bureaucratic hierarchies, of both the centralized and decentralized varieties, have almost inevitably proved structurally static and have rarely been predisposed to rapid change. Earlier this century this was of little concern as product lifecycles were measured in years if not decades. Technological progress in manufacturing was also relatively stable and minor, whilst most markets exhibited fairly consistent patterns of consumer demand. However, since the late-1970s, such a stability of consumer-driven economics has no longer proved to be the case.

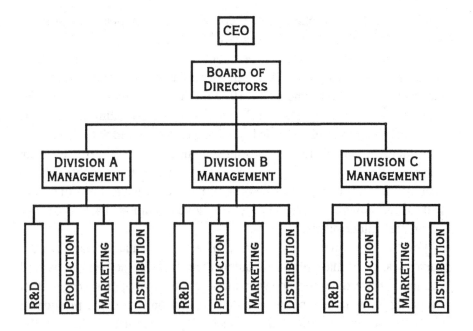

Figure 15.2 A Decentralized Multidivisional Form

As discussed in Part IV, in recent decades many markets and media have globalized. In addition, product lifecycles have often come to be measured in months, whilst technological progress has permitted manufacturing plant to be programmable rather than dedicated. In recent years consumers have also become increasingly fickle and selective in their tastes. Bouts of recession have additionally hit many traditional industries and organizations hard. In many instances, bureaucratic productive forms with slow moving, top down patterns of planning and communications have therefore become unwieldy legacies of better, more stable days.

Changes in the automobile industry in recent decades serve well to highlight wider industrial and organizational trends in the decline of the mass-production paradigm of 'big is best'. In the early 1970s, for example, the Ford Motor Company had built a plant to produce 500,000 tons of iron engine blocks a year. A true monolith of stone, the plant was solely designed to reap economies of scale. Whilst the size of seventy-two football fields, the plant was therefore only equipped to produce specialized, fuel-guzzling V-8 engines.[403]

Unfortunately for Ford, between 1960 and 1980 the geographic span of the automobile industry had transformed from national to global.[404] Consequently, by the time of the 1979 oil crisis, Japanese cars with far more fuel-efficient engines than Ford's V-8s were flooding the market. With massive sunk-costs in a dedicated plant, Ford found that it could not react quickly enough to new customer demands for more fuel-efficient vehicles. Retooling of its vast V-8 engine plant to make lighter, more fuel-efficient engines proved be prohibitively expensive. Ford therefore had to shut down the entire factory and move operations back to a range of smaller, older plants.[405]

For the first time, the dedication of a vast production facility to a narrow range of mass produced outputs had failed to deliver the desired economic reward. Across the world it began to dawn upon managers that investing in the largest possible scale of operations no longer provided a guarantee for profitability. As new technologies accrued, and especially as *programmable* plant became available which did not need to be dedicated to the production of a specific item, so *flexibility* became the new watchword for effective organizational construction.

THE FIRST ORGANIC ORGANIZATIONS

The development of flexible or 'organic' forms of productive structure was researched in the early 1960s by several teams including that of Tom Burns and G.M. Stalker.[406] After studying a range of successful Scottish manufacturing firms, these two researchers suggested the existence of a continuum of organizational forms. At one end of this spectrum were firms with inflexible productive structures which Burns and Stalker labelled 'mechanistic'. These all exhibited rigid, bureaucratic hierarchies, dedicated plant, and were most common in industries with stable technologies and well-defined markets. A typical example was a firm which produced the man-made fibre rayon.

At the other end of the scale were the firms which Burns and Stalker labelled 'organic'. These thrived upon fluid organizational relationships with few rigid authority patterns. The absence of any clear or extensive hierarchy was vital in organic organizations—for example within those involved in electronics manufacturing. In place of a well-defined bureaucracy, flexibility was paramount for coping with unpredictable, expansive markets, and rapid technological advancement. Project teams in organic organizations also needed to be rapidly created and disbanded in accordance with changing market conditions. Indeed, Burns and Stalker found deliberate attempts in electronics manufacturing not to specify individual tasks and roles but instead to rely upon jobs defined through worker interaction.

It is, almost by definition, difficult to pin down the exact structure of any organic productive form. However, as markets have become more turbulent and even 'hyper-competitive' in recent decades, several attempts have been made to conceptualize a 'standardized' organic organizational structure capable of responding rapidly to changing technologies and product market conditions. In the 1960s and 1970s, chief amongst such models was the 'matrix organization'.

Within matrix organizational structures Henri Fayol's principle of unity command is sacrificed. Rather than having a single boss, workers are instead split into project teams and made responsible to more than one manager. Usually this involves workers being responsible to a traditional functional manager *as well as* to a manager responsible for a particular project team, product brand, or geographic region. With authority lines vague, the assumption is that workers will cooperate to get the job done most effectively. Team membership is also fluid as the needs of changing market conditions dictate.

Burns and Stalker found matrix structures in existence within the Scottish electronics manufacturing firms they surveyed. Also in the 1960s, the giant defence contractor TRW Systems used a matrix structure to develop the sophisticated Atlas and Titan rockets for the US space programme.[407] Today, the British chemicals giant ICI is organized on matrix lines by territory and then by product/business.[408] Many universities and research institutions are also organized upon the arrangements of a loose matrix. A schematic of a manufacturing matrix organization indicating patterns of dual responsibility appears in **figure 15.3**.

Matrix structures have enabled a variety of companies—and in particular high technology companies—to become more flexible. This said, within many other organizations matrix forms have been tried and

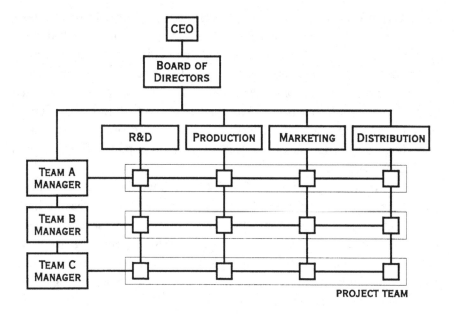

Figure 15.3 Dual Authority in a Matrix Organization

abandoned. The failure of matrix initiatives has largely been due to problems with multiple authorities which have outweighed any gains in flexibility. Indeed, with up to six levels of management superimposed in some matrix organizations, it often became unclear who was responsible for what, where orders came from, and exactly how many bosses there were.[409]

NETWORKS EMERGE

Matrix structures appear to work best in industries and organizations which have traditionally operated loosely-autonomous project teams. Certainly, experience has proven that matrix forms are not suitable for all firms seeking increased flexibility. However, despite this fact, since the 1980s it has also become increasingly obvious that large, bureaucratic organizations are similarly incapable of coping with many new market realities. Indeed, as we explored in **chapter 6**, it was in the 1980s that organizations began to alter their work/command relationships to make use of more temporary, part-time, and sub-contractual workers, in order to benefit from increased labour flexibilities.

As early as 1982 Peters and Waterman were noting that in 'excellent' firms a 'small is beautiful, small is effective' philosophy was starting to replace that of 'big is best'.[410] Conventional wisdoms were being challenged, with structures 'a lot more divided up and a lot less tidy' than would have traditionally been the case.[411] What more and more companies were beginning to understand was that once they exceeded a certain size, diseconomies of scale began to set in with a vengeance. Decentralization was therefore being taken as far as possible in order to maximize flexibility. Internal markets within firms were also starting to appear, so permitting different divisions to trade both with and against each other in order to retain their competitive edge.

In the middle of the 1980s more and more firms began to disaggregate and/or to outsource non-core activities. This helped to reduce sunk capital and labour costs within those areas in which many firms possessed no comparative advantage. For example, many firms sold-off and bought-in distribution, cleaning, computing, and plant maintenance. Any previous logic of striving for total vertical integration thereby came to be abandoned.

In their seminal 1986 paper *Organizations: New Concepts for New Forms*, Raymond Miles and Charles Snow proposed that a new form of productive structure was emerging to cope with the increasingly turbulent, 'competitive jungle'.[412] They labelled this new form the 'dynamic network', and noted that it was both a cause and a result of a more competitive business environment. Miles and Snow's hypothesis was that specialist organizations (with highly-dedicated plant and knowledge) would only survive in narrower and narrower market segments or niches. 'Generalist' organizations wishing to span a wide variety of business environments therefore needed to adopt highly flexible structures capable of being rapidly reconfigured in the face of changing technologies and market conditions. Such organizational structures were likely to be dynamic networks, an example of which is illustrated in **figure 15.4**.

As indicated in the figure, a dynamic network consists of a central co-ordinating core (or 'broker') which draws upon the services of different

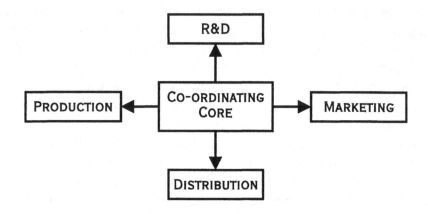

Figure 15.4 A Network Production Structure

specialist 'agents'. Such agents may either be internal to the parent organization or, more commonly, other firms from the marketplace. Either way, the productive partners tied to the core in a dynamic network are only coupled-in as and when required on the basis of each project undertaken. Unlike in a vertically-integrated hierarchy, by operating in an 'outsourcing mode' the core organization may remain small with minimal sunk costs in dedicated productive resources. It may be, for example, that by outsourcing production, the core organization gains the freedom to use different manufacturing facilities for different projects over time. As a result, it may use the most suitable and up-to-date technology in each instance, rather than having to rely upon any one internal plant. Similarly, the core may call upon the services of different distributors, marketing teams, and other agents, tailored specifically to selected projects or product lines.

Miles and Snow identified the emergence of networked organizations from an increased incidence of joint ventures, subcontracting, and licensing activities. They also noted that vertical disaggregation, the use of brokers to play the lead role in linking together partners, and an increased reliance upon market mechanisms, were all key characteristics of dynamically-networked productive forms. Full disclosure information systems were also viewed as critical in enabling contracts to be monitored and to permit each network agent to optimize its value added.[413] Indeed, towards this end, advanced computing and communications technologies are often considered critical in the establishment of an effective organizational network. Some have even suggested that it is no coincidence that network organizations closely resemble the configuration of a modern information system. To cite Mark Daniell:

> Every business unit, serving local demand, communicates extensively with other units; and every unit is guided by operating protocols, central priorities and investment decisions laid down at the centre. The network is truly interdependent, drawing on the capabilities of each unit to strengthen their collective performance. It does not waste programmes, or individuals which can make a contribution to it.[414]

Miles and Snow identified network organizations in the construction industry and in textbook publishing. In the latter case it was (and remains) common for the publishing house (the network core) to outsource copyediting, design, typesetting, printing, binding, and distribution, to a range of external partners on a project basis.[415] Dynamic networks have also been identified in studies of the fashion industry (where Benetton provides a prime example of such a mode of organization), as well as within the media sectors of film and television production.[416]

It should be noted that the network model is significant not only in terms of its impact upon any particular individual organization. Perhaps even more importantly, dynamically-networked productive forms change the nature of entire industries. Once networks are in operation, no longer may firms be identified as discrete black boxes. Instead, a whole host of resources intermingle across entire industries in complex and constantly shifting alliances of broker cores and specialist agents. Indeed, we may describe networks as 'dynamic' due to the way in which resources are continually coupled and uncoupled from the core as and when required. A network organization is therefore rarely likely to be structurally static. Rather, the range and number of partners involved is likely to be in a constant state of flux.

Across industries, the continuous coupling and uncoupling of productive capacity and labour resources may well prove unsettling. However, the complementarity of the different firms and portfolio individuals involved in a network will permit elaborate organizations to be created capable of handling complex projects way beyond the competencies of any single, individual player. In some ways, dynamic networks therefore represent the evolution of 'supra-organizations' across industries—or of alliances of companies finally learning to work together as one.

TOWARDS THE FUTURE ORGANIZATION

In their book *The Second Industrial Divide*,[417] Michael Piore and Charles Sabel suggest that the emergence of new technologies and market conditions will lead to a transition in our dominant mode of production. Since large scale enterprises first came into being, they contend that the most popular organizational model has been that of mass production. However, as technologies and business environments change, their proposition is that we are now entering an era to be dominated by a production paradigm labelled 'flexible specialization'.

As often exemplified by the dynamic network model, flexible specialization involves the use of an adaptable workforce, and/or the flexible application of production technology, in order to reap economies of scope rather than of scale. Whereas economies of scale are derived from lower costs in mass production, economies of scope are those enabling the effective production of a variety of products from the same resource base. At the very least, it is now becoming necessary for businesses to balance economies of scope and scale.[418] One effective way to do this is to outsource production wherever possible as in the dynamic network model. Another may be to invest in highly programmable plant capable of customizing each item produced to individual customer specification.

An acceptance of Piore and Sabel's hypothesis invokes a final clarity of understanding in our analysis of the evolution of productive form. For a start, the paradigm shift from mass production to flexible specialization reminds us why lumbering, bureaucratic organizations are in decline. Remembering that these giants were predicated upon a logic of mass production, it becomes obvious that in a world of flexible specialization they will find themselves outmoded. Further, if due to changing tastes, prosperities, and technologies, mass-produced homogeneous goods are no longer acceptable (as current Western demand suggests), then we ought also not to be too surprised that the safe, static organizational models which produced them are now also no longer sufficient. Or, in other words, it may well be that it is the Western taste for increased variety in consumption which is responsible for a similarly increased (if feared) variety in working patterns and organizational relationships.

Organizations are inevitably products of ourselves. As what we demand of them has changed, so their make-up has also altered, and so in turn must the patterns of our lives and expectations. Tapestries of consumption have always driven the fabrics of organizational construction. In a capitalist society, we can only be engaged by organizations to produce what, in aggregation, we all demand.

In the final chapter of Part V we shall further investigate the many issues associated with the rise of future organic organizations. In particular, we will address the concern that future organizational arrangements may curtail many of the certainties and social foundations of our current working lives. New technologies already enable the flexibly-specialized coupling of telecommuters and other remote workers into so-termed 'virtual organizations'. As the ultimate in organic organizational forms, these productive mechanisms may prove to be both powerful and productive. Yet they may also rapidly become inhuman and cold.

Perhaps unfortunately, the transition from past to present informs us that it would be folly to try to swim against the tide of organizational evolution. Our challenge, then, may be to avoid becoming cocooned as isolated free agents within the organic, organizational networks of the future.

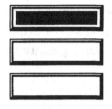

16
Of Networks
& Cocoons

FOR MILLIONS OF YEARS dinosaurs ruled the Earth. Lumbering beasts, they had no apparent competition. Indeed, in comparison with ferocious giants like Tyrannosaurus Rex, the scrawny mammals of Jurassic and Cretaceous ages must have appeared extremely puny and almost insignificant. Any suggestion that mammals would one day dominate the planet would therefore have been treated with scepticism by any roaming extraterrestrial or time traveller who happened to be passing by.

Of course, as we all know, the dinosaurs were nethertheless destined for extinction. Their smaller and nimbler cousins did also indeed survive to inherit the Earth. More explicitly, in an evolutionary battle against changing climatic conditions, huge creatures of great muscle and scale lost out, whilst smaller entities thriving upon higher brain capacities and adaptability managed to prosper against the odds.

Two hundred millions years later the war of nimble intelligence against solid might continues to rage. At the end of the 20th century the 'nimble intelligence' is that of flexibly-specialized, organic organizations. In opposition, the baton of 'solid might' has been handed down to bureaucratic productive forms.

Given our knowledge of the past, it would seem stupid to suppose that David will lose out this round to Goliath. Apparently, however, many managers are still placing their bets upon the rising meek being crushed by the previously strong. Of course, such a vision goes against much past experience. Comfortably or not, history has an uncanny knack of repeating itself. Once again, we ought therefore predict that intelligence in small packages will triumph over slow-adapting muscle. Just as the dinosaurs are no more, so, in perhaps only a few decades, the rigid, large-scale bureaucracies which have characterized the Present Age are also likely to be extinct. Intelligence will win out over sheer size; flexible processes over rigid structures; and raw imagination over ingenuity or awe.

FUTURE ORGANIZATIONS IN CONTEXT

This final chapter before the presentation of my Future Mindset assesses likely tools, pressures, and structures, for the Future Organization. In the previous two chapters, we have furthered our analysis of past and present productive forms by first considering the broader organizational context of the period. **Table 16.1** completes this cycle by listing the dominant future characteristics of achievement focus, member status, knowledge media, and geographic span. The table thereby highlights the key organizational context of the future. And taking even a very cursory glance at the table, it should immediately become apparent that the future business environment is likely to be very different from that of the past or the present.

Almost all business analysts agree that competition is becoming more and more cut-throat. Indeed, the phrase 'hyper-competition' has been coined to describe such a state of affairs. In the last chapter we noted how new forms of organization, like the dynamic network, are both a cause and an effect of increasingly hyper-competitive environments. Now, over the following sections, I shall further contend that a shift from bureaucratic to organic productive forms is both driving, and being driven by, broader changes in the other four facets of reality.

Specifically, my list of 'tools and pressures for organic organization' encompasses *digital systems*, *portfolio lives*, *advanced groupware* and *borderless economies*. Each of these relates in sequence to a major future attribute of either achievement focus, member status, knowledge media, or geographic span. By exploring these instruments of change for organic organization, we will therefore begin to draw together many previous threads of analysis.

Having progressed this far into *Challenging Reality*, most readers should already have some understanding of digital systems, portfolio

Reality Facet	Typical Nature
Achievement focus	Raw imagination (the value of ideas)
Member status	Free agents (portfolio individuals)
Knowledge media	Metachannel (metamedia of VR and controlled reality environments)
Geographic span	Unlimited (global and beyond)

Table 16.1 The Organizational Context of the Future

lives, advanced groupware, and borderless economies. This said, the following sections do briefly recap upon previous arguments and definitions. More importantly, they also highlight how the four tools and pressures for organic organization interact. The basis of such interactions is also illustrated in **figure 16.1**.

DIGITAL SYSTEMS

Digital systems include those technologies which permit the encoding of previously physical products and information media into an electronic format. As noted in **chapter 4**, digital systems are therefore playing a key role in our transition of achievement focus from ingenuity to imagination. Indeed, in future it will in part be digital systems which empower the realization of almost any dream. As more and more products and services 'go virtual', so there will be fewer and fewer limits upon what we can afford to create.

Digital systems may also be used to automate the manufacturing of items—such as food, furniture, cars and clothing—which must continue to be produced in the physical world. As a consequence, digital systems

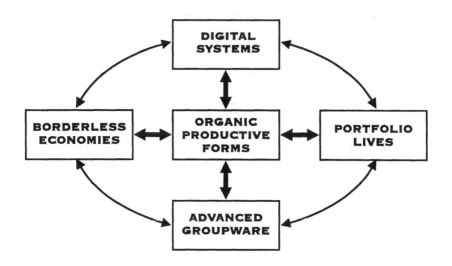

Figure 16.1 Tools & Pressures for Organic Organization

have become integral to all forms of programmable productive plant. In fact, without digital systems, production lines would still be dedicated to the manufacture of a single item, such as Henry Ford's infamous 'black only' Model 'T'. Today, many manufacturers can change what they produce by altering a computer program. In the past, they would have had to physically retool the line.

At more advanced levels, digital systems enable the customization of individual items of assembly-line output. For example, digital systems now permit some car manufacturers to tailor each vehicle to individual specification. Customers enter their requirements for colour, upholstery, and so on, into a showroom computer console. Their name is then associated with a particular vehicle throughout its period of manufacture.[419] Similarly, digital systems now allow jeans to be 'mass produced' according to customer measurements entered into a touch-screen or supplied over the Internet.[420]

Looking further ahead, digital systems will soon allow many processes to be integrated or 'internetworked' *across* organizations.[421] This will permit the most rapid response to market events. Signs of internetworking are already apparent in the retail sector, where the placement of a fresh order with a supplier by an automatic stock-control system is now commonplace. However, retail giant Wal Mart has already taken internetworking one stage further by developing a system which permits a predictive data model to be shared with its suppliers. As a result, not only may actual sales patterns directly drive fresh stock orders and delivery. In addition, sales data may also influence the specification and manufacture of replacement product. For example, the system can monitor how different clothes fashions are selling in different states and re-supply accordingly. Sharing linked data models, Wal Mart and its partners thereby boost their combined 'corporate IQ'.[422]

In short, digital systems may add value and flexibility in almost every stage of product or service design, creation, administration and distribution.[423] Of particular significance, digital systems are usually a prerequisite for flexible specialization. Without digital systems, organizations would almost certainly not be able to develop environmentally-adaptive organic productive forms. Indeed, without electronic lines of co-ordination, many dynamic networks would not be able handle the complexity of data, information, and knowledge, involved in their web. Nor would organic organizations be able to flexibly program their productive plant.

In the reverse direction, the desire to develop more organic organizations also continues to breed pressures for more and more sophisticated digital systems.[424] Chief amongst these pressures is a rising demand for corporate digital infrastructures capable of permitting twenty-four-hour global operations within companies which never sleep. The desire to integrate the expertise of a wider and wider genre of portfolio individuals into 'virtual' organizations is also driving some frontiers of digital systems research.

PORTFOLIO LIVES

Portfolio lives are those lived by workers who are no longer the long-term employees of a single organization. For some people this may solely involve an acceptance that no job will be for life, and hence that sooner or later they will need to move on from their present organizational home. However, for others, portfolio lives already involve new freelance, free-agent working relationships with flexible and shifting organizational ties. Portfolio lives may therefore result from either mental or contractual changes in the work/command relationship, and quite possibly both.

As with digital systems, portfolio lives constitute both a tool of, and a pressure for, more organic productive forms. As discussed in **chapter 6**, organizations in pursuit of more organic modes of operation are seeking an increasing number of sub-contractual, temporary, part-time and outsourced workers. Willingly or not, these individuals will need to have adopted a portfolio working status. Quite obviously, flexible firms, and in particular numerical labour flexibilities, are contingent upon the existence of a portfolio workforce. Organizations may only evolve organically as far as the workers whom they can attract and retain will allow them to go.

The other way around, people seeking more flexibility in their own working arrangements are also demanding that organizations move away from employment patterns constituted around a fixed, nine-to-five working schedule. For example, parents with young children may only wish to work in the middle of the day, or perhaps only within school terms. A growing number of healthy fifty- and sixty-year-olds— 'discarded' from full-time, core employment—are similarly demanding the flexibility to labour part-time. As discussed in **chapter 6**, there is also a small but growing trend towards individual 'downshifting'. This is where people dictate their own conditions of organizational engagement to jigsaw with other life plans. To the surprise of some employers, flexibility in hours worked is now becoming more important than pay or promotion prospects for those individuals keen to enjoy a quality 'flexilife'.

All labourforce movements towards portfolio lives challenge old-style bureaucracies and their stringent role demarcations. Due to the very flexibilities upon which they are contingent, portfolio lives and subsequent working arrangements are also often beneficial to both worker and organization. Additionally, new digital systems are now enabling those with advanced technology skills to become 'virtual' teleworkers with the freedom to labour remotely from home. As 'digital work' proliferates, portfolio individuals may increasingly sell their energies and skills electronically to a wider and wider range of internetworked, organic organizational forms.

ADVANCED GROUPWARE

'Groupware' encompasses all computer applications designed to benefit many users working together, rather than just lone individuals. So, for example, whilst a word processor or a drawing package may be labelled as 'individual-ware', electronic mail is purely a groupware application. You have to be very sad indeed to only send electronic mail to yourself.

A more rigorous, business definition of the concept comes from Lotus Development. They define groupware as software which 'uniquely enables organizations to communicate, to collaborate, and to coordinate business processes'. As the Lotus world-wide web site further explains:

> Groupware is so compelling because it allows businesses to create organizational memory and [to] share knowledge and expertise across time zones, geographies, and networks. It draws together the collective intelligence found in unstructured information sources . . . . Companies using groupware find that the barriers to high-performance teamwork that have plagued them fall away.[425]

By allowing groups of individuals (remote or otherwise) to work together smarter, faster, and in more productive ways, groupware has become a key tool and enabler of organic organization. Conversely, groupware proliferation has also been identified as a pressure forcing many organizations to become more organic. Even 'lowly' groupware tools like electronic mail may decimate formal hierarchies.[426] Freed of conventional lines of paper-based, 'snail-mail' communication, ideas and information soon find their own best electronic route to flow. Temporary interdepartmental project teams usually also spawn far more easily, and operate far more effectively, within companies which operate electronic mail networks. Indeed, it seems unlikely that electronic mail will ever become bureaucracy's ally. Already electronic mail and access to the sprawling datasphere of the world-wide web are commonplace. And, of course, there is also far more to groupware today than just electronic mail.

Until recently public domain networks, such as the Internet, together with systems for electronic data interchange (EDI),[427] defined the scope of inter- and intra-organizational connectivity.[428] However, whilst the Internet and EDI prove effective for basic data exchanges and structured transactions, they are not well suited for collaborative intra-business dealings. As a result, secure, private, internal organizational 'intranets' are now being devised. These often make use of the computer hardware, internal network infrastructure, and Internet software tools, in which many organizations have already invested. Intranets may therefore provide significant improvements in organizational communications, database access, and collaborative team working, for a minimal outlay. Intranets also enable organizations to become far more organic, as operations may be focused within an electronic space (rather than a physical building) which may then be accessed by any worker in any location at any time.

The market leader for total groupware solutions is *Lotus Notes*. This offers the broadest range of intranet facilities. Specifically, *Notes* allows workers to communicate securely across both internal networks and remote telecommunications links. It also allows the collaborative sharing of documents and data files from a central database. A sophisticated custom applications development environment is also included.[429]

Using *Notes*, users sat at computers strewn around an office, country— or even the planet—can hold interactive, electronic conversations whilst working together on documents and other files. Already there are around 1.5 million *Notes* users world-wide within 9000 organizations. Applications include improving the quality of business processes in product development, customer service, sales, and account management. Market sectors involved also range from hazardous waste disposal, to insurance and financial services.[430] Some universities are now even using *Notes* to support degree courses offered remotely to anybody with a computer and a modem (telephone) link.[431]

The groupware of the mid- to late-1990s permits most work capable of being digitally encoded to be shared and swapped near-effortlessly between several individuals and organizations. However, groupware systems capable of mediating more advanced forms of social interaction are also starting to emerge. Today videophones, and/or rudimentary computer video-conferencing links, may be set up for between a few hundred and a few thousand dollars. Industry standards—such as 'T.120' —are also finally being agreed by consortia of leading market players.[432]

With video-enabled groupware tools, workers remote from a common organizational home are likely to feel less isolated and should hence prove more productive. Electronic interactions may also take on a more 'human' feel when remote individuals can be seen as well as being heard and/or experienced in text. Approaching 60 per cent of human communication is non-verbal. It is therefore hardly surprising that the development of advanced groupware systems capable of conveying non-verbal messages is being pursued with vigour by a myriad of research teams worldwide.

As discussed in **chapter 10**, beyond video, audio, and data link-ups, future groupware metamedia will marry the technologies of virtual reality (VR) with those of network communications. The result will be 'virtu-commuting'. Rather than boarding a car, train or plane—or settling before a video camera and screen—remote individuals desiring a meeting will instead don a range of VR clothing to interface over a computer link. Using a head-mounted display (HMD) and a dataglove, participants in currently-developmental distributed VR systems may share a virtual office within which a meeting can be held. Those without VR links may attend on 'virtual TV monitors'. Tables, whiteboards, and virtual papers, are also available to mediate successful human interaction.[433] As also noted in **chapter 10**, future VR systems are likely to be able to blanket all of our senses without the need for cumbersome headsets and body suits.

Business meetings in groupware virtual realities may sound like science fiction, especially given the primitive nature of many contemporary VR systems. Yet the technologies involved are about to explode in power and plummet in cost. Indeed, we can be confident that it will not just be designers, but also managers, company representatives, and homeworkers of all genres, who will regularly meet in cyberspace in the next decade. Controlled-reality environments (CREs) in the physical world may also soon be developed as tools for fostering certain forms of group interaction. At their most basic, groupware CREs may simply be customized meeting and training spaces available for hire by free agents or their parent organization. As Charles Handy notes in *The Empty Raincoat*, every organizational network 'needs a club at its hub to add the human face to the electronic impulse'.[434] In future, such clubs may exist most effectively in CRE space.

BORDERLESS ECONOMIES

As organizations interconnect into the emerging global hardware platform of modern business, so many barriers of time and space are becoming transparent. As Don Tapscott puts it in *The Digital Economy*, 'technology is eliminating the "place" in workplace. Home may be where the heart is, but increasingly the office is anywhere the head can be connected'.[435]

As detailed in **chapters 12** and **13**, many of the major challenges before humanity are global rather than regional or national. Indeed, the popularity of expanding global networks such as the Internet continues to prove that borders between nations have only ever been artificial. As digital systems and advanced groupware proliferate, so any economy choosing survival will be unable to exist within meaningful economic boundaries. Indeed, now that many kinds of work may be shifted electronically around the globe, no economy can afford to erect economic barriers which may significantly impede trade into and out of its sphere. Culturally, and perhaps even politically, the nation state may still be alive and kicking. Yet, as the third millennium prepares to dawn, economic nationalism looks set to expire. To the alarm of many governments, electronic business knows no national boundaries nor tax regimes. And no longer may restrictions at ports and airports prevent the flow of money, services, or even goods, across regional or national divides.

Borderless economies, however, do exhibit pressures for organic organization. Indeed, rigid, bureaucratic productive forms have proved largely ineffective in taking on the world. For success, the global companies which operate across borderless economies need to be capable of rapidly adapting to local needs. As Douglas Adams of *Hitch Hiker's Guide to the Galaxy* fame enthuses, one of the pet phrases for his multimedia company The Digital Village is to be 'globally local and locally global'.[436] To be either (or both) organizations need to be inherently flexible. Such flexibility also needs to be mental as well as structural. Borderless economies require organizations which no longer either think or act in a mindset smaller than that of the whole planet or beyond.

The other way around, organic organizations are themselves using borderless economies as tools in order to maximize their scope of operations and resource base. For a start, organic organizations are likely to want to engage the services of the best portfolio individuals, regardless of where they happen to be located around the planet. As we have increasingly witnessed over the past few decades, organizations seeking to maximize their market potential are also pursuing as wide a geographic span as it is possible for them to maintain. And today, even 'basic' digital systems and groupware make the management of a global geographic span near-child's play.

NEW ORGANIZATIONAL FORMS

Utilizing the tools, and caught within the interactions, of digital systems, portfolio lives, advanced groupware, and borderless economies, new breeds of organic organization are beginning to spawn. In the last chapter we explored the 'dynamic network' as just one model of emerging organic organization. Within such a web, a slim core of 'brokers' coordinates a wider periphery of 'agent' partners who provide design, production, distribution, and so forth, only as and when required on a project basis. Such a model of flexible resource utilization is undoubtedly proving successful in many market sectors. Indeed, examples may be found from publishing and broadcasting to soft-toy manufacture. However, in other industries, the dynamic network model is likely to be too radical, or perhaps not even radical enough.

Figure 16.2 illustrates what we may term an 'organic hierarchy' for a future manufacturing organization. In terms of flexibility, this project-based productive form lies somewhere between the rigid bureaucratic structure of a strict hierarchy, and the fluidity of a dynamic network. The model (which may be usefully compared with the hierarchies presented in **figures 15.1** and **15.2**) is based upon three levels of organization. Each of these is characterized by a shifting cluster of loosely-structured individuals held together by task and process demands, rather than by a bureaucratic role framework. Members of clusters may be dispersed geographically and even organizationally. However, common members will serve as links between adjacent clusters. Digital systems and advanced groupware will also permit each team to function as a cohesive whole.

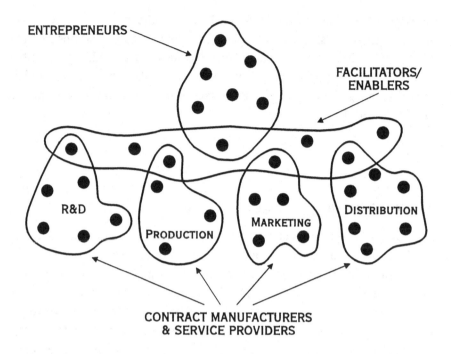

Figure 16.2 An Organic Hierarchy

At the 'top' of the organic hierarchy comes a cluster of *entrepreneurs*. This loose grouping is responsible for sparking fresh ideas and for raising the resources to bring the wider organization into existence. The entrepreneurial cluster will also provide strategic direction and will engage (either internally or externally) the services of the middle cluster of *facilitators* or *enablers*.

The facilitators/enablers group is responsible for translating entrepreneurial detail into action. It does this by engaging and coordinating a range of *contract manufacturers & service providers* who will actually build or deliver final products and services. Effectively, therefore, an organic hierarchy is an organizational model wherein 'thinkers' (the entrepreneurial cluster) engage 'connectors' (the facilitating/enabling cluster) who in turn locate and manage the 'doers' (manufacturers and service providers) required to bring visions and plans into actuality.

As a simple example, consider the chain of events involved when a company wishes to organize a conference, product launch, or other trade event. Almost certainly it will establish an 'entrepreneurial' team. This cluster of individuals will first develop ideas and funding. It is then likely to engage the services of a specialist conference organizer or public relations agency capable of supplying a complete event 'package'. However, almost certainly such a package will be put together by drawing upon the services of a range of other parties, such as hotels, caterers, graphics designers, and so forth. As another example, organizations in need of new buildings may establish a management (entrepreneurial) team who will in turn engage architects (facilitators/enablers) who will then sub-contract actual building work to a range of contractors (manufacturers/service providers). In yet another instance, a research company may engage the services of a consultant (facilitator) to provide the business links required to bring a new innovation to market, and/or to arrange manufacture and distribution by a range of third parties.

The organic hierarchy may be seen as a transitory model between the bureaucratic hierarchy and dynamic network, as each loosely-defined cluster (possibly itself a network) may be internal or external to a larger organization. The former may especially prove the case when the organic hierarchy constitutes part of a multi-divisional enterprise. Within, one entrepreneurial cluster (the centre) may link with several facilitator/enabler groupings, each of which manages the activities of a particular product line or business. Manufacturing and service clusters may then be run intra-organizationally as cost or profit centres utilized by a range of facilitating/enabling clusters as appropriate.

Alternatively, organic hierarchies may further emerge as many networked organizations integrate, and/or seek an extended funding base. It could be, for example, that the entrepreneurial cluster comprises a venture capitalist or holding company. The range of organizational networks which constitute every investment portfolio may then each be run by a team of consultant facilitators/enablers. Effectively operating as remote network cores, such teams will in turn outsource most manufacturing and service-provision to the marketplace. Already some venture capitalists seeking to spawn a range of new business activities may be observed establishing organizational structures akin to the organic hierarchy model.

VIRTUAL CLUSTERS & RUBBER BANDS

To some companies the thought of adopting an organic hierarchical structure comprised of shifting project clusters may seem adventurous. However, to others further down the track of organic progression, the organic hierarchy may already appear rather tame.

Much as been written in recent years upon 'virtual organizations' as the ultimate form of organic organization.[437] Lacking even the agent-broker rigidity of the dynamic network, such organizations pull together requisite individuals, capital, and technologies, in a transitory fashion only as and when required. Therefore, whilst at least the core of a dynamic network may endure for years or even decades, virtual organizations will have no identifiable existence over time. The organizations of the future may therefore not be readily identifiable as such.[438]

Virtual organizations depend for their very existence upon the four tools for organic organization as previously discussed. By definition, virtual organizations will be those with little or no dedicated infrastructure and few (if any) employees. Instead, both labour and capital will be contracted minimally as required. Virtual organizations may therefore be just 'boxes of contracts'—data stores, or lists of business acquaintances. Virtual organizations will also route much of their business through the electronic domain of cyberspace. Their 'structures' may therefore be most readily exhibited upon a computer screen.[439]

One way to define a virtual organization is as a computer-networked social mechanism capable of temporarily bringing together people, capital, and technologies, to engage in a collaborative, productive activity.[440] As such, virtual organizations may operate as groupware overlays across existing productive structures. Alternatively, they may be comprised of loose clusterings of individuals and technologies with few formal traditional organizational ties.

In *Cyber Business* I illustrated a virtual organization as a 'rubber band' which lassoes individuals from within a range of less ephemeral organizations via groupware links.[441] This model of virtual organization is reproduced in **figure 16.3**. Most importantly, it should remind us that even the most organic and 'virtual' of organizations will depend upon the provision of a physical business infrastructure by other, more traditional organizations. Not all business activity can take place in cyberspace.

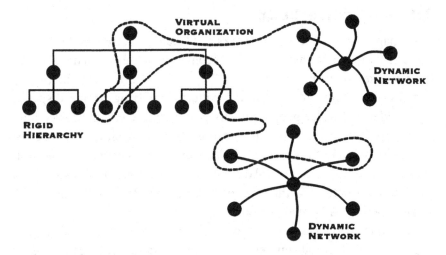

Figure 16.3 Virtual Organization as a Rubber Band
[From *Cyber Business: Mindsets for a Wired Age*]

However, it may be that virtual organizations spawn as 'rubber bands'—as groupware teams—to oil the wheels both within and across more traditional productive forms. This may especially be the case when smart or 'intelligent' software-agent 'servants' emerge to automate and monitor the complexity of short-term inter- and intra-organizational sub-contractual activity.[442]

As an alternative to the 'rubber band' scenario, some virtual organizations may be loose clusters of free-agent individuals who access global markets across digital systems using advanced groupware. Under this second model, virtual organizations may trade solely in knowledge and information (ie in 'virtual product'). Alternatively, they may outsource manufacturing and physical service-rendering activities to their more capital-intensive cousins as and when required. Regardless—and to the frustration of many—the structures and functioning of most virtual productive forms will never be opaque. Indeed, there will never be any universal virtual organizational forms.[443] As a consequence, there will also never be any definitive guidelines for constructing a virtual organization.[444] For unlike bureaucracies, virtual organizations exist to get work done, not to pre-structure and hence constrain its progression.

THE AGE OF THE BLOB

This chapter is entitled 'Of Networks and Cocoons' to reflect the fact that the more organic productive forms become, the more isolated and lonely their workers may be. All four of the tools and pressures for organic organization imply future working patterns involving people dispersed over wider and wider geographic areas and with fewer and fewer long-term organizational ties. Communications between such workers are also increasingly likely to be mediated electronically rather than in the flesh. Indeed, one of the most critical differences between networked and virtual productive structures is the level of human contact and affiliation likely to be experienced by their workers.

Dynamic networks, whilst organic, are focused around a core organization which outsources specific sub-tasks to other agent *organizations*. Both the network core and its outsourcing partners may therefore offer contracts for workers as long-term employees. In contrast, virtual organizations involve a very loose coupling of free-agent *individuals* to a very lean management centre. There are therefore no long-term jobs—let alone traditional employee positions—to be had *anywhere* within a virtual organization. Rather, every individual is 'cocooned' as a resource to trade themselves in their own right. This makes the organizations they serve extremely flexible, as they bear no sunk labour costs. However, it also leaves the people who work for such organic organizations very much alone.

In a recent end-of-class discussion, one of my MBA students summarized our current period of organizational transition as being 'from hierarchies to blobs'. With this observation he was noting how most of the organizational structures which I had drawn early in the session had included many solid, interconnecting lines. In contrast, the more modern organic organizations which I had later scribbled on the flip-chart had been built from rough clusters of single individuals loosely associated with vague dotted lines or rubber bands. The more I thought about it, the more the 'hierarchies to blobs' sentiment fitted perfectly.

John Donne once declared that 'no man is an island'. However, as the 21st century approaches, his famous pronouncement is sadly no longer the case. Today digital systems, portfolio lives, advanced groupware, and digital economies, are heralding the dawn of a new organizational reality in which *every* man or woman will be an island. Or, in the words of my MBA student, everyone will be their own blob. How such cocooned individuals will fare in the new world of work raises a great many social concerns which few societies have begun to significantly address. A labourforce dominated by portfolio individuals interfacing electronically any time and anywhere also presents a great challenge for the Future Organization. Almost certainly, the best way to tackle this challenge will be to evolve as organic a productive form as market conditions in any particular industry will allow.

In the next and final chapter, I shall present a framework for surviving the harsh, new economic, technological and social reality of the 21st century. Some of the elements of my ten-point 'Future Mindset' will appear obvious. Others obscure or far fetched. Yet all of my conclusions are to be derived from our study of reality facet transformations past, present and future.

Almost regardless of whether you choose to buy-in to my particular judgements or not, one more general point surely has to be a certainty. For both organizations and individuals to prosper, they will now have to concentrate upon adopting a new *mindset*, rather than any particular new set of skills. Today's and tomorrow's skillsets—like today's and tomorrow's technologies—will become obsolete in only a few years if not months. Only mindsets—or 'mental frameworks' for future strategies and vision—have any hope of longevity. Some form of mindset containing enough room for growth therefore has to be paramount for future success.

17
The Future Mindset

How we choose to shape our future, and how we choose to realize our dreams, greatly depends upon where we decide to draw the line between present and future fantasy and reality. If we do not believe that some of the predicted developments of the New Age will be achieved, then our closed minds will inevitably condemn them to remain as residents of the Land of Fiction. Across the cyberspace medium, new 'virtual' realities will soon come to be experienced. New social patterns will also emerge, whilst new forms of business organization will rise to craft the information of the world toward the accomplishment of previously undreamt of crusades. In the New Age, *Cyber Business* developments will not only change how we perceive reality, they will also alter the nature of reality itself.[445]

THE ABOVE PARAGRAPH CLOSED the prequel to this volume. In capturing the idea that reality is something we may ourselves create, it also served as the foundation for this book. It therefore seemed only fitting to quote the above words once again to open this final chapter of *Challenging Reality*.

As my self-citation hopefully conveys—and indeed as I argued way back in **chapter 1**—we may think of reality as a fictional cage. Being largely make-believe, the boundaries of this prison have always been open to interpretation. Indeed today, more than in any other age, the limits upon both individual and organizational accomplishment are now largely determined by what we will accept as possible. With ubiquitous digital systems, groupware, genetic engineering, biotechnology, borderless economies, and portfolio lives, we already have many of the tools of the future in our hands. It therefore only remains for us to decide if and how we wish to survive, and what kind of future we want to create.

THE TRIANGULAR PARADOX

At the end of the 20th century, the business world is caught within a triangular paradox. Such a state of affairs is illustrated in **figure 17.1**. On the first of the triangle's sides, change has become the norm. No longer are periods of transition punctuated by static passages of time. The old change-management model of 'unfreezing', 'movement' and then 're-freezing' every year or three has therefore become redundant.[446] In its place, the 'movement' phase is now constant, with no time required for us to 'unfreeze' from present habits into which we never get the chance to become frozen. To cope with this new adaptive reality, we need to *learn how to continually learn* as effectively as possible. In fact, the job of many managers is now that of coping with a constant barrage of new ideas, technologies, and processes, which become obsolete long before they are fully understood.

On the second side of the paradox triangle, business is increasingly focusing upon short-term horizons. Often this is due to rigorous financial pressures from shareholders, and/or executive remuneration packages based upon year-end performance bonuses. Organizations may have more opportunities than ever before to mould the clay of our future. However, few seem willing to try or even care. Shamefully, in the me-first profit-horizon of the here-and-how, long range planning has gone out of the window.[447]

The final side of the triangular paradox concerns the 'ostrich reaction' which many organizations now exhibit towards *radical* transformation. Such a defensive, Luddite blindness often breeds unconscious short-termism. Today, changes which may be too great or troubling frequently go unseen. Indeed, many an organization has now placed its head in the sand in the hope that our rising whirlwind of economic, social and technological transition will pass it by. And what, some of you think that this doesn't happen? Then just look around—and you'll watch it occurring every day.

The ostrich reaction is particularly surprising given that most businesses now accept change as constant. The problem, or so it appears, is that the level of change most can see (let alone accept) is incremental rather than radical. Incremental changes—an odd world-wide web site here, a teleworker there, or the occasional use of electronic mail—are

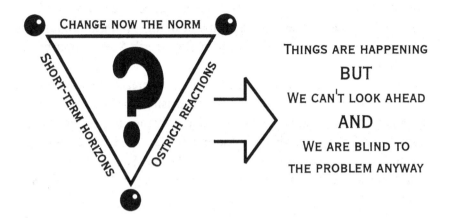

Figure 17.1 The Triangular Paradox

comfortably taken on board without pain or complaint. Radical transform-ations—such as the rise of imagination-focused organic organizations, the application of virtual reality, or future geographic spans beyond the Earth—are most definitely not. Instead, most pending revolutions are blissfully ignored by blinkered dinosaurs waddling home in search of cardigans and slippers. The paradox therefore prevails of a business community which, whilst accepting constant change, also refuses to look beyond the end of its nose, and which seldom manages to see (yet alone accept) the inevitability of radical transformation.

To make matters worse, it's not just the business world which is resistant to radically-different future realities. Academics—those pamper-ed public servants supposedly employed to safeguard human advance-ment—are usually even less open minded. For example, one well-known lecturer who reviewed *Cyber Business* described its content as varying from the 'questionable' to the 'dubious' to the 'incredulous' to the 'ridiculous'.[448] Yet *every* technological development so dismissed was *already* in the research lab when the book was written. Indeed, just two years on, many of the 'predictions' of *Cyber Business* have begun to take form in actuality. At the very least most have now become the subject of frequent popular debate. Another early, anonymous reviewer—and a professor of information systems in a 'leading business school'—chose to dismiss the whole idea of 'software agent' servants as unworkable.[449] However, the week his comments hit my desk, the *Financial Times* cited a survey predicting a software agent market worth $2.6 billion by the year 2000.[450]

With such 'learned' individuals pretending to preach the cutting-edge in our universities, it is perhaps hardly surprising that business remains unprepared to accept radical transition. Certainly the time is long overdue for many academics—particularly those in the 'social' sciences—to open their eyes to the world *outside* of the Ivory Tower. Such an action would at least constitute an opening shot in the war against the frictions of paradox.

METAMORPHOSIS PAST, PRESENT & FUTURE

The previous fifteen chapters have explored just some of the radical transformations which have taken place in our five facets of reality past, present and future. However, as this book nears its conclusion, it is now time to pull all of the facets back together as one. As an initial step, let us first summarise the main concepts, happenings and dilemmas which our studies of each reality facet progression have brought to our attention.

Achievement Focus

Through the ages, our achievement focus has progressed from *awe* through *ingenuity* and towards *imagination*. In Part I we began our exploration of this metamorphosis by considering the nature of the ancient Wonders of the World. Indeed, by reflecting upon the awe associated with great physical constructions like the Egyptian Pyramids, we sought to be reminded of a human spirit and a *passion* of value to the Future Organization.

In contrast to the past, the Present Age has been characterized by a mass faith in the *cleverness* or the *process* of science and technology. Never more was this the case than when we raced to the Moon. This greatest of modern ventures was conceived as a political dream. Yet the ingenuity of science delivered it as a shared reality in which the whole world could take pride.

With technology increasingly able to deliver almost any reality, humanity now faces a future of creativity or decay. Already, the 'why' of any great achievement is becoming more important than any physical 'what' produced or the ingenious 'how' of its realization. Future Organizations will therefore need to cleave purpose from purposeless. With the cost of digital and genetic technologies high, they also have the challenge of maintaining the stability of a society segmented by an economic underclass/overclass divide.

At present, knowledge and expertise are becoming more important than raw data or information. Yet, as new technologies make any act of achievement theoretically possible, even knowledge and expertise may be devalued. Henceforth, *imagination* will become the critical organizational resource of the future. Achievement focus may be our most abstract facet. Yet its future transition carries with it very real implications.

Member Status

Our dominant work/command relationship was once based upon owned *serfs or slaves* who had no rights and no freedoms. It then progressed to involve *employees* paid to fulfil organizational roles, and who came to possess many rights if still few freedoms. However, if current labour market transitions continue, Future Organizations are likely to demand a great many lone *free agents* or 'portfolio individuals'. Such future workers will be increasingly free to organize their own lives, yet as a consequence will have few (if any) traditional employment rights at all.

In Part II we commenced our history of member status by highlighting the plight of the 'tools that talked' and upon whose backs most ancient empires were forged. We then noted how slavery was eventually abolished in the 19th century not out of social choice or moral outrage, but due to economic necessity as cheap labour became available and capitalism spread.

Post slavery and serfdom, workers traded their time, bodies and souls in return for the economic rewards of a mechanistic, organizational role. Over many decades working conditions substantially improved. Then came the depressions of the 1980s which gave rise to new modes of flexible employment. With 'core' and 'periphery' segmented, so the labourmarket has now divided and worker power has waned. Times may still be rosy at the centre. However, upon the periphery rim, work is once again both harsh and uncertain.

The implication of the rise of new forms of flexible work is likely to be a shift away from a labourmarket based upon times and places, and towards one focused upon tasks and value added. In future work will be something you do, not somewhere you go. Digital technologies, changing expectations of the welfare state, and our shifting achievement focus, are all driving such a transformation. In future some portfolio workers may 'downshift' for a higher quality of life. Symbiotic worker–organization relationships may also replace the 'you're lucky to be here' mentality. The best future workers may even be members of the flexible periphery rather than the permanent labour core. However for all, the concept of a 'career' looks certain to take on a whole new meaning.

Knowledge Media

Since early humans formed tribes, the means used to replicate ideas have utilized an increasing-wide range of communications forms. Our dominant knowledge media have therefore progressed from the *single channel*, to the *multi-channel*, and on towards ubiquitous, *metachannel* 'metamedia.'

As we noted in Part III, this incredible evolution began with the birth of language itself. Then came the development of writing and printing. Across the Present Age, the telephone, sound recording, photography, movies, television, and more recently computer networks, also emerged to permit multiple or 'multimedia' knowledge replication.

Today, as computers are used more and more 'interpersonally', so the Internet, the forthcoming information superhighway, and distributed virtual reality, all look set to evolve into future metamedia. Physical 'controlled reality environments' may also become significant organizational tools for pooling group skills. All such metamedia will allow human *experiences* to be shared. They will additionally enable reality to be distorted and our senses augmented. Future digital media will also make information so widely available that—like air—it becomes a worthless or 'dead' resource incapable of adding significant value.

Geographic Span

Partially as a result of knowledge media transformation, humanity's geographic span has widened across history from the *constrained* to the *relaxed* and beyond. Our exploration of this shift commenced in Part IV with an explanation of the Second Law of Thermodynamics. This certainty of physics condemns all isolated communities to decay unless they seek resources further afield. For this reason we noted how early empires flourished in regions with networks of waterways which enabled easy trade and transportation. We also noted how sea-faring nations subsequently dominated the world up until the Present Age. Indeed, it was not until the arrival of railways, steamships—and then automobiles—that the majority ceased to be immobile. Sadly, such mobility was initially experienced by many during the first global events of the two world wars.

Post-1945, the Cold War held back the great technological potential for globalization. Indeed, only with the fall of communism and the rise of global causes in the 1980s did any sense of global citizenship begin to surface. In particular, digital mass media played a significant role in permitting the emergence of today's 'global village'. However, globalism is already leading to isolation, a loss of individual identity, and mass-cultural homogeneity as mighty organizations peddle global products.

Into the future, the superorganism of humanity will also need fresh resources. Just as our ancestors shrunk the Earth with ships and planes, so technologies are now thankfully being developed to shrink the wider frontier of the solar system.

Productive Form

Since the earliest days of civilization, *feudal or craft based* productive structures have given way to *bureaucratic* organizational machines. And now, today, more flexible, *organic* organizations are starting to replace the static monoliths of bureaucracy.

As Part V commenced we noted how in ancient times large-scale organizations were autocratic, if rare. We subsequently noted how, at the dawn of the Present Age, bureaucratic organizations became essential to administer growing and more geographically dispersed business undertakings.

Mighty hierarchies dominated organizations of mass production, vertical integration, and mass consolidation, well into the 20th century. Indeed, only in recent decades have markets become turbulent enough to challenge the 'big is best' logic of 'Fordism'. In turn leaner, more intelligent, and more flexible organic productive forms, are now emerging with increasing success.

Today, whole industries are being transformed as large, 'black box' organizations are confronted by new 'virtual' productive forms utilizing the tools of digital systems, portfolio lives, and advanced groupware. With organizations transforming from 'hierarchies to blobs' in the face of radical transformation on all sides, so skillsets will increasingly erode. As a result, wide mental frameworks may now offer the best hope for long-term future success.

THE FUTURE MINDSET

Without a detailed analysis of every situation, it is impossible for any futurist to advise any specific industry or organization upon how best to cope with uncertainties ahead. This book can therefore not hope to provide a *detailed* schematic for the future of your own particular life or organization. Indeed, you should hardly expect it to do so. Such a schematic will demand the specification of a range of skills which will inevitably degrade or evolve rapidly over time. It will also best be drafted by yourself, given your own unique, specialist knowledge of your own individual situation.

Having noted the above rider, what a book such as this may do is to supply a broad mental framework—or a 'mindset'—as a general guide for coping with future transition. How this mindset will relate to your own circumstances only you can decide. However, relate it most certainly will.

In providing an executive summary of the entire book to date, the previous section effectively defined where humanity has come from, that upon which we may build, and the many problems we all have to face. It is unlikely in the extreme that either you and/or your organization will remain unaffected by at least some of the dilemmas which ***Challenging Reality*** has outlined within its pages. Subsequently, I can but hope that the mindset derived from our shared journey will at least make your future a little easier and more exciting. The ten, specific Future Mindset elements are listed as follows:

- ☐ Look through your hardware
- ☐ Beware incrementalism
- ☐ Question the conventional
- ☐ Learn tomorrow's technology today
- ☐ Accept incomplete knowledge
- ☐ Benchmark the future beyond the present
- ☐ Direct the hyper-real
- ☐ Opt for action
- ☐ Propagate radical memes
- ☐ Live for today, plan for tomorrow, and build for the future

The Future Mindset's first two elements—*look through your hardware* and *beware incrementalism*—are intended to highlight extremely broad agendas for long-term success. The next four—*question the conventional, learn tomorrow's technology today, accept incomplete knowledge,* and *benchmark the future beyond the present*—then supply some detail to bring the first two agendas into focus. Finally *direct the hyper-real, opt for action, propagate radical memes,* and *live for today, plan for tomorrow, and build for the future,* involve specific avenues of action. Please read and think about the list above for a moment before delving into the more explicit explanations of each element to follow.

Look through your hardware

This first general agenda applies upon two levels. Initially we may think of it just in terms of computing. In such a context, 'look through your hardware' reminds us that computers are merely tools. Yet many people forget this simple fact. Ask around a low-tech office and you may be told that Sarah and Harry are doing the accounts, writing letters, or drafting new designs. However, ask around many a modern office, and you may well be informed that the happy duo are both 'working on the computers'.

Many people allow the technology of the microchip to mask tasks from their vision. They see screens, mice and keyboards, not documents, ledgers or works of art. Just as sculptors worth *with* chisels but *in* stone, so today office workers labour *with* computers but *in* the electronic medium of cyberspace. *We therefore need to think our technology transparent.* As a result, a focus shift ought to occur away from technical and software skills and back towards tasks, value-for-money, and processes. Don't evaluate what a new computer can do. Instead, speculate what you or your workers (wherever they may be) can do with a new computer.

A level up, there is also a wider, organizational agenda to be gleaned from this first Future Mindset element. In this broader context, 'look through your hardware' should make us all think about the move towards organic organizations focused upon processes rather than structures. Like computers, organizations are merely tools. Social and cultural rather than technological, organizations are just a slightly different kind of machine. As such, organizations need to be viewed as means rather than ends in themselves. Yet again this often does not happen.

Bureaucracy and hierarchy often become more important than the job they are supposed to get done. Just as we need to stop seeing computers, so we also need to stop thinking about the structures of our organizations. Instead we should concentrate upon the tasks with which we are charged. As we explored by studying the transformation of achievement focus across the whole of Part I, imagination and *ideas* are destined to become the key resources of the future. Machines and structures will therefore come to play a secondary, if necessary, role within our lives. They must therefore not be allowed to clog our vision.

Beware Incrementalism

This second general agenda picks up upon the dilemma of the triangular paradox. 'Incrementalism' occurs when people or organizations are only receptive to minor rather than radical change. In being 'beware of incrementalism', we need to ensure that we are open to radical new ideas, and not just to small incremental concepts which won't stretch us too far beyond the present.

Great changes and economic transitions occur gradually. However, those who come out on top are almost always those who first accept and adapt to where we are going not just tomorrow, but years or even decades hence. Across history, all great accomplishments have involved radical rather than incremental leaps. Indeed, those who have tried to extrapolate just a little from the present have almost always failed. As we noted in Part III, Marconi succeeded with an electronically-scanning television system. In contrast, John Logie Baird failed with a simpler mechanical apparatus based upon a physically rotating disk. Similarly, those who succeed in the future will be those who put their all into *radically* different undertakings.

Question the conventional

This point, together with the three to follow, starts to bring our two broader Mindset agendas into specific focus. 'Question the conventional' implies that we should not just strive to improve that which is currently being done. Instead, it ought to make us consider whether we would be better off doing something different entirely. Questioning the conventional is therefore all about maximizing process *effectiveness*. In contrast, the more common objective of achieving increases in *efficiency* may only lead to improvements in inappropriate actions.

Often questioning the conventional demands taking a radical leap of faith. Today, do banks and insurance companies need highstreet branches or even roving advisors to interface with their customers? Phone-based financial services like First Direct and Direct Line have in recent years proved that they do not. Similarly, do all shops still need physical stores? Or would some retail businesses prove more effective if they traded down the information superhighway? In the age of the Internet, CD-ROMs and digitization, do libraries still need multitudinous shelves stuffed full of paper volumes? And do salespeople and other reps really need to spend their lives on planes or in traffic jams now that groupware links can shrink the world onto their desktop or even into their pocket?

Since Imhotep first dared to be different and trusted *stone* as a reliable building material, so great accomplishments have been founded upon leaps of faith which have questioned soon-to-crumble norms. So be there first. Don't just buy some new hardware for the office or move the furniture around. Question whether you really still need the office in the first place.

Learn tomorrow's technology today

The information superhighway, virtual reality, ubiquitous computing, genetic engineering, controlled reality environments, nanotechnology, software agents *et al*, really are all just around the corner.[451] Some firms are already thinking about them. A select few are even planning and profiting from their application. All organizations should therefore at least be aware of what is going on, and hence how the world of current convention will change as the technology of tomorrow becomes the hardware and software of today.

As all of our reality facet progressions have demonstrated, almost any technological advancement has the capacity to impact significantly upon patterns of human activity. Indeed, no other force other than technology has so significantly altered our achievement focus and working patterns, advanced our knowledge media, widened our geographic span, or permitted the rise of new organizational paradigms such as 'flexible specialization'. Technological progress, even if apparently of no *immediate* relevance, therefore ought not to be ignored. This said, note how this Mindset point refers to 'learning', rather than to immediately *applying*, the latest innovations. As indicated by the first Future Mindset element, we have a need to look *through* our hardware—to become effective technology users, rather than techies who only wish to hoard and polish the latest kit. There is a fine line indeed to be walked between questioning the conventional and using new technologies before the bugs have been ironed out. To cite the Managing Director of one leading design consultancy:

My philosophy is that I want to be a pioneer in every area . . . [of this business] . . . other than technology, where I'm happy to come second, and not have to pay for the costly mistakes that others can make for me.[452]

The message with new technology is therefore to learn—to study and evaluate possibilities—and hence to become *aware* of the treasures which future technology may deliver. Only then should you risk all. And of course, as you quietly climb a background learning curve, some other poor sod will be left to dip the first toe into that magic lake which may turn out to be acid.

Accept incomplete knowledge

To many, this Future Mindset point is a real sore. As we noted in our study of knowledge media in Part III, today there is simply too much to know. It is therefore no longer possible to become an expert in even a small knowledge domain. As a result, many people become stressed—doomed to drown in a bottomless infobog within which they can only ever tire and sink. Procrastination often results, with decisions delayed until the situation becomes more certain. It won't. It can't. And the world would be a less interesting place if it did.

Perhaps the biggest challenge for the control freaks of the 1990s is to learn to accept incomplete knowledge. Granted, it is now wise to source information from a wide range of sources in order to obtain some degree of integrity. However, at the back of the mind, we all need to remember that information is fast becoming a dead resource. Like air, we now live and breath information. However, it is not paramount in our lives and business dealings—regardless of what many a management information systems manager may preach. Vision and imagination remain what is most important for success. Indeed this has always been the case.

When President Kennedy gave the famous speech which popped the gun on the race to the Moon, nobody knew how such a goal would or could be achieved. Indeed, many of the top NASA scientists who eventually triumphed in this incredible feat were initially sceptical. Their problem? Only that Kennedy had not chosen to wait for complete knowledge. Instead, he had gambled upon the ability of his people to overcome.

The message from the above is clear. Don't opt to drown or hide in figures and reports. All that any literature review or market research can now really tell you is how much more there is that you will never, ever know. Today, information raises new questions as much as it provides answers. Indeed, even when cyberspace is awash with smart software agents to mask their biological masters from infocomplexity, we will only ever top-slice the surface of 'relevant knowledge'. There is also the risk that today's raw data will only point towards futures down the safe pathway of today, rather than indicating any radical road ahead. Gut instinct will always be of value. Indeed, in the near future, those taken least seriously may well be those claiming to know the most.

Benchmark the future beyond the present

When planning ahead it has always been foolhardy to extrapolate forward from current good practice. This said, many have done so in the past, with more destined to follow them into failure in the future.

Benchmarking the future beyond the present involves questioning the conventional, becoming acutely aware of incrementalism, and looking right through any hardware involved. Across history, when this has not taken place the results have been disastrous. Take the example of the Ford Motor Company's manufacturing strategy in the 1960s. With its massive plant at River Rough built solely for mass production, the company placed a single bet upon the future becoming a bigger and brighter extension of the present. Unfortunately, as we noted in Part V, this was not to be the case. Instead the oil crisis hit, programmable production plant empowered flexible specialization, and the Japanese cut in on the American car market.

One often critical element for benchmarking the future beyond the present is to utilize your knowledge of tomorrow's technology today. Take the education sector as an example. Some universities are now putting up more and more buildings to cope with hoped expansions in student numbers. Those smarter appreciate that 21st century students will increasingly access higher education on a distance-learning basis via advanced groupware. With students to spend less and less time in physical lecture theatres, many educational buildings are destined to become a liability. By questioning their conventional operational paradigms in the light of tomorrow's technology, forward-looking universities—particularly in the United States—are therefore benchmarking their future beyond the present. In other industries, similar foresight is being demonstrated by those organizations already opting for radical, free-agent-based working patterns and/or even virtual productive forms. Just two such cases include Chiat Day and Cavendish Management Resources as discussed in **chapter 7**.

Direct the hyper-real

'Direct the hyper-real' is the first Future Mindset element to highlight a specific avenue for action. As discussed in Part III, hyper-realities are created when multimedia, or even emerging metamedia, abstract humanity from 'reality' itself. Around the planet, data and myth are already distorted by mass medias painting black-and-white images in technicolour on fading phosphor. Today it is important not to bound your view of the future by exhibiting the ostrich reaction of incrementalism. However, as hyper-reality spreads, so it is also becoming vital not to believe too strongly in information and resultant perceptions from any one source.

Be careful not to see, hear—and believe—only that which you wish to know. The world is awash with data. However, little of it is processed into information without considerable bias and colouration. A digital infosphere can never be believed. As a result, question everything, everyone, everywhere. Remember that a picture is now worth a thousand lies. A great many of our entertainments—our business, our realities—are now hyper-real. In itself this is not dangerous. Rather, hyper-reality only becomes dangerous when you are unaware of it.

On the positive side, once the nature of hyper-reality becomes appreciated, the direction of such fictions may present many a Future Organization with a new and powerful competitive weapon. Or in other words, whilst it may be potentially dangerous to permit your own window upon reality to be manipulated, there may be great benefits to be gained by distorting the perceptions of others. Of course, effective advertising agencies have known this for years.

By controlling present multimedia and future metamedia, Future Organizations are sure to learn to direct hyper-reality to their own advantage. Already companies like Disney, McDonald's, and Nike, are blazing such a trail in exporting not just products, but also the hyper-real expectations which then demand more of them. A few years hence, all successful organizations may similarly be trading not just in products and services, but also in their own unique perceptions of the world.

Opt for action

If there is one clear factor which has always distinguished those who have proved successful from those who have not, then it has been their bias for action. Having weighted the seven points above, there will never be a good time to make radical decisions. As has already been noted, reality is continually shifting, whilst knowledge will always be incomplete. Yet, across history, doing something has usually proved better than doing nothing.

The primary reason to adopt an action bias—if only at the individual level—is not so much to be right, as to be learning. Today, new opportunities for the application of cutting-edge technologies or new working practices often only present themselves some way down the line. Early adopters—even those who plump for the 'wrong' standard—tend to stay in business. Those who don't adopt early sometimes never even get into the game.

A few pages back I cautioned against becoming one of the first gamblers in the new-technology stakes. However, it is important here to differentiate between *today's* cutting-edge systems (which already work and may usefully be adopted), and those technologies likely to be cutting-edge *tomorrow* (but which today may still be full of holes).

The most sensible way to proceed seems to be to adopt a bias for action once somebody else has proved the water safe. In other words, become a 'fast follower'. Then, even if you dive into the wrong technological pool, at least there should be no major disasters. At worst, you'll gain some valuable experience with new systems which may prevent you drowning in ventures ahead. Admittedly, the balance of when to jump may be incredibly fine. However, those who wait to see just exactly what will become standard almost always end up using second-rate technological hand-me-downs. As many surveys show, over three-quarters of the costs of investing in even a simple technology like a personal computer now attribute to time spent climbing the learning curve, rather than to hardware and software purchase. It therefore pays to be doing *something*, if perhaps not quite at the cutting edge.

So, for example, get on line and get an e-mail address to use the established technologies of the Internet now, even if you can't quite see the point. Create a web site, even if you're not quite sure why you're doing so. In the near future there will be no time for contemplation; no luxury to work with 'complete' information. In place of such traditional crutches, there will only be transparent work systems and rapidly evolving technologies through which processes will flow. The future is exciting and liberating, yet it will not come knocking on the front door, or even a-beeping in an e-mail across your monitor screen. The future needs to be actively grabbed with the mind.

Propagate radical memes

Innovative ideas need to permeate all levels of organization if they are to survive and reap their just rewards. To encourage this, managers may need to engage in overt acts of 'memetic engineering' in order to ensure that radical memes spread. But how may this be done? One answer may be to manipulate the hyper-real by launching both memes and 'anti-memes' into open debate.

In many organizations the problem of the ostrich reaction to radical change needs to be overcome. As a result, if somebody proposes a really *radical* idea as 'something to think about for the future' then it is unlikely to be remembered, much less debated. Why? Because if the idea is too radical then nobody else will be prepared to refute it with a logical argument lengthy enough to grant the idea a fair airing. The idea—the radical meme—will therefore not get discussed further, and is extremely likely to die. If, however, after a radical idea has been proposed, somebody else (prearranged) immediately presents a passionate case against it, then debate will ensue. Third parties will subsequently get drawn into the drama, and the idea will be remembered and may spread.

The introduction of a 'antimeme' in order to permit a radical meme's merits to be more openly debated lies at the heart of memetic engineering. Although often successful, such debates may, of course, also prove dangerous. After all, there is always some risk that the 'antimeme' will win. Fortunately, this danger may be somewhat reduced by making sure that the initial 'advocate' of the antimeme quickly changes sides once argument has begun to rage. So don't just commission a report advocating radical change. Additionally, let somebody else write a document stating why no radical changes are required. Then simply let the two clash in public. Exciting and experimental, memetic engineering is likely to become a key future managerial weapon.

Live for today, plan for tomorrow, and build for the future

To round off the Future Mindset, this final point is the one which I most hope will be remembered. 'Live for today, plan for tomorrow, and build for the future' is really all about *balance*. It involves accepting that life is a short-term phenomenon; that effective business operations demand the short- to medium-term planning of a year or so hence; and yet that great achievements may only be realized within the far-flung reaches of the long-term.

As noted when I first introduced this concept in **chapter 2**, many of our ancestors laboured upon great undertakings which consumed multiple human lifespans. Yet today we usually shy away from even *conceiving* great projects for completion beyond the grave. However, as we shall discuss in the following section, there are potentially great turmoils ahead whose resolution will require humankind to labour for the long-term good. Early civilizations frequently planned decades or even centuries hence whilst living for the present. We need to recapture such a spirit of collective humanity and with some urgency.

LIFE BEYOND THE BLIP

The most common argument I hear against any further development of new technologies or working practices is that they are not 'fair' or 'liked'. They will therefore, I am frequently told, not be 'allowed' to take place. For example, a future workforce of portfolio individuals tending for themselves with no clear organizational home and little job security? No! Not a chance! 'They' won't allow it. 'They' won't be able to afford it. 'The Government' will act to make everything OK. Sorry chaps, but the happenings of the present, let alone past histories, show such argument not to be the case. Life is not fair. It never has been and it never will be. Nor has the collective functioning of humanity ever been directed by mass-compliance with any universal, caring-and-sharing moral code.

Recently I found myself discussing the implications of future DNA screening with a friend who researches ethics in financial services. When the Humane Genome Project is completed, simple tests will be able to pinpoint genetic 'disorders' and hence likely candidates for premature death. However, my friend assured me that governments will 'simply not permit' insurance to be refused to those individuals shown to be cursed with fatal genetic ailments. However, unfortunately for such people, I fear that my friend is wrong.

Governments already allow three-quarters of the world to live in poverty. They also continue to finance wars in the face of hunger, and effectively decide who is to live or die on the basis of political whim. The human race is at best only locally moral. Nobody is therefore now waiting in the wings to make life fair and cosy for all. Those of us living in currently-prosperous nations are just lucky to have enjoyed the certainty of our luxurious lifestyles for so long.

Perhaps the gravest conclusion which I have to draw from my study of **Challenging Reality** is that we are now living at the tail of what I term 'the blip'. By this I refer to the fifty year period of post-war Western prosperity which, from around the late-1980s onwards, has significantly begun to wane.

The blip has been a wonderful period of Western history within which to reside. It has been characterized by the rising might of industrialization, resources aplenty, great technological wonders in both work and entertainment, and living standards far exceeding those of our recent ancestors. Security and individual freedom have also characterized a half-century within which many have been supported by the friendly monster of the now-fading-fiction of a sustainable welfare state. Such prosperity has, I believe, been maintained by a scandalous rape of our planet, the waste of the great surplus of humanity's industrial rise, and (more recently) the mortgaging of our future to sustain the society of the present. Yet now the blip is coming to an end. And with its lingering death, so too individual security—not to mention fairness for all handed down from above—also face extinction in the West. Such delights are, of course, niceties which most Third World countries have never, ever known.

As we noted in Part II, the periphery labourforce of the late-20th century already has much in common with that of its early dawn. Additionally, governments around the world are now painfully aware that their deficits are too high. There is also no possibility for our entire aging population to enjoy the welfare benefits and medical care which the naïve politicians of the 1940s and 1950s preached that all 'deserved'.

The years to follow the blip are almost certain to be harsh and socially bitter. Within, those Future Organizations which survive will have to make many difficult choices which will impact severely upon millions of lives. Realism will have to replace right as societies come to work out what they can actually afford to sustain for their citizens long-term. This may sound a sorry conclusion as this book draws to a close. However in life unpleasantness often has to be faced. History, after all, does at least inform us that humankind *will overcome*. It may also be that we have another chance for untold prosperity waiting just around the corner.

The blip of the 20th century exploded as technology finally enabled the resources of Mother Earth to be exploited to their fullest, short-term potential. In the near future, a second 'blip' may therefore arise when and if humanity decides to roam further to exploit the resources of the solar system. The prospect of this opportunity for the 21st century should at least begin to charge us with hope. However, any effective exploitation of space will demand massive economic sacrifices in the here-and-now. Effective space exploitation will also require the mass-adoption of the meme of living for today, planning for tomorrow, and building for the future. We also need to make certain that when—or if—the potential blip of century 21 starts to occur, that we are ready to use its wealth as a long-term staging post for *future* prosperity. It would be a shame indeed if once again we squandered away so many opportunities purely for the short-term horizons of the 'never had it so good'.

* * *

FANTASY'S BEGINNING, FANTASY'S END

1978 saw the release of the movie *Superman*.[453] The film was promoted with the hype of any multi-million dollar blockbuster of its genre and period. However, as the movie opened the audience was presented with a rather unrewarding tracking shot over the surface of the planet Krypton. The landscape of this alien planet looked cheap, polystyrene white, and was definitely not up to audience expectation. The whole thing just appeared too much like the model it so clearly was. Indeed, I can remember thinking that the planetscapes of the original *Star Trek* series had been more convincing.

The camera eventually approached an area of black void within which superman's father—played by Marlon Brando—was picked-out by a solitary spotlight. To a hushed and apprehensive audience, this impressive character then delivered one of the most powerful opening lines in movie history. Amid an environment of perspex and plastic, Marlon stated quite categorically that 'This is no fantasy. No careless product of wild imagination'.

Superman's dad then went on to address the crimes of General Zod. However, by this time the audience was already reassured that everything was OK. In the cinema you could almost *feel* people settle after they had been firmly told that everything was real. After all the guy up on the screen had recently been the Godfather. His assertion that 'this was no fantasy' was therefore not to be trifled with.

The power of the opening line in *Superman* to cement a common belief to a shared fantasy more broadly reminds us how reality itself is just a common fiction. However, it is an extremely important fantasy in which most people desperately need to believe. It is therefore little wonder that looming transitions destined to destroy many present norms are being so strongly resisted in some quarters.

Today, our organizations are our dominant fictional tools. They empower our lives and permit the realization of our dreams. They provide stability and yet may also take it away. Bastions of our very humanity, it is up to Future Organizations to reassure us—like galactic Marlon Brandos—that the realities of the future will be certain and OK.

This book itself is likely to be discounted as a fiction by some individuals. In particular, many academics will discount *Challenging Reality* for being based upon sweeping histories, a multitude of secondary source data, and far too much 'blue-sky thought'. Yet, to my mind, such features are unashamedly *Challenging Reality*'s strengths, not weaknesses. I therefore have no apologies to make regarding the nature of my work.

Many still try to craft fresh organizational theory from 'rigorous' quantitative analysis. They breathe meaning into the abstract and rely upon low-response-rate surveys to deliver 'hard' data and cold 'facts'. The figures they derive may clearly be of value to some within the me-now horizons of the short-term. However, what quantitative organizational analysis invariably misses is that organizations are ultimately human affairs.

Empowered by technologics and their fictions of reality, organizations enable us to survive and to realize our passions of collective will. Like the organizations of the past, those of the future will therefore be pillars of successful aspiration. They will also evolve erratically to greatness from competitions of love and hate; from dreams lost and hopes won. As such, Future Organizations will mostly redefine our realities not of economics or technology, but of what it really means to be human.

Epilogue
Earthfall in the Dust

THE AIRLOCK FINALLY SEPARATED and she stepped out onto the surface. The Earth hung before her over two hundred thousand miles out in space. Even after five years it was still an awe inspiring sight. Like the earliest of moonwalkers she once again raised her thumb at arm's length and the planet disappeared. All that her ancestors had ever known obscured by a single digit.

She covered the dead terrain rapidly as she headed towards the rise with the great but graceful bounds of an experienced lunar orienteer. Her new suit really was amazing. Unlike the old models of rigid plastic and metal, it fitted like a second skin—its smart, biomolecular structure constantly reforming itself to allow a total freedom of movement.

Fine white particles gently rose and settled around her footfalls as she climbed towards the summit. It was strange to be able to vaguely feel the lunar shale through the shifting membrane of living nanotech which clung to her soles. As predicted, they had come a very long way in a very few decades and only just in time. Yet the best was still to come. The solar system was finally shrinking for the rule of humanity. Some of the Martian colonists were even predicting that they would now vegetate their world in mere decades, rather than the first estimates of several thousand years. Though, of course, that had to be impossible.

Reaching the top of the rise, she paused to behold the enormity of the construction site. Ten times the size of her own home, when completed the Third Dome would be the single greatest structure ever to be built by humanity. Tirelessly efficient, the army of builder drones continued to labour before her as far as a non-augmented eye could distinguish in the fading Earthlight. Breathing deeply before descending to inspect their latest fabrications of metal and living plastic, her mind could not help but return to the wildest of the popular fantasies to be experienced in the VR metasuites. A green Mars by 2100? Never. Something in the red dust must be addling her distant comrades' brains.

Raising a smile, she took the first of many sliding steps down the dusty slope towards the coming labours of the day. A second home where human beings could live and love and play without even the gentle constraints of a biosuit was indeed a wonderful dream. But then you had to draw the line somewhere between fantasy and reality . . .

Further Reading

IN PREPARING A BOOK like *Challenging Reality* I am, of course, indebted to all of those who have written before me on such a wide range of topics. Whilst a full listing of references and other endnotes follows, below are just some of those books which have most informed my thoughts over the past few years, and which I would most heartily recommend.

Artificial Reality II, Myron W. Krueger (Reading, MA: Addison-Wesley, 1991).

Being Digital, Nicholas Negroponte (London: Hodder & Stoughton, 1995).

Beyond Certainty: The Changing World of Organizations, Charles Handy (London: Hutchinson, 1995).

Chaos & Cyberculture, Timothy Leary (Berkeley, CA: Ronin, 1994).

Computers as Theatre, Brenda Laurel (Reading, MA: Addison-Wesley, 1993).

Creative Organizational Theory: A Resourcebook, Gareth Morgan (Newbury Park, CA: Sage, 1989).

Cyberia: Life in the Trenches of Hyperspace, Douglas Rushkoff (London: HarperCollins, 1994).

Cyberspace: First Steps, Michael Benedikt (ed) (Cambridge, MA: MIT Press, 1993).

Egyptian Pyramids and Tombs, Philip J. Watson (Aylesbury: Shire Publications, 1987).

From Post-Industrial to Post-Modern Society: New Theories of the Contemporary World, Krishan Kumar (Oxford: Blackwell, 1995).

Gaia: A New Look at Life on Earth, James Lovelock (Oxford: Oxford University Press, 1979).

Glimpses of Heaven, Visions of Hell: Virtual Reality and its Implications, Barrie Sherman and Phil Judkins (London: Coronet, 1993).

Globalization, Malcolm Waters (London: Routledge, 1995).

Images of Organization, Gareth Morgan (Beverley Hills, CA: Sage, 1986).

Macro Engineering: Global Infrastructure Solutions, Frank P. Davidson and C. Lawrence Meador (eds) (Chichester: Ellis Horwood, 1992).

Metaman: Humans, Machines and the Birth of a Global Super-organism, Gregory Stock (London: Bantam Press, 1993).

Mirror Worlds: The Day Software Puts the Universe in a Shoebox: How it Will Happen and What it Will Mean, David Gelernter (New York: Oxford University Press, 1992).

Monarchs of the Nile, Aidan Dodson (London: The Rubicon Press, 1995).

Mondo 2000: A User's Guide to the New Edge, Rudy Rucker, R.U. Sirus and Queen Mu (London: Thames & Hudson, 1993).

Moon Shot: The Inside Story of America's Race to the Moon, Alan Shepard and Deke Slayton (London: Virgin, 1995).

Organization Theory: Selected Readings—3rd Edition, D.S. Pugh (ed) (London: Penguin, 1990).

People's Century: From the Dawn of the Century to the Start of the Cold War, Godfrey Hodgson (London: BBC Books, 1995).

Space, Time and Man: A Prehistorian's View, Grahame Clark (Cambridge: Cambridge University Press, 1992).

Technology in the Ancient World, Henry Hodges (London: Michael O'Mara Books, 1996).

Technotrends: How to Use Technology to Go Beyond Your Competition, Daniel Burrus, with Roger Gittines (New York: HarperCollins, 1993).

The Digital Economy: Promise and Peril in the Age of Networked Intelligence, Don Tapscott (New York: McGraw-Hill, 1995).

The Empty Raincoat: Making Sense of the Future, Charles Handy (London: Arrow, 1995).

The Industrial Revolution, T.S. Ashton (Oxford: Oxford University Press, 1968).

The Media Lab: Inventing the Future at MIT, Stuart Brand (New York: Penguin, 1988).

The Metaphysics of Virtual Reality, Michael Heim (New York: Oxford University Press, 1993).

The Mode of Information, Mark Poster (Cambridge: Polity Press, 1990).

The Penguin History of the World, J.M. Roberts (London: Penguin, 1995).

The Power of the Machine: The Impact of Technology from 1700 to the Present, R.A. Buchanan (London: Penguin, 1994).

The Road Ahead, Bill Gates with Nathan Myhrvold and Peter Rinearson (New York: Penguin, 1995).

The Search for Meaning, Charles Handy (London: Lemos & Crane, 1996).

The Second Industrial Divide: Possibilities for Prosperity, Michael J. Piore and Charles F. Sabel (New York: Basic Books, 1984).

The Selfish Gene, Richard Dawkins (Oxford: Oxford University Press, 1989).

The Snows of Olympus: A Garden on Mars, Arthur C. Clarke (London: Victor Gollancz, 1994).

The Third Wave, Alvin Toffler (London: Collins, 1980).

The Virtual Community, Howard Rheingold (London: Secker & Warburg, 1994).

The War of Desire and Technology at the Close of the Mechanical Age, Allucquère Rosanne Stone (Cambridge, MA: MIT Press, 1995).

The Wisdom of Ancient Egypt: Writings from the Time of the Pharaohs, Joseph Kaster (London: Michael O'Mara, 1995—first published by Barnes & Noble, 1968).

Understanding Organizations—4th Edition, Charles Handy (London: Penguin, 1993).

Virtual Reality and the Exploration of Cyberspace, Francis Hamit (Carmel, IN: Sams Publishing, 1993).

War of the Worlds: Cyberspace and the High-tech Assault on Reality, Mark Slouka (London: Abacus, 1996).

References & Notes to All Chapters

Preface

1. Within his most recent anthology, veteran techno-philosopher Timothy Leary contends that in future person-to-person 'flesh encounters' will be 'rarer yet more thrilling', as interlinked 'cyberexchanges' between remote individuals increasingly become the norm. *Chaos and Cyberculture* (Berkeley, CA: Ronin, 1994): 5.
2. For a broader discussion of the role of dramatic enactment in reality manipulation, *see* Brenda Laurel *Computers as Theatre* (Reading, MA: Addison-Wesley, 1993): 187.

Chapter 1: Prelude

3. Arthur C. Clarke *The City and the Stars* (London: Frederick Muller, 1956): 11.
4. Alvin Toffler *Future Shock* (London: The Bodley Head, 1970): 430.
5. Charles Handy *Beyond Certainty: The Changing World of Organizations* (London: Hutchinson, 1995): cover quote.
6. Christopher Barnatt *Cyber Business: Mindsets for a Wired Age* (Chichester: John Wiley & Sons, 1995).
7. For a fuller discussion of the mechanistic (and alternative) origins and metaphors of organizations *see* Gareth Morgan's *Images of Organization* (Beverley Hills, CA: Sage Publications, 1986).
8. Charles Handy, op.cit.
9. Timothy Leary *Chaos and Cyberculture* (Berkeley, CA: Ronin, 1994): 19.
10. Richard Dawkins *The Selfish Gene* (Oxford: Oxford University Press, 1976, revised 1989).
11. Ibid.: 192 (1989 edition).
12. Alvin Toffler *The Third Wave* (London: Collins, 1980).
13. Michael J. Piore and Charles F. Sabel *The Second Industrial Divide: Possibilities for Prosperity* (New York: Basic Books, 1984).
14. The Statue of Zeus at Olympia in Greece dominated the interior of the Temple of Zeus, and is listed as one of the Seven Wonders of the ancient world.
15. Somewhere between 1507 and 1515, Polish astronomer Nicolaus Copernicus wrote the *Commentariolus*, an astronomical treatise proposing heliocentricity. This is a paradigm wherein the Sun is believed to rest at the centre of the universe, with the Earth and other planets revolving around it. Prior to the *Commentariolus*, earlier cosmologies had always been based upon a geocentric universe, with the most important celestial body—the Earth —stationary at its centre.

16. Gagarin's flight in Vostok 1 consisted of a single orbit of the Earth, and lasted only 1 hour 48 minutes. However, by 1988 Soviet cosmonauts Vladimir Titov and Musa Manarov had spent over one continuous year in orbit aboard the Mir space station.
17. Cited from Gary Osborne's lyrics for 'Brave New World' within Jeff Wayne's musical version of the *War of the Worlds* (CBS, 1978; Columbia/Sony Music, 1985).
18. Boy King Tutankhamen died in Egypt in 1325 BC, aged a mere 18. He rested in peace for over 3,200 years until, in 1922, his tomb was unearthed by archaeologists Howard Carter and Lord Carnarvon. The sarcophagus and other treasures they plundered have since become popular icons of ancient Egyptian civilization.
19. Or in other words **chapters 4, 7, 10, 13, 16** and **17**.

Chapter 2: An Archaeology of Wonder

20. The Pyramids at Giza in Egypt were constructed around 2500 BC. The Statue of Zeus sat on his throne within the Temple of Zeus at Olympia in Greece, and was sculpted by Phidias around 450 BC. The Temple of Artemis was to be found within the city of Ephesus in Turkey around 550 BC. The Mausoleum of Halicarnassus was also located in Turkey, with its completion occurring around 350 BC. The Pharos of Alexandria that guided sailors safely towards the great Egyptian city was built around 280 BC, and stood over 440 feet high. Also dated to around 280 BC was the Colossus of Rhodes, located upon the island of Rhodes in Greece. The Hanging Gardens of Babylon are believed to have been situated somewhere on the east bank of the Euphrates, and are usually associated with King Nebuchadnezzar II, who lived between 604 and 562 BC.
21. There is some debate regarding whether all of the Pyramids of Egypt, just the three Great Pyramids at Giza, or indeed solely the Great Pyramid of Khufu, constitute the first of the Seven Wonders.
22. To cite just a few examples, pyramids mirroring those of ancient Egypt exist in modern cities from Paris to Las Vegas (the former of which boasts Pei's Glass Pyramid at the entrance to the Louvre, whilst the latter possesses a pyramid topped with a beam of light so bright that it can be seen from space). The Statue of Liberty bears a resemblance in size and role to the Colossus of Rhodes, whilst there are lighthouses (like that at Alexandria) around the world. The Pyramids of Egypt and the light of the Pharos at Alexandria even feature on the American dollar bill.
23. Citation from the opening sequence of John Romer's series of four documentaries entitled *The Seven Wonders of the World*, produced by Discovery Productions with Agran Barton Television for Channel Four: MCMXCIV. The title of **chapter 2**—*An Archaeology of Wonder*, and referring to the story of the Seven Wonders being more than one of 'stone and bone'—is also a phrase attributable to John Romer within this series.
24. *Raiders of the Lost Ark* (Lucasfilm, 1981).
25. Philip J. Watson *Egyptian Pyramids and Tombs* (Aylesbury: Shire Publications, 1987): 7.
26. Joseph Kaster *The Wisdom of Ancient Egypt: Writings from the Time of the Pharaohs* (London: Michael O'Mara, 1995—first published by Barnes & Noble, 1968): 4.
27. A 'mastaba' refers to a burial place with a mound, funerary house or other construction built over it. Early mastabas were the forerunners of the Pyramids, and

consisted of a mud brick superstructure or 'bench' constructed on top of a set of subterranean rooms cut into the rock. Typical mastabas were some 40 to 60 yards long by 15 to 25 yards wide. For further information *see* Philip Watson; op.cit.: 9–17.

28. Joseph Kaster, op.cit.

29. Pyramid tombs were constructed by the Pharaohs of the Third to the Sixth Dynasties, whose reigns spanned from around 2650–2200 BC. This timespan is now known as the period of the Old Kingdom. It was also one of the most secure and peaceful phases of ancient Egyptian civilization, and produced some of ancient Egypt's greatest achievements in engineering, political organization, and the arts.

30. The reference here is to *Microsoft Encarta*, the best-selling multimedia encyclopedia supplied on a CD-ROM disk for either IBM or Apple compatible personal computers. Corbis, a company owned by Microsoft founder Bill Gates, is also currently engaged in the digitization and archiving of the one million or more most famous images in the world.

31. The Step Pyramid has sides containing six great 'steps', as opposed to the smooth walls of later pyramids beyond the Fourth Dynasty. This is probably due to the fact that the design was changed several times during construction, with the tomb originally being a square mastaba 'bench', which subsequently became part of the lowest step level. Cut into the bedrock 27 metres below the Step Pyramid was King Djoser's tomb. For further detail upon both this structure and the four stepped pyramids which followed (the last of which was eventually filled in to form a smooth-faced true-pyramid for King Snefru), *see* Philip Watson, op.cit.: Chapter 3.

32. The Bent Pyramid at Dahshur was so called due to the radical change of angle of its sides—from the usual 54 degrees to a shallower 43—about half way up. This change in angle is usually taken to imply that the pyramid had to be finished in haste, with the shallower upper portion requiring a smaller volume of stone.

33. Khufu is often still referred to by his Greek name of Cheops. Indeed, it is only recently that many of the ancient Egyptian kings have come to be known by their Egyptian rather than Greek names. Within this book all names are in their most common Egyptian format, unless otherwise stated.

34. In ancient times Giza was the Egyptian capital of Memphis, and is today part of Greater Cairo.

35. It is hotly debated whether the shafts leading up from both the King's chamber, and from the supposedly abandoned Queen's chamber below, were constructed for practical reasons of ventilation, or whether they instead played a ritualistic role as 'star shafts' permitting the spirit of the deceased to reach out to the heavens.

36. Philip Watson, op.cit.: 57–58.

37. Ibid.: 31.

38. The case for the Sphinx being several thousand years older than the Pyramids at Giza (and hence being a relic of a far more ancient and as yet unknown civilization) largely focuses upon the fact that the stones of the monument appear to have suffered erosion by water and rain, rather than by the wind, as with other rock structures at the site. If this case is ever conclusively proven, then the notion of ancient Egypt as the oldest of civilizations—and as the first to build in stone—would almost certainly have to be revised.

39. It should be noted that, whilst today we know the largest of the Giza Pyramids (that of Khufu) as the 'Great Pyramid', that the ancient Egyptians themselves knew Khaefre's Pyramid (built on higher ground, and hence in some ways more dominating) by this name.

To the Egyptians, Khufu's tomb was known as the 'Pyramid Which is the Horizon', whilst the third pyramid of the Giza trio (that of Menkaure) was known as the 'Divine Pyramid'.

40. Grahame Clark *Space, Time and Man* (Cambridge: Cambridge University Press, 1992): 89.

41. For a discussion of the concept of 'modernity' *see* Krishan Kumar *From Post-Industrial to Post-Modern Society: New Theories of the Contemporary World* (Oxford: Blackwell, 1995): Chapter 4.

42. Ibid.

43. Richard Dawkins *The Selfish Gene* (Oxford: Oxford University Press, 1976 and 1989): 199.

44. Grahame Clark, op.cit.: 90–91.

45. In this context, it is perhaps interesting to note that, in the past five years, over 400 books upon the Pyramids and the Pharaohs of ancient Egypt have been published in the United Kingdom alone. *Source: Timewatch* (London: BBC Television, 19th August 1996).

46. Joseph Kaster, op.cit.: ix.

47. Ibid: 105.

Chapter 3: The Age of Invention

48. Cited from Neil Armstrong's introduction to *Moon Shot: The Inside Story of America's Race to the Moon* by Alan Shepard and Deke Slayton (London: Virgin, 1995): 2.

49. Egon Larsen *Atomic Energy: The Layman's Guide to the Nuclear Age* (London: Pan Books, 1958).

50. Ibid: 108.

51. Ibid: 141

52. Ibid: 146–152

53. Ibid: 152–154.

54. R.A. Buchanan *The Power of the Machine: The Impact of Technology from 1700 to the Present* (London: Penguin, 1994): 25. The most obvious structure supportive of invention and inventors is the patent system, as discussed in **chapter 4**.

55. John Romer, cited from the opening sequence of the fourth and final documentary in his television series entitled *The Seven Wonders of the World*, produced by Discovery Productions with Agran Barton Television for Channel Four: MCMXCIV.

56. Thomas Alva Edison (1847–1931) is most certainly one of the most significant individuals to have shaped the Present Age. Amassing more than 1000 patents during his lifetime, Edison is credited for the invention of the incandescent filament lamp (the first practical electric light bulb), the first electrical generating system, sound recording (via his phonograph device), and for the first motion picture projector.

57. R.A. Buchanan; op.cit.: 255.

58. Literally, 'Sputnik' translates as 'fellow traveller'. The satellite circled the globe every 96 minutes, transmitting a simple radio beacon picked up around the planet as it flew hundreds of miles overhead.

59. Alan Shepard became the first US space traveller upon the 4th of May 1961 aboard his spacecraft Freedom Seven.

60. In the summer of 1960, America's 'invulnerable' U2 spy plane had been shot down by the Russians, whilst earlier in the year there had been Castro's communist victory in Cuba. American intervention in Cuba just days before Yuri Gagarin became the first man in space had also proved a humiliating failure.

61. *See* Roger Diski *Apollo: When the World Held its Breath,* booklet written to accompany the Central Independent Television, WGBH/Boston and TV Asahi documentary of the same title (London: Screen Guides, 1994): 4–5.

62. A manned moonlanding was one of just many goals considered. Others included the setting up of the first space station. However, in this the Americans already considered themselves to be at a disadvantage in comparison with Soviet space science.

63. In setting a goal for the US space programme that could take nearly nine years to reach completion, President Kennedy was not taking any personal risks. Even if reelected, he knew he would be out of the White House before any launch to the Moon. In fact, due to his assassination in November 1963, John F. Kennedy never lived to see the achievement of the great goal which he set for his country.

64. Alan Shepard and Deke Slayton *Moon Shot: The Inside Story of America's Race to the Moon* (London: Virgin, 1995): 245–246.

65. Ibid.: 152.

66. Early Mercury missions—such as that flown by America's first astronaut Alan Shepard—were not designed to achieve Earth orbit due to the relatively low power of their Redstone launch boosters. However, later Mercury missions made use of newer, more powerful Atlas boosters. Upon the first of these flights on the 20th of February 1962, John Glenn became the first American to orbit the Earth.

67. Perhaps most notably, Gemini 5 stretched long flight duration to eight days, whilst Gemini 7 extended this record to fourteen. Geminis 6 and 7 were the first ever spacecraft to make a rendezvous, whilst Gemini 8 achieved the first space docking (with an unmanned test satellite named Agena).

68. Alan Shepard and Deke Slayton, op.cit.: 223.

69. Ibid.: chapter 15.

70. Ibid.: 249–250.

71. Two variants of Saturn rocket were used to launch Apollo missions. The smaller were Saturn 1Bs, used to launch Apollo craft into earth orbit for equipment tests. The much larger Saturn V was only needed when Apollo capsules were actually fired to the Moon.

72. After the unmanned Zond success, the Soviet lunar programme was beset by failure after failure. Indeed, Zond itself was only a brief reprise after the tragic failure of the earlier manned flight of Soyuz 1, during which cosmonaut Vladimir Komarov was killed upon reentry.

73. With no wind on the Moon, the *Stars and Stripes* was stiffened with a wire to hold it in place. Unfortunately, the blast-off of the lunar module caused the flag to fall over upon the *Eagle*'s departure.

74. The elaborate media coverage undoubtedly helped to boost public support for the moonlandings programme by making remote events seem very 'real'. Cameras were somehow in position to record Neil Armstrong stepping down onto the lunar surface, the lunar module in space, and even the launch of the *Eagle*'s ascent stage away from the Moon. When Saturn rockets were launched, colour images of empty fuel stages being jettisoned Earthwards were also recorded. In the days when we now take superb movie and TV special effects for granted, it is easy to forget the ingenuity behind the recording

of the Apollo missions for posterity. Indeed, TV and film coverage was so comprehensive that it caused some to question whether the entire moonlandings programme had in fact been staged in a movie studio.

75. An electrical fault caused one of Apollo 13's liquid oxygen tanks to explode, ripping open one side of its service module. In order to survive, commander Jim Lovell and his two fellow astronauts had to transfer into the tiny lunar module. They then performed a 'slingshot' around the Moon to put them on a heading back to Earth. With power severely rationed, their spacecraft became extremely cold and damp with condensation, and indeed it is a wonder that they survived to tell the tale. Whilst Lovell later described the mission as a 'successful failure', Apollo 13 was nevertheless a major blow for NASA, and one which caused many Americans to question the value, as well as the safety, of the moonlandings programme.

76. The Skylab programme was vital to allow NASA to maintain functioning technical crews and an astronaut training programme before the Space Shuttle became a reality. The programme was also relatively cheap, due to the fact that the hardware from the cancelled Apollo 18, 19 and 20 remained in storage. In fact, the Skylab station itself was a converted Saturn V third stage, launched into orbit by the first two stages of the rocket.

77. J.M. Roberts *The Penguin History of the World* (London: Penguin, 1992): 980.

78. Charles Augustus Lindbergh set off from New York on the 20th of May 1927 in his single-engined plane *The Spirit of St. Louis*. Thirty-three hours and thirty-two minutes later he arrived in Le Bourget airport in Paris, the first man to fly non-stop across an ocean.

79. As cited in Alan Shepard and Deke Slayton, op.cit.: 246.

80. Buzz Aldrin, cited from the television documentary *As it Happened: Moonlanding*, produced by George Carey (London: Barraclough Carey Productions for Channel Four Television and Discovery Productions, 1994).

81. Gene Kranz, cited from *As it Happened: Moonlanding*, ibid.

82. The first light bulb was revealed to the world by Thomas Edison in 1879. The first microprocessor (a device comprising the main components of a computer upon a single silicon chip) was coded the 4004 and launched by Intel in 1971.

Chapter 4: Creativity & Decay

83. Lucasfilm *Star Wars—Return of the Jedi: Official Collector's Edition* (Newtown, CT: Paradise Press, 1983): 29–30.

84. These comments come from an interview with Phil Tippett entitled 'In the Tracks of Jurassic Park' conducted by Iain A. Boal, and contained within James Brook and Iain A. Boal (eds) *Resisting the Virtual Life: The Culture and Politics of Information* (San Francisco, CA: City Lights, 1995): 253–262.

85. For a fuller account of the work of Lucasfilm *see* Mark Cotta Vaz and Shinhi Hata *The Star Wars Archives* (London: Virgin, 1995). Also published in the United States as *From Star Wars to Indiana Jones: The Best of the Lucasfilm Archives* by Chronicle Books.

86. The way in which the Apollo 1 tragedy spurred those working upon the moonlandings programme towards eventual success is just one of many cases demonstrating how humanity may flourish in the face of adversity. Similarly, threats, real or imagined,

always pull people together—whether they concern an enemy invasion or the proposed building of a new bypass.

87.   Daniel Burrus with Roger Gittines *Techno Trends: How to Use Technology to go Beyond your Competition* (New York: HarperCollins, 1993).

88.   The transhuman mailbase is one of the busiest on the Internet, generating hundreds of responses per week. For more information on some transhuman agendas *see* Timothy Leary *Chaos and Cyberculture* (Berkeley, CA: Ronin, 1994).

89.   Virtual reality (VR) cyberspace access most commonly involves participants donning a head-mounted display (HMD), together with a dataglove or other 3-D pointing device, in order that they may both witness and manipulate a 3-D graphics world. The term VR was first coined in 1989 by Jaron Lanier, the CEO of the pioneering Virtual Products Limited (VPL).

90.   *See*, for example, Timothy Leary *Chaos and Cyberculture* (Berkeley, CA: Ronin, 1994); Barry Sherman and Philip Judkins *Glimpses of Heaven, Visions of Hell: Virtual Reality and its Implications* (London: Hodder & Stoughton, 1993); Benjamin Woolley *Virtual Worlds* (Oxford: Blackwell, 1992); Howard Rheingold *Virtual Reality* (London: Mandarin, 1993); Christopher Barnatt *Cyber Business: Mindsets for a Wired Age* (Chichester: John Wiley & Sons, 1995).

91.   Christopher Barnatt *Cyber Business: Mindsets for a Wired Age* (Chichester: John Wiley & Sons, 1995).

92.   Nicholas Negroponte *Being Digital* (London: Hodder & Stoughton, 1995).

93.   Myron W. Krueger *Artificial Reality II* (Reading, MA: Addison-Wesley, 1991): xiv.

94.   This theme is one of many developed by R.A. Buchanan in *The Power of the Machine* (London: Penguin, 1994).

95.   The Internet is an international conglomeration of computer networks into which anybody may connect over a telephone link. The world-wide web provides an easy-to-use, graphical 'point-and-click' interface to the Internet. Most web pages contain both text and graphics. Tens of thousands of individuals, in addition to businesses and other organizations, now have their own web pages. Even a cursory browse of the web reveals that many such pages feature material digitized from copyrighted sources such as popular films and TV shows.

96.   Barry Sherman and Philip Judkins *Glimpses of Heaven, Visions of Hell: Virtual Reality and its Implications* (London: Hodder & Stoughton, 1993): 86.

97.   Physical achievements, of course, have always been protectable not just by laws but by physical barriers (such as doors, locks and castles), as well as by brute force.

98.   Esther Dyson 'The Price of Knowledge—Intellectual Property on the Internet', *Siemens Nixdorf DIALOGUE Magazine* (March 1st 1996): 5–7.

99.   Mark Slouka *War of the Worlds: Cyberspace and the High-Tech Assault on Reality* (London: Abacus, 1996): 69.

100.   Ibid.: 94.

101.   Yet to be realized in reality, the 'information superhighway' encapsulates the *idea* of a high-capacity computer-and-video communications network linking every organization and every home. The highway may therefore develop out of today's more modest Internet network infrastructure (*see* note 95). However, as Microsoft guru Bill Gates notes, the 'information highway' is a bad metaphor, as it implies geography and travelling. Instead, we would be better served to think of the highway as a new marketplace. *See* Bill Gates

with Nathan Myhrvold and Peter Rinearson *The Road Ahead* (NY: Penguin Books, 1995): 5-6.

102. One could discuss for pages whether in future computerized products and softwares will become either 'smart' or truly 'intelligent'. In practice, any such distinction will be irrelevant. One thing of which we can be certain is that in future many digital systems will become very, very *clever* indeed.

103. Nicholas Negroponte, op.cit.: 75.

104. Ibid: 148.

105. In contrast to many popular misconceptions, artists have almost always been at the forefront of the adoption of new technologies. Cave painters, after all, were almost certainly amongst the first to use the new media tools of their day. Those who built cathedrals also founded their accomplishments on the back of cutting-edge technological prowess. Virtual reality is similarly a technology to have first been adopted (and developed) by artists ahead of the business community. *See* Myron Krueger, op.cit: xii & 2.

106. Traditionally, insulin has been obtained from the pancreas tissue of animals. Factor VIII for haemophiliacs has traditionally been produced from donated human blood. Unfortunately, a great many of the haemophiliacs who received Factor VIII produced from human blood before the mid-1980s contracted hepatitis or acquired immune deficiency syndrome (AIDS) due to a lack of screening for such viruses within contaminated donor material.

107. Aside from using genetic engineering to alter living organisms, scientists are now also using biotechnological processes in the synthesis and reengineering of new chemicals and compounds. However, the most extreme level of molecular manipulation is associated with the embryonic science of nanotechnology. This involves the physical manipulation of the structure of matter (via the movement of individual atoms), and may therefore one day become widespread in the synthesis of designer molecular structures. Within his book *The Engines of Creation* (Anchor/Doubleday, 1986) Eric Drexler predicts that 'self-replicating assemblers'—tiny virus-sized robots—will in future to able to synthesize *anything* we desire (including new, more complex assemblers) from the likes of carbon and water. Nanomachines may even be able to be injected into the human body to undertake tissue repairs, unclog cholesterol-clogged arteries, and so forth.

108. Deoxyribonucleic acid (DNA) is the very building block of life, with each DNA molecule encoded with the billions of bits of chemical information that determine each individual's physical make-up. The nucleus of every one of our body cells is thought to contain a single DNA molecule in the shape of a double helix which, if unwound, would be a staggering sixteen inches long. (*See* Rudy Rucker et al, *Mondo 2000: A User's Guide to the New Edge* (London: Thames & Hudson, 1993): 82.

109. The Human Genome Project is run under the auspices of the Human Genome Organization (HUGO), and at the time of writing involved the collaboration of formal genome programmes in the United States, Japan, the former Soviet Union, Denmark, France, Germany, Italy and the United Kingdom.

110. The cloning technique pioneered at the Roslin Institute involved sucking the DNA out of an infertile sheep's egg. This genetically barren egg was then 'reprogrammed' by implanting it with alternative sheep DNA derived from a foetus, and which had previously been cultured (potentially limitlessly) within the laboratory. An electrical pulse was used to release the genetic material from the implanted cells so that they would 'take over' their

new host egg. Finally, the reengineered egg was implanted into a surrogate mother within whose womb it could develop to maturity.

111. As reported by Gina Kolata in her article 'A Vat of DNA may become the Computer of the Future' (New York Times News Service, 1995).

112. Nicholas Negroponte, op.cit.: 211.

113. Mark Slouka, op.cit.: 61.

114. Francis Fukuyama *The End of History and the Last Man* (London: Hamish Hamilton, 1992).

115. Allucquère Rosanne Stone 'Will the Real Body Please Stand up?: Boundary Stories about Virtual Cultures' in Michael Benedikt (ed) *Cyberspace: First Steps* (Cambridge, MA: MIT Press, 1991): 110.

116. When microprocessor chips were first being launched, it is interesting to note that journalists were eager to discover how such tiny devices would be repaired in the event of any failure. Many could simply not accept that microelectronic components would become so cheap that they would be disposable.

Chapter 5: Tools that Talked

117. John Romer *The Seven Wonders of the World*—television documentary series produced by Discovery Productions with Agran Barton Television for Channel Four: MCMXCIV: programme 1, part III.

118. Whilst agricultural, building and manufacturing technologies were not advanced, the people of Pergamon did set forth to extend Greek culture and to advance and diffuse civilization. Perhaps most notably parchment (known as pergameme) was perfected in the city's schools when papyrus came to be in short supply. *See* J.M. Roberts *The Penguin History of the World* (London: Penguin, 1995): 212.

119. John Romer, op.cit.

120. Gregory Stock *Metaman: Humans, Machines and the Birth of a Global Super-organism* (London: Bantam Press, 1993): 90.

121. A United Nations committee on slavery in 1951 reported that whilst the practice was rapidly declining, various vestiges of human servitude were still widespread in some quarters. A Geneva convention in 1956 subsequently adopted a new convention relating to the abolition of slavery and similar practices, which widened definitions of human servitude previously enshrined by the League of Nations International Slavery Convention of 1926.

122. The psychological contract is not a written document, but instead encompasses all of the implicit, mutual expectations—of rights and privileges, duties and obligations—arising from an employment relationship. These may all have a significant influence upon employee and employer performance and other behaviour. For example, employees may expect a pleasant working environment, job security, satisfying work, equitable personnel policies, opportunities for development, and to be consulted within certain decision making processes. Employers, on the other hand, may expect employees to accept their ideology, to work diligently, not to abuse goodwill, to show loyalty, and not to betray trust or to reflect the organization in a bad light. *See*, for example, Laurie J. Mullins *Management and Organisational Behaviour* (London: Pitman, 1993) 3rd edition: 11–13.

123. The concept of organizational broker cores drawing services from free agents within industry marketplaces is discussed by Raymond Miles and Charles Snow in their paper 'Organizations: New Concepts for New Forms' in the *California Management Review* XXVII: 62–73.

124. J.M. Roberts *The Penguin History of the World* (London: Penguin, 1992): 61.

125. Ibid.

126. Robin Sowerby *The Greeks: An Introduction to their Culture* (London: Routledge, 1995): 29.

127. J.M. Roberts, op.cit.: 247.

128. Information sourced from the Africa Reparations Movement Information Sheet *A Brief Chronology of Slavery, Colonialism and Neo-Colonialism*.

129. J.M. Roberts, op.cit.: 644.

130. America declared independence from Great Britain in the July of 1776—an independence finally recognized by the British in 1783.

131. For example the Presbyterians, the Methodist Episcopal church, and the Society of Friends (Quakers), all made declarations against slavery from the late-18th century onwards.

132. Lincoln's election signalled the end of various compromises over the slavery issue between the Northern and Southern states which had been agreed in 1820, 1832 and 1850. Lincoln represented the Republicans as the first purely sectional political party, and did not receive a single Southern electoral vote. *See* Michael Lind *The Next American Nation: New Nationalism and the Fourth American Revolution* (New York: The Free Press, 1995): 36–38.

133. For a far more complete account of the events leading up to the abolition of slavery in the United States, *see* J.M. Roberts, op.cit.: 744–51.

134. Gregory Stock, op.cit.: 90–91.

135. Thomas Sowell *Ethnic America: A History* (New York: Basic Books, 1981): 27.

136. Gareth Morgan *Images of Organization* (Newbury Park, CA: Sage, 1986): 275.

Chapter 6: Willing Cogs in the Machine?

137. J.M. Roberts in the Foreword of Godfrey Hodgson's *People's Century* (London: BBC Books, 1995): 6.

138. Godfrey Hodgson *People's Century* (London: BBC Books, 1995): 20.

139. Indeed, the concept of man as a 'rational economic' animal whose behaviour may be predicted by simple rules of demand and supply still dominates much economic thinking to this day.

140. At the beginning of the 20th century, tractors had already brought mass production to the land. Once they owned a tractor, farmers not only needed far fewer workers, but could also cultivate the land previously used to grow fodder for their horses.

141. Godfrey Hodgson, op.cit.: 99.

142. Renault worker Arthur Herbaux, cited in Godfrey Hodgson, op.cit.: 99.

143. *See* F.W. Taylor *Scientific Management* (New York: Harper & Row, 1947).

144. Time and motion study involves researchers with notepads, rulers and stop watches observing, measuring and recording all of the salient details of any work activity in order that an optimal method of working may be calculated.

145. Taylor was keen to highlight the importance of bringing together the science of the 'one best way' with 'scientifically selected and trained workmen'. *See* F.W. Taylor *Scientific Management*, op.cit.

146. Taylor's ultimate system of managerial task specialization involved workers being responsible to two groups of foremen. The first group consisted of individual *planning supervisors* concerned with work ordering, instruction methods, work timing and costing. The second 'functional foremen' group were *performance supervisors* with responsibilities for group control, speed, repair work and work inspection. Unfortunately, such a system (wherein a labourer could be under the jurisdiction of up to *eight* different supervisors at any one time), proved overly complex, and hence was eventually scrapped. Indeed, it was not until the 1960s that such methods of 'matrix management' entered the mainstream.

147. For more information upon Taylor's experiments at Bethlehem and elsewhere, *see* F.W. Taylor *Scientific Management*, op.cit.

148. Indeed, Taylor's engineering-inspired management methods even came to be investigated by a House of Representatives Special Committee in 1911 following worker unrest after an attempt to introduce Scientific Management into a government arsenal.

149. The Great Depression was triggered by the crash of the Wall Street stock exchange on the 24th of October 1929, and lasted for around a decade.

150. Godfrey Hodgson, op.cit: 112.

151. Ford worker Paul Boatin, cited in Godfrey Hodgson, op.cit.: 113.

152. Godfrey Hodgson, op.cit: 115.

153. Although perhaps obvious today, the results of the Hawthorne experiments were a revelation at the time, and indeed marked a watershed in the study of management and the social sciences. Elton Mayo and his team of researchers had set out to identify optimal physical working conditions for assembly staff via a series of experiments in which they observed workers and their output whilst factors such as illumination levels and the timing of rest breaks were changed. However, it soon became apparent that the act of observing —of showing an interest in—workers at the plant had just as great an impact upon their productivity as did their physical working environment. This phenomena was subsequently termed the 'Hawthorne effect'. *See* (for example) E. Mayo 'Hawthorne and the Western Electric Company' in D.S. Pugh (Ed) *Organization Theory: Selected Readings*, 3rd edn (London: Penguin, 1990): 345–357.

154. *The Sunday Times Business Supplement*, 24th November 1985.

155. In the UK, several studies were undertaken to determine the roots of the new trend towards flexible manning. The CBI Employment Affairs Directorate published the results of a survey entitled *Managing Change: The Organization of Work* in 1985. Manpower, at the time the UK's largest temporary agency, also published a survey on *The Changing Face of Work* in the same year. In association with the Department of Employment and the Institute for Manpower Studies, the National Economic Development Office (NEDO) also published a detailed report on *Changing Working Patterns: How Companies Achieve Flexibility to Meet New Needs* in 1986.

156. Indeed, prior to the birth of a host of new TV companies in the mid-1980s (most notably those producing low-cost programmes for Channel 4 and for the breakfast audience), the television industry in the UK was described by Margaret Thatcher as the 'last bastion of restrictive practices'.

157. The Flexible Firm model was first introduced by John Atkinson in *The Flexibility Factor* (Sussex University: Institute for Manpower Studies, 1985).

158. Functional flexibility may occur in two directions. Horizontal functional flexibility will involve a worker becoming capable of undertaking different tasks at the same skill level. For example, an assembly worker may be trained to operate a wide range of assembly machines. Vertical functional flexibility, on the other hand, will involve workers being capable of taking on jobs at different skill levels. It may be, for example, that a machine operator also undertakes the cleaning of his or her machine, or perhaps even takes on responsibility for the machine's repair and maintenance.

Chapter 7: Totally Free to Fly & Totally Free to Fall

159. *Visions of Heaven & Hell*, written and produced by Mark Harrison (London: Barraclough Carey Productions for Channel 4 Television, 1995).
160. Ibid.
161. Cited from Charles Handy *Beyond Certainty: The Changing World of Organizations* (London: Hutchinson, 1995): 212.
162. Nicholas Negroponte *Being Digital* (London: Hodder & Stoughton, 1995): 237.
163. Ibid: 228.
164. I say '*in theory at least*' as there are important mindset and skillset limitations to be considered when making such bold and optimistic statements! Accepting the abstraction of work processes across computer network systems represents a great mental challenge for many people. Future workers will also need to be highly 'digitally literate' in order to work across such networks. For a far broader discussion of the likely development of electronic business systems, readers should consult my previous book *Cyber Business: Mindsets for a Wired Age* (Chichester: John Wiley & Sons, 1995).
165. Nicholas Negroponte, op.cit.: 237.
166. Peter Cochrane, cited in *Visions of Heaven & Hell: Will Technology Deliver us a Bright New Future?*, booklet to accompany the television series of the same name (London: Broadcasting Support Services for Channel Four Television, 1995): 3.
167. 'Discover a Better Way to Work: Highlights from Telework UK 95 Conference', *New Ways to Work Newsletter* (March 1996): 16.
168. Dom Pancucci 'Remote Control', *Management Today* (April 1995): 78.
169. Burger King, American Express and British Telecom are just some of the companies to have reaped major cost savings from teleworking arrangements; ibid.
170. This concept is explored in far greater detail within Michael Lind's *The Next American Nation: New Nationalism and the Fourth American Revolution* (New York: The Free Press, 1995).
171. Charles Handy *Beyond Certainty* (London: Hutchinson, 1995): 8.
172. Ibid: 31.
173. *Changing Work Patterns and the Consumer—A Crisis for the Millennium* (Mintel, April 1996).
174. Ibid.
175. In some service industries (such as healthcare) the employment of human beings to undertake dexterous physical tasks is likely to remain prevalent for a long time to come. However, in others, such as further and higher education and training, we are increasingly likely to see traditional employees replaced with interactive, technology-based systems. By no means all service sectors are 'safe' from computerized automation.

176. According to Ovum, by the year 2000 the market for intelligent agent software will be worth $2.6bn per annum. For more information upon the software agent phenomenon *see* Christopher Barnatt *Cyber Business: Mindsets for a Wired Age* (Chichester: John Wiley & Sons, 1995): chapter 4.
177. Thomas J. Peters and Robert W. Waterman *In Search of Excellence: Lessons from America's Best-Run Companies* (New York: Harper & Row, 1982).
178. For a broader discussion of different types of 'power', 'role', 'task' and 'person' (professional) employment cultures, *see* R. Harrison 'How to Describe Your Organization', *Harvard Business Review* (September–October 1972).
179. 'Equitable Flexibility—A Way Forward?', *New Ways to Work Newsletter* (March 1996): 2.
180. Charles Handy, op.cit.: 25.

Chapter 8: Escapes from the Here & Now

181. Indeed, within his book *Organizational Culture*, Andrew D. Brown even contends (perhaps with some bias!) that the study of corporate culture has now become the single most important active research area in management (London: Pitman, 1995): 3.
182. The noun 'meme' was first defined by Richard Dawkins in *The Selfish Gene* (Oxford: Oxford University Press, 1976, revised 1989): 192.
183. Mark Poster *The Mode of Information: Post Structuralism and Social Context* (Cambridge: Polity Press, 1992).
184. Ibid.: 6.
185. Grahame Clark *Space, Time and Man* (Cambridge: Cambridge University Press, 1992): 6.
186. The establishment of hunting parties which returned their kill to a communal home for *future* consumption was probably also significant in the evolution of time awareness.
187. Talk of 'early human beings' is, by its very nature, somewhat contentious. Patterns of spoken language may have first been evolved by the tribal communities of our pre-human ancestor homo erectus before (or during) its lengthy evolutionary transition into homo sapiens.
188. This particular hypothesis is presented within J.M. Roberts' *The Penguin History of the World* (London: Penguin, 1995): 18. Some linguists, however, now consider that human language is more akin to bird songs that animal calls, and may hence have very different foundations. *See*, for example Jean Aitchison *The Seeds of Speech: Language Origin and Evolution* (Cambridge: Cambridge University Press, 1996).
189. *See* Grahame Clark, op.cit.: 42–44. Further to the discussion in the text it should also be noted that whilst language gave preliterate peoples an awareness of time, and an ability to communicate across it, it did not cause them to be concerned with events other than those of the immediate present. In other words, whilst communications across time became possible and took place, they were not conscious. It is worth bearing this point in mind considering our analysis of cyclical versus linear time in **chapter 2**.
190. The Palaeolithic Age (the 'Stone Age') is divided into three periods: the Lower Palaeolithic Age (from around 600,000 to 100,000 BC), the Middle Palaeolithic Age (dated at around 100,000 to 40,000 BC), and the Upper Palaeolithic Age (which lasted from around 40,000 to 10,000 BC). It was during the Upper Palaeolithic Age that the first

homo sapiens appeared. The finest cave paintings of this period date from between 15,000 and 11,000 years ago, with some of the best examples having been discovered in Lascaux in Southern France and Altamira in Northern Spain. *See* Herman Kinder and Werner Hilgermann *The Penguin Atlas of World History: Volume One* (London: Penguin, 1974): 13, and Giovanni Caselli *The History of Everyday Things: Our World Through the Ages* (Hemel Hempstead: Simon & Schuster, 1993): 12.

191. Grahame Clark, op.cit.: 16.

192. Ibid.: 87.

193. Such seals—also known as 'signet stones'—represent the first incarnation of printing technology. Often formed as part of a ring, they were used to mark surfaces either with signatures, or with various religious symbols.

194. Around 3000 BC, and indeed for several thousands of years afterwards, the peoples of Egypt and of Mesopotamia were frequent trading partners.

195. Grahame Clark, op.cit.

196. An example of a determinative could be a little man placed after a man's name, or an eye placed after a verb for seeing. For more detail upon hieroglyphics and their complex decipherment, *see* Joseph Kaster *The Wisdom of Ancient Egypt: Writings from the Time of the Pharaohs* (London: Michael O'Mara Books, 1995): chapter 2.

197. Ibid.: 190.

198. Information upon the development of early forms of writing is sourced from a variety of references, including *Microsoft Encarta*, Grahame Clark (op.cit.), and Michael Wood's television series *Legacy: Origins of Civilization* (Central Independent Television in association with Maryland Public Television and NHK Enterprises, 1991).

199. J.M. Roberts *The Penguin History of the World* (London: Penguin, 1992): 51.

200. In ancient Rome, literate slaves also copied texts—allowing some volumes to be issued in their thousands.

201. In 972 AD the Tripitaka (sacred Buddhist scriptures comprising over 130,000 pages) had been printed in China entirely from wooden blocks.

202. An adequate supply of cheap, quality paper was essential in printing's development, as more ancient writing surfaces—such as papyrus or vellum—were either too fragile or too expensive to be used in the process. Fortunately, the art of paper making (introduced into Europe in the 12th century) had been sufficiently perfected by the 15th century to allow for the abundant availability of an adequate paper supply made from pulped rags.

203. J.M. Roberts, op.cit.: 523.

204. *See* Bill Gates with Nathan Myhrvold and Peter Rinearson *The Road Ahead* (London: Viking, 1995): 9.

205. Charles Handy *The Search for Meaning* (London: Lemos & Crane in association with the London International Festival of Theatre, 1996): 23.

206. J.M. Roberts, op.cit.: 523.

207. R.A. Buchanan *The Power of the Machine: The Impact of Technology from 1700 to the Present* (London: Penguin, 1994): 174.

208. Whilst the speed of early-19th century presses (using sprung levers to force the platen against the bed rather than more primitive screw thread mechanisms) was only around 300 impressions per hour, such printers could print far larger forme areas than previous printing mechanisms, hence enabling four, eight or even sixteen final pages to be printed at the same time.

209. The first steam-driven press was invented in 1814 by Friedrich König.

210. *The Times* installed such a machine in 1856. *See* R.A. Buchanan, op.cit.: 174.

211. Stewart Brand *The Media Lab: Creating the Future at MIT* (New York: Penguin, 1988): 42.

212. I am, of course, setting aside here more subtle media for human communicative interplay—such as those involving gesture, touch and taste, as well as those permitting the transmission of memes in the form of music or by pictures (though neither of the latter could be replicated and/or communicated outside of direct human experience at this point in time).

Chapter 9: Cyberia: First Steps

213. Cited in Stewart Brand *The Media Lab: Inventing the Future at MIT* (New York: Penguin, 1990): 63.

214. The first of these definitions comes from William Gibson's novel *Neuromancer*, wherein the term cyberspace was coined for an unsuspecting world (New York: Ace Books, 1984): 67. Those definitions which follow are selected from across my own previous book *Cyber Business: Mindsets for a Wired Age* (Chichester: John Wiley & Sons, 1995), save for the last, which was concocted solely for this volume!

215. Michael Benedikt *Cyberspace: First Steps* (Cambridge, MA: MIT Press, 1991): 3.

216. *See* note 214.

217. Douglas Rushkoff *Cyberia: Life in the Trenches of Hyperspace* (London: HarperCollins, 1994): 16–17.

218. R.A. Buchanan *The Power of the Machine: The Impact of Technology from 1700 to the Present* (London: Penguin, 1992): 159–161.

219. The coding system of dots and dashes invented by Samuel Morse was incorporated into United States' legislation in 1843, and quickly became an American and then a world telegraph standard.

220. The 'telegraphone', a device for recording sound by magnetizing steel tape, was invented by V. Poulsen in 1889.

221. The cassette tape format was developed by Norelco and Philips, and replaced earlier 8-track, 4-track and 'PlayTape' cartridge formats. Cassettes were test marketed across Europe in 1966, over a year before their introduction into the United States.

222. A scientific paper by Peter Mark Roget suggested that motion could be portrayed by presenting the human eye with a number of still images in rapid succession as early as 1824. One of the first devices to make use of this 'persistence of vision' was the zoetrope. This consisted of a series of drawings mounted on the inside of a spinning drum. When viewed through slits in its sides, the still images contained within the drum appeared to move. As soon as photography became a practical process, experiments began with zoetrope-style devices using photographs rather than hand drawn images. One such apparatus was the Kinematoscope, patented in America by Coleman Sellers in 1861, and which animated images mounted on a paddle wheel. In the 1870s English photographer Eadweard Muybridge also experimented with motion capture, and, using banks of still cameras fired in quick succession, managed to record sequences of photographs showing galloping horses and then other animals.

223. In contrast to the Lumière brothers' cinèmatographe combination printer, camera and projector, Edison's viewing box Kinetoscope machines of 1894 only allowed one person at a time to view a movie.

224. *See* Godfrey Hodgson *People's Century* (London: BBC Books, 1995): 172.

225. Ibid.: 19.

226. From the early-19th century onwards the reliability and organization of postal services improved greatly in many countries. This was largely due to the development of road and rail transportation systems. As early as the 18th century, standardized postal rates had been implemented in Great Britain.

227. Or as Daniel Bell contends, via mass media, the number of people and/or places one knows accelerates at a 'steeply exponential rate'—*The Coming of Postindustrial Society, The Cultural Contradictions of Capitalism* (New York: Harper & Row, 1976): 172.

228. Whilst *The Jazz Singer* was the first publicly screened film with synchronized sound, it perhaps ought to be noted that Thomas Edison managed to produce a rudimentary talking picture with his Kinetoscope as early as 1889.

229. CD-ROM (or Compact Disk Read Only Memory) drives are used to access the hundreds of megabytes (or hundreds of millions of characters) of data which may now be stored on a 5″ laser disk. Computer CD-ROM applications already range from encyclopedias to games, databases to photo albums and even movies.

230. The key difference between the systems created by Baird and Marconi was that, whilst the former used a camera which scanned images 'mechanically' through slits in a rotating disk, the latter was based upon a totally electronic (and hence more effective) camera apparatus.

231. Colour television was first invented in 1950 by Peter Carl Goldmark. However, it took several decades before the majority of the television audience had colour sets.

232. Ithiel de Sola Pool *Technologies of Freedom: On Free Speech in an Electronic Age* (Cambridge, MA: Harvard, 1983).

233. Even to this day, a significant proportion of each Eurovision Song Contest broadcast is devoted to informing viewers about regions of other countries.

234. It is perhaps interesting to note that, whilst several science fiction writers had told tales of a manned lunar landing well before 1969, none had predicted that such an event would be witnessed live by so many fellow human beings back home.

235. Cited from Nicholas Negroponte's *Being Digital* (London: Hodder & Stoughton, 1995): 82.

236. Mark Poster *The Mode of Information: Poststructuralism and Social Context* (Cambridge: Polity Press, 1990): 47.

237. JVC introduced the VHS format video cassette recorder in 1976, and by early 1977 had been joined by four other Japanese electronics manufacturers and RCA. By the January of 1981 VHS had a 75 per cent market share, and by January 1988 95 per cent.

238. Also known as Digital Versatile Disk by the computer community, DVD looks set to become the de facto standard for video playback and recording, as well as for computer-based multimedia, by the turn of the century. At the time of writing, the maximum capacity of a DVD was 4.7 Gb—over seven times greater than a standard CD-ROM—and enough to store a high quality digital copy of most movies.

239. Nicholas Negroponte *Being Digital* (London: Hodder & Stoughton, 1995): 164 & 84–85.

240. Ibid.: 55.

241. The world's first electronic computer, ENIAC—the Electronic Numerical Integrator And Computer—was built from value technology at the University of Pennsylvania. For further information upon the history of computer evolution from ENIAC to PC and beyond, *see*, for example, Christopher Barnatt *Cyber Business: Mindsets for a Wired Age* (Chichester: John Wiley & Sons, 1995): 31–38.

242. Don Tapscott *The Digital Economy: Promise and Peril in the Age of Networked Intelligence* (New York: McGraw-Hill, 1995): 16.

243. Ibid.: 26.

244. It should be noted that nobody 'owns' the Internet—the system is a loose conglomeration of networks under the jurisdiction of a wide number of administrators who have chosen to operate with common communications standards (or 'protocols') for the common good.

245. This statistic has been reported by John Perry Barlow, and is cited from Mark Slouka's *War of the Worlds: Cyberspace and the High-tech Assault on Reality* (London: Abacus, 1996): 38.

246. Howard Rheingold *The Virtual Community* (London: Secker & Warburg, 1994).

247. Via the virtual reality mark-up language (VRML), it is now possible to construct world-wide web pages based upon an interactive, 3-D virtual reality interface.

248. Bill Gates simply refers to 'the highway' within his book *The Road Ahead* written with Nathan Myhrvold and Peter Rinearson (New York: Penguin Books, 1995).

249. The 'I-way' is the abbreviation for the information superhighway used by Don Tapscott, op.cit.

250. Bill Gates with Nathan Myhrvold and Peter Rinearson *The Road Ahead* (New York: Penguin Books, 1995): 66.

251. Don Tapscott, op.cit.: 106.

252. Ibid.: 34.

253. As reported by Stewart Brand in *The Media Lab: Inventing the Future at MIT* (New York: Penguin, 1988): 219–220. Other examples of digital retouching provided in Brand's review include a photograph of tennis rivals Bjorn Borg and John McEnroe standing back to back which was totally faked, together with a *Whole Earth Review* cover featuring three flying saucers buzzing downtown San Francisco.

254. Mark Slouka *War of the Worlds: Cyberspace and the High-tech Assault on Reality* (London: Abacus, 1996): 107.

255. I hasten to add that I am by no means implying here that everything on television in these two decades was necessarily true—only that, whilst broadcasters and governments in these times could be *selective* in what they showed, they had little power to create or pervert images which did not exist.

Chapter 10: Shared Nightmares, Shared Dreams

256. *See* notes 229 and 238.

257. For the distinction between data, information and knowledge *see* **chapter 8**, pp. 106–107.

258. The convergence of these three sectors of the media has been discussed in depth by a range of authors. *See*, for example, Don Tapscott *The Digital Economy: Promise and Peril in the Age of Networked Intelligence* (New York: McGraw-Hill, 1996), Nicholas

Negroponte *Being Digital* (London: Hodder & Stoughton, 1995), or Stewart Brand *The Media Lab: Inventing the Future at MIT* (New York: Penguin, 1988).

259. In addition to text and still images, world-wide web pages are increasingly also incorporating a digital collage of sound recordings, video images and virtual reality models.

260. My own *The Computers in Business Blueprint* (Oxford: Blackwell, 1994) is as guilty as a whole host of other texts in this respect.

261. Timothy Leary *Chaos and Cyberculture* (Berkeley, CA: Ronin Publishing, 1994): 7.

262. Myron W. Krueger *Artificial Reality II* (Reading, MA: Addison-Wesley, 1991): 3.

263. For more information upon on virtual reality hardware and its development *see*, for example, Francis Hamit *Virtual Reality and the Exploration of Cyberspace* (Carmel, IN: Sams Publishing, 1993), Howard Rheingold *Virtual Reality* (London: Mandarin, 1993), or Benjamin Woolly *Virtual Worlds* (London: Penguin, 1992).

264. Typical VR headset resolutions are only in the order of around 320×200 pixels. 3-D wands or 'flying mice' are used just like ordinary computer rodents save for the fact their position and motion may be detected within 3-D rather than only 2-D space. Datagloves, however, are far more sophisticated input devices. Actually worn rather than held, they not only track the position of a user's hand in space, but in addition determine finger position and orientation.

265. Most rudimentary force-feedback systems today rely upon arrays of tiny air bladders positioned within VR clothing such as datagloves or bodysuits. By inflating and deflating these bladders as appropriate, pressures can be artificially registered against a VR user's body, hence allowing them to 'feel' surfaces in VR. Unfortunately, only relatively small forces may be mimicked by air bladder technologies. More complex force-feedback systems therefore need to rely upon complex exosceletal structures of servomotors which encase the user.

266. Advancements in head mounted display (HMD) technology are likely to be most rapid as liquid crystal and other flat-screen colour display systems are perfected and fall in cost. The improvement of motion sensing technologies is likely to prove a little more problematic, with some perceivable (if minor) delay between the motion of the body and resultant actions in VR being almost inevitable regardless of the computer power applied to the problem. However, systems for permitting effective force-feedback are likely to be the most difficult to develop, with complex servomotor 'cages' at present thought to be able to produce the most likely solution as opposed to air bladder clothing (*see* note 265).

267. Timothy Leary, op.cit.: 8.

268. Ibid.: 19.

269. For more information upon direct retinal imaging, phosphotronic optical stimulation, and direct electronic links into the brain, *see* Christopher Barnatt *Cyber Business: Mindsets for a Wired Age* (Chichester: John Wiley & Sons, 1995): 135–139.

270. Interestingly, most of those who argue that direct human–computer linkages will *always* remain pure fiction tend to be academics in computing-related areas such as management information systems (MIS). Ironically, we can therefore be grateful that blue-sky thinking in computer development and application is still alive and kicking outside of the stifled inertia of the Ivory Tower. Staggering advancements in computing and genetic and molecular engineering have taken place over just the last five to ten years. To close

one's mind towards possibilities for the 'ultimate' form of human–computer interface therefore has to be nothing short of absurd.

271. Systems allowing for emergency surgery to be undertaken on the battlefield by a remote surgeon operating via distributed VR are already in development by the US army.

272. *See* Steve Pruit and Tom Barrett 'Corporate Virtual Workspace' in Michael Benedikt (ed) *Cyberspace: First Steps* (Cambridge, MA: MIT Press, 1993): 383–409.

273. *See* S. Benford, J. Bowers, S. Gray, T. Roden, G. Ryan, and V. Stanger 'The Virtuosi Project' in *Proceeding of VR 94* (London: Virtual Reality Expo).

274. Such a notion is explored by Francis Hamit within *Virtual Reality and the Exploration of Cyberspace* (Carmel, IN: Sams Publishing, 1993).

275. For example in *Virtual Reality* (London: Mandarin, 1993) Howard Rheingold devotes a chapter to 'Teledildonics and Beyond'. In *Cyberia: Life in the Trenches of Hyperspace* (London: HarperCollins, 1994), Douglas Rushkoff also discusses some of the more outlandish possibilities for virtual sex, including the potential ability for virtual lovers to program the feel of their bodies. Virtual sex is also a topic for discussion within Barrie Sherman and Phil Judkins, *Glimpses of Heaven, Visions of Hell: Virtual Reality and its Implications* (London: Hodder & Stoughton, 1993), and Francis Hamit *Virtual Reality and the Exploration of Cyberspace* (Carmel, IN: Sams Publishing, 1993), amongst others.

276. Timothy Leary, op.cit.: 3.

277. Umberto Eco *Travels in Hyperreality* (New York: Harcourt Brace Jovanovich, 1986).

278. *See* Alison Sprout 'Moving into the Virtual Office' *Fortune International* (2nd May 1994): 67.

279. Howard Rheingold *The Virtual Community* (London: Secker & Warburg, 1994).

280. The first use of the term simulacra is generally attributed Jean Baudrillard, and arose from his investigation of the 'hyper-realism' of television advertisements.

281. The term 'hyper-reality' refers to a state of affairs wherein passively accepted ubiquitous technologies and social veneers effectively mask the 'true' nature of the world from its citizens.

282. Allucquère Rosanne Stone *The War of Desire and Technology at the Close of the Mechanical Age* (Cambridge, MA: MIT Press, 1995): 177.

283. Groupware simply refers to any form of software productivity tool used to enable team working and to allow work exchange over a computer network. The most common examples of groupware are e-mail and multi-participant computer conferencing. *See* chapter 16, pp. 229–231.

284. Timothy Leary, op.cit.: 84.

285. Don Tapscott *The Digital Economy: Promise and Peril in the Age of Networked Intelligence* (New York: McGraw-Hill, 1996): 320.

Chapter 11: Within These Walls

286. Entropy is a critical concept associated with the Second Law of Thermodynamics, and is defined as a precise mathematical measure of the rate of dissipation of any system's thermal energy. Or, in other words, entropy is a measure of the level of disorder within

a system. It should be noted that the all-too-common notion that entropy itself is a force of disorder, rather than a measure thereof, needs to be avoided.

287. Lars Skyttner *General Systems Theory: An Introduction* (Basingstoke: Macmillan Press, 1996): 13.

288. In his 1776 book *The Wealth of Nations*, Adam Smith suggested that all nations would benefit from trade if each specialized in the production of just those goods in which they enjoyed an *absolute* economic advantage. So, for example, if Worksville was better at producing clothing rather than food, and Greentown was better at producing food rather than clothing, then Worksville should produce only clothing and Greentown only food, for by trading together each could benefit from obtaining both more food and more clothing. However, such a concept of absolute advantage as the only basis for rational trade was modified by economist David Ricardo in the early-1800s. Ricardo proposed that even if some regions were more efficient at producing all types of produce, then they could still be *comparatively* better at producing some goods rather than others. As most modern economists now accept, by concentrating upon those activities in which they possess *comparative* advantage, it therefore becomes rational for economies to engage in trade even if some of their partners prove less efficient in all areas of production.

289. Between about 1650 and 1950 the population of the world expanded from around 500 million to around 2.5 billion. Population increase was also most marked in those regions witness to the greatest influences of industrialization.

290. Malcolm Waters *Globalization* (London: Routledge, 1995): 1.

291. This quotation comes from a far longer passage detailing the effects of entropy increases upon the Universe as explained by The Doctor in Episode One of the *Doctor Who* story 'Logopolis' (London: BBC Television, 1981).

292. Malcolm Waters, op.cit.: 9.

293. The remains of Çatal Hüyük were discovered on the edge of the Konya plateau in south central Turkey in the 1950s. For more information *see* Giovanni Caselli *History of Everyday Things: Our World through the Ages* (Hemel Hempstead: Simon & Schuster, 1993): 18–21.

294. Known as the Proto-Dynastic, or Archaic, Period of the First and Second Dynasties. Within some sources Narmer is still referred to by his Greek name of Menes.

295. Grahame Clark *Space, Time and Man* (Cambridge: Cambridge University Press, 1992): 62.

296. Henry Hodges: *Technology in the Ancient World* (London: Michael O'Mara Books, 1996): 14–17.

297. Ibid.: 250.

298. Ibid.: 158–162.

299. It is unfortunately beyond the limits of the text to even briefly detail all of the early seafaring races, and their transportation developments, aside from the Egyptians, Mesopotamians, Greeks and Romans. However, the Phoenicians and the Aegeans, the Vikings and the Chinese, to name but a few other races and empires, were also famous for their early sailing craft and maritime trade and/or explorations.

300. Indeed, it should be noted that, up until the end of the Middle Ages, clear distinctions were rarely made between the merchant and naval ships of most nations.

301. Henry Hodges, op.cit.: 203.

302. Ibid.: 222.

303. Grahame Clark, op.cit.: 70–74.

304. Rome finally fell in the 5th century AD.

305. Short canals were constructed in Italy, France and the Netherlands from the 16th century onwards. However, it was not until 1692 that the Canal du Midi—the first really modern artificial waterway—was completed in France to connect the Atlantic with the Mediterranean. The first totally artificial inland British waterway was the Bridgewater canal, completed in 1761, which was built to transport coal from Worsley to Manchester. Many other commercial inland waterways followed, with canal construction peaking in Britain in the 1790s. Builders and engineers such as Thomas Telford then went on to work on enclosed docks to ease the congestion at ports, as well as to construct or improve roads, although the latter often proved difficult to finance. In the United States canal building had a slightly later heyday from around 1815 to 1840.

306. R.A. Buchanan *The Power of the Machine: The Impact of Technology from 1700 to the Present* (London: Penguin, 1994): 123.

307. Steam engines had first emerged in the West in the late-17th century, although the Greek inventor Hero had invented a rudimentary steam turbine when working at the Museum of Alexandria in the fourth century BC. By 1712 steam engines were in service for pumping water, with the first effective steam engine being used at a coal mine in Dudley in the English Midlands in 1712. However, it was not until boilers could be forged capable of withstanding high pressures that steam powered transportation became a possibility.

308. Just one of the many innovations utilized by Stephenson was the use of sleepers beneath the rails in order to prevent them cracking under the impact of the locomotive.

309. In the strictest sense the first passenger railway was that built by George Stephenson between Stockton and Darlington, and which first carried passengers (some 600 of them) on the 27th of September 1825.

310. As a notable example, the Institution of Mechanical Engineers was formed in 1847, and was dominated by engineers employed by railway companies. Its first president was George Stephenson.

311. R.A. Buchanan, op.cit.: 138.

312. American inventor John Fitch launched the first recorded steam boat on the Delaware River in 1786.

313. Clippers—the fastest and most sea-worthy sailing ships ever built—were introduced in the mid-19th century.

314. Studies suggest that between 65 and 98 per cent of the tools used by Neanderthal groups were made from materials taken from within about a three mile radius, with the remainder drawn from within about twelve miles. *See* Grahame Clark, op.cit.: 30.

Chapter 12: The Rise & Demise of Nations

315. *Monty Python's Life of Brian* (London: Handmade Films, 1979).

316. Don Tapscott *The Digital Economy: Promise and Peril in the Age of Networked Intelligence* (New York: McGraw-Hill, 1996): 64–65.

317. R.A. Buchanan *The Power of the Machine: The Impact of Technology from 1700 to the Present* (London: Penguin, 1994): 64–65.

318. Ibid.: 153.

319. In a response to the rise of Germany an alliance or *entente* had been formed between France, Britain and Russia. A counter-alliance between Germany, Italy and the Austro-Hungarian empire had also been forged.

320. It should be noted that since the latter half of the 19th century the Balkan states of Southeast Europe had become increasingly politically unstable, and that power-struggles and then two wars in these territories had been stirred up by several other European nations.

321. Marcel Batreau, cited from Godfrey Hodgson *People's Century* (London: BBC Books, 1995): 40.

322. J.M. Roberts *The Penguin History of the World* (London: Penguin, 1995): 860.

323. Godfrey Hodgson, op.cit.: 231–232.

324. Rationing of some foods continued in Britain until as late as 1954.

325. This figure represented around five per cent of the annual gross domestic product of the United States at that time.

326. Will Hutton *The State We're In* (London: Vintage, 1996): 49.

327. It is estimated that nearly twenty million Russians died during WWII.

328. Although segmented into Eastern and Western sectors, Berlin remained a city deep inside the communist Soviet sector of Germany. In 1948 and 1949 the Russians tried to starve out its Western inhabitants. However, the Americans and the British refused to go and organized an airlift. Over 321 days around 272,000 flights were made into West Berlin and the Soviets finally admitted defeat.

329. The international situation which arose when the Soviet Union stationed nuclear weapons in Cuba probably came the closest to sparking a global conflict between the NATO Alliance and those countries under Soviet influence.

330. Malcolm Waters *Globalization* (London: Routledge, 1995): 107.

331. Specifically the Vienna Convention of 1985, and the Montreal Protocol of 1987, dealt with the limiting of CFC and carbon monoxide emissions.

332. Marshal McLuhan *Understanding Media* (London: Routledge, 1964).

333. The distinction between the unifying rather than the integrative forces of globalization is clearly expanded upon by Malcolm Waters, op.cit.: 42.

334. Kenichi Ohmae 'Putting Global Logic First' *Harvard Business Review* (January –February 1995): 119–124.

335. It is, of course, somewhat ironic that in demonstrating the relative decline of nation state boundaries that we rely upon trade statistics amalgamated at a national level.

336. G. Barraclough (ed) *The Times Atlas of World History* (London: Times, 1978): 256.

337. Funk & Wagnall's Corporation, cited in *Microsoft Encarta 95*.

338. R. Walters and D. Blake *The Politics of Global Economic Relations* (Englewood Cliffs, NJ: Prentice Hall, 1992): 16.

339. GATT, the organization for the General Agreement on Tariffs and Trade, was established in 1947 and currently boasts over 100 members. Its goals are to restrict import protection to tariff barriers as opposed to quotas, and then to seek a consensus on tariff reductions.

340. Kenichi Ohmae, op.cit.: 120.

341. *See* George Ritzer *The McDonaldization of Society* (Thousand Oaks, CA: Pine Forge, 1993). The concept of 'McDisneyization' was discussed more recently by George in an internal seminar during a visit to the University of Nottingham in the Summer of 1996.

342. Mark Slouka *War of the Worlds: Cyberspace and the High-tech Assault on Reality* (London: Abacus, 1996): 2–3; 86.
343. Kenichi Ohmae, op.cit.: 120.
344. Ibid.
345. Don Tapscott, op.cit.: 311.
346. The two-phase development and crisis of the modern state is discussed by Malcolm Waters, op.cit.: 98–101.
347. Malcolm Waters, op.cit.: 183.
348. Ibid.: 17.

Chapter 13: Our Island Earth

349. Konstantin E. Tsiolkovsky was the Russian scientist who first envisioned the use of rockets in space travel. His words are cited from Alan Shepard and Deke Slayton's *Moon Shot: The Inside Story of America's Race to the Moon* (London: Virgin, 1995): 433–434.
350. James Lovelock *Gaia: A New Look at Life on Earth* (Oxford: Oxford University Press, 1995): xvii.
351. Ibid.: x.
352. Ibid.: xiv–xv.
353. Ibid.: 32–34.
354. In scientific usage an aeon equates to one thousand million years.
355. James Lovelock, op.cit.: 18.
356. Gregory Stock *Metaman: Humans, Machines & the Birth of a Global Super-Organism* (New York: Bantam Press, 1993).
357. James Lovelock, op.cit.: 3.
358. *Cited from* Frank P. Davidson and C. Lawrence Meador (eds) *Macro-Engineering: Global Infrastructure Solutions* (New York: Ellis Horwood, 1992): 144.
359. In business today one year plans, three year plans, five year plans and ten year plans tend to dominate. However, when you ask many managers—or indeed many students of business—how they expect their career to develop it is still not uncommon to find people who are looking twenty to thirty years ahead.
360. A local area network (or LAN) is used to connect computers within a single office or building. In contrast wide area networks (or WANs) link computers over much longer distances, and most usually via telephone connections. In this sense the Internet is the largest wide area network in the world.
361. This estimate is cited from Juan Antonio Blanco *Tercer Milenio: Apuntes para una reflexion* (Third Millennium: Notes for Reflection), (NPG Centro Felix Varela, Havana: October 1994).
362. The World Commission on Environment and Development *Our Common Future* (Oxford: Oxford University Press, 1987).
363. Richard Welford *Environmental Strategy and Sustainable Development: The Corporate Challenge for the 21st Century* (London: Routledge, 1995): 6.
364. James Lovelock, op.cit.: 25.
365. Ibid.: 27.

366. K. Eric Drexler *Engines of Creation* (London: Fourth Estate, 1996): 83.

367. Ibid.: 84.

368. Ibid.: 88.

369. Ibid.: 95.

370. Alan Shepard and Deke Slayton *Moon Shot: The Inside Story of America's Race to the Moon* (London: Virgin, 1995): 428.

371. At the time of writing NASA's space shuttle fleet consisted of the *Discovery*, *Atlantis*, *Columbia*, and the *Endeavour*.

372. K. Eric Drexler, op.cit.: 85.

373. Ibid.: 88.

374. Anybody who thinks that self-replicating, self-repairing construction robots are pure fantasy is advised to read K. Eric Drexler's excellent *Engines of Creation*, op.cit.

375. The idea of terraforming Mars goes back at least fifty years, and is both discussed and illustrated with virtual reality modelling within Arthur C. Clarke's *The Snows of Olympus: A Garden on Mars* (London: Victor Gollancz, 1994). James Lovelock has also co-authored a book on the subject with Michael Allaby entitled *The Greening of Mars* (London: Andre Deutch, 1984). Papers on terraforming have also appeared in *Nature* (Vol. 352 No. 6335) as well as in the *Journal of the British Interplanetary Society* (Vol. 45 No. 8).

376. At the time of writing the website for NASA's reusable launch vehicle programme was located at: http://rlv.msfc.nasa.gov/

377. If you are reading this book and you don't think that searching the Internet for information is child's play then you should get yourself (and your organization) a connection to the Internet *and fast*.

378. I am indebted to Dr Roy Bradshaw for this observation.

379. *Cited from* Mark Poster *The Mode of Information: Post Structuralism and Social Context* (Cambridge: Polity Press, 1992): 125.

Chapter 14: Tools of the Overlord

380. The farmers of ancient Egypt effectively faced a year split into three seasons each of four months. During the season of 'Akhet' (or inundation'), which occurred between July and October, the Nile flooded the fields. It is therefore almost certainly during this time of year that a great deal of pyramid construction work would have taken place.

381. We could debate for many pages exactly how and when capital technologies became concentrated within urban rather than rural centres of population. Some claim that this process was already under way in the late-18th century during the first phases of the industrial revolution. However, others note that in some countries mass industrialization (and hence urban concentration) has yet to occur even in the late-20th century.

382. Other notable members of the task or 'classical' school of management included Urwick, Brech, and Mooney & Reiley.

383. Fayol's full list of his fourteen principles of management comprised of division of work, authority, discipline, unity of command, unity of direction, subordination of individual interest to the general interest, remuneration, centralization, scalar chain (line of authority), order, equity, stability of tenure of personnel, initiative, and *esprit de corps*.

For further detail *see* Henri Fayol *General and Industrial Management* (London: Pitman, 1949—translated from the 1916 French original by Constance Storrs).
384. Robert P. Vecchio *Organizational Behaviour* (Chicago: Dryden Press, 1991): 9.
385. Ibid.
386. Gareth Morgan *Images of Organization* (Newbury Park, CA: Sage, 1986): 23.
387. Ibid.: 24.
388. For a detailed coverage of the process of the industrial revolution *see* T.S. Ashton *The Industrial Revolution 1760-1830* (Oxford: Oxford University Press, 1968).
389. Ibid.: 75.
390. Gareth Morgan, op.cit.: 24.
391. As detailed in his book *The Wealth of Nations* (1776).
392. Gareth Morgan, op.cit.: 24.
393. Max Weber 'Legitimate Authority and Bureaucracy' from *The Theory of Social and Economic Organization* (Free Press, 1947—German original of 1924 translated and edited by A.M. Henderson and T. Parsons), reproduced in D.S. Pugh *Organization Theory: Selected Readings* (London: Penguin, 1990): 14.
394. Ibid.: 12.
395. Charles Handy *The Empty Raincoat: Making Sense of the Future* (London: Arrow, 1995).

Chapter 15: Monoliths of Stone

396. A.D. Chandler, Jr 'Managerial Hierarchies', reproduced in D.S. Pugh (ed) *Organization Theory: Selected Readings*—3rd Edition (London: Penguin, 1990): 100.
397. Large batch and process production first appeared in refining and distilling industries, where the liquid or semi-liquid nature of the inputs and outputs permitted the construction of highly-integrated manufacturing facilities.
398. A.D. Chandler, op.cit.: 108.
399. It should be noted that growth by merger in the late-19th and early-20th centuries was most common in the United States due to the deregulated nature of its rising economy.
400. Ken Starkey and Alan McKinlay *Strategy and the Human Resource: Ford and the Search for Competitive Advantage* (Oxford: Blackwell, 1993): 15.
401. A.D. Chandler, op.cit.: 113.
402. United States Federal Trade Commission *Report on Corporate Mergers* (1969): 176.
403. Thomas J. Peters and Robert R. Waterman *In Search of Excellence: Lessons From America's Best-Run Companies* (New York: Harper & Row, 1982): 112.
404. Peter F. Drucker *Innovation and Entrepreneurship: Practice and Principles* (London: Pan, 1986): 95.
405. Thomas J. Peters and Robert R. Waterman, op.cit.
406. *See* Tom Burns and G.M. Stalker *The Management of Innovation* (London: Tavistock, 1961).
407. For a comprehensive discussion of the nature, advantages and disadvantages of matrix organizations *see* Gareth R. Jones *Organizational Theory: Text and Cases* (Reading, MA: Addison-Wesley, 1995): 154-160.

408. Laurie J. Mullins *Management and Organizational Behaviour—Third Edition* (London: Pitman, 1993): 326.
409. S.A. Bergen *R&D Management: Managing Projects and New Products* (Oxford: Blackwell, 1990): 145.
410. Thomas J. Peters and Robert R. Waterman, op.cit.: 111.
411. Ibid.
412. Raymond E. Miles and Charles C. Snow 'Organizations: New Concepts for New Forms' *California Management Review* (Vol. XXXVIII, No. 3, Spring 1986).
413. Ibid.: 64–65.
414. Mark Daniell 'Webs we Weave' *Management Today* (February 1990): 83.
415. Raymond Miles and Charles Snow, op.cit.: 69.
416. In *Creative Organization Theory: A Resourcebook* (Newbury Park, CA: Sage, 1988): 67, Gareth Morgan discusses 'organic networks' 'operationalizing the ideas' of a fashion label created by a broker core. Within the British Broadcasting Corporation an initiative known as 'Producer Choice' now allows producers to become the brokers of networks drawing facilities and talent from both inside and outside of the Corporation as they so wish. For more details of networked organizational structures in film and television production *see* Christopher Barnatt and Ken Starkey 'The Emergence of Flexible Networks in the UK Television Industry' *British Journal of Management* 5(4) (1994).
417. Michael J. Piore and Charles F. Sabel *The Second Industrial Divide: Possibilities for Prosperity* (New York: Basic Books, 1984).
418. Ken Starkey and Alan McKinlay, op.cit.: 16.

Chapter 16: Of Networks & Cocoons

419. For a wider review of the impact of the 'microprocessor revolution' upon production *see* Michel Liu, Hélène Denis, Harvey Kolodny and Bengt Stymne 'Organizational Design for Technological Change' *Human Relations* Vol. 43, No. 1 (1990): 7–22.
420. Apparently the 'hardest problem in clothing fit' is women's jeans, with only 27% of customers being happy. The system to electronically link the retailers, cutters, stickers and washers of Levi jeans was pioneered by Sung Park, a former IBM software engineer. *See* Don Tapscott *The Digital Economy: Promise and Peril in the Age of Networked Intelligence* (New York: McGraw-Hill, 1996): 91–92.
421. The term 'internetworking' was introduced by Don Tapscott who contends in *The Digital Economy* that future organizations will, in the main, be 'internetworked enterprises' (New York: McGraw-Hill, 1996).
422. Learning loop links between Wal Mart and other organizations are explored by Stephan Haeckel and Richard Nolan in 'Managing by Wire', *Harvard Business Review* (September–October 1993): 122–132.
423. For example, computer aided design (CAD) and/or VR modelling may augment innovation and design, whilst computer aided manufacturing (CAM) utilizing computer numerically controlled (CNC) machine tools or robots may automate production. Marketing and distribution may then be assisted with electronic data interchange (EDI), database customer profiling, or perhaps even the use of the Internet's world-wide web. *See* Christopher Barnatt *Management Strategy and Information Technology: Text and Readings* (London: International Thomson Business Press, 1996): chapter 2.

424. It is perhaps interesting to note that, since 1991, in aggregate companies have spent more on computing and communications hardware and software than on industrial and agricultural plant. *Source*: Thomas A. Stewart 'The Information Age in Charts', *Fortune International* (April 1994): 55.

425. Lotus Development's world-wide web site is located at http://www.lotus.com. The citation presented in the text was downloaded as of 22/8/1996.

426. *See*, for example, Thomas A. Stewart 'Managing in a Wired Company', *Fortune International* (11th July 1994): 20–28.

427. Electronic data interchange is defined as the 'transfer of structured data from computer to computer using agreed communications standards'. Key to the operation of any EDI system must be the transfer of data in a *directly usable* electronic form which will prevent its future human re-keying. *See*, for example, Joe Peppard (ed) *IT Strategy for Business* (London: Pitman, 1993): 144–159.

428. Lotus Development, op.cit.

429. Information from the Lotus Development world-wide web site, op.cit.

430. Ibid.

431. As just one example, the Henley Management College in the UK uses *Lotus Notes* to support 7000 postgraduate students on distance-learning programmes worldwide.

432. Geoffrey Wheelwright 'Kingpins focus on a standard' (Videoconferencing), *Financial Times Review of Information Technology* (6th March 1996): 16.

433. For more detail upon pilot 'virtual office' developments *see* S. Benford, J. Bowers, S. Gray, T. Roden, G. Ryan, and V. Stanger 'The Virtuosi Project' in *Proceeding of VR 94* (London: Virtual Reality Expo).

434. Charles Handy *The Empty Raincoat: Making Sense of the Future* (London: Arrow Books, 1995): 218.

435. Don Tapscott *The Digital Economy: Promise and Peril in the Age of Networked Intelligence* (New York: McGraw Hill, 1996): 65.

436. Douglas Adams, from his 'Global Hero' interview in *Creative Technology* (September 1996): 31.

437. For a review *see*, for example, Christopher Barnatt, 'Office Space, Cyberspace and Virtual Organization' in the *Journal of General Management* (Summer 1995).

438. Charles Handy, op.cit.: 38.

439. Ibid.: 39.

440. A similar definition appears in *Cyber Business* wherein I defined a virtual organization as 'any pattern of organization based around information technology systems that enable geographically remote individuals to work together' (Chichester: John Wiley & Sons, 1995): 215.

441. Christopher Barnatt *Cyber Business: Mindsets for a Wired Age* (Chichester: John Wiley & Sons, 1995): 83.

442. Software agents are autonomous pieces of computer code capable of roaming networks to undertake instructions supplied by their human masters. Software agents are also usually capable of learning both from their master's actions, and from the outcomes of previous business dealings. The market for agent technology is expected to exceed $2bn by the year 2000. *See*, for example, Paul Taylor 'Help is on Hand from Intelligent Agents', *Financial Times Review of Information Technology* (March 6th 1996): 1, or chapter 4—'Agents, Ghosts & Other Virtual Monsters' in *Cyber Business*, ibid.

443. Christopher Barnatt, op.cit.: 74.

444. This noted, lots of invoice-wielding consultants are very eager to offer help!

Chapter 17: The Future Mindset

445. Christopher Barnatt *Cyber Business: Mindsets for a Wired Age* (Chichester: John Wiley & Sons, 1995): 208.

446. For an explanation of this model *see* Andrew D. Brown 'Transformational Leadership in Tackling Technological Change' *Journal of General Management* (Volume 19, Number 4, 1994).

447. Granted, most companies still profess to preparing 'long range plans'—yet with one, three, five or possibly ten years taken as a 'long time'.

448. These comments are cited from a review of *Cyber Business: Mindsets for a Wired Age* written by Joe Peppard to appear in the *Middle East Business Review*. With thanks to John Denton, Reviews Editor, for the advance copy of the text.

449. *See* note 442.

450. Philip Manchester 'Agent Software' *Financial Times A–Z of Computing* (26th April 1994): 3.

451. All of these new technologies have been explored within previous chapters. However, for a more detailed review *see* (for example) Daniel Burrus with Roger Gittines, *Technotrends: 24 Technologies that will Revolutionize Our Lives* (New York: HarperCollins, 1993).

452. Cited from 'Who Needs More Technology?', *Creative Technology* (January 1995): 27.

453. *Superman: The Movie* (Warner Brothers, 1978).

Index